World Atlas of Elections

VOTING PATTERNS IN 39 DEMOCRACIES

Dedication

To
Mark and Miriam Leonard
and
Sheila Natkiel

World Atlas of Elections

VOTING PATTERNS IN 39 DEMOCRACIES

Dick Leonard and Richard Natkiel

The Economist Publications Ltd
PO Box 1DW
40 Duke Street
London W1A 1DW

© 1986: in the text, Dick Leonard; in the maps and charts, Richard Natkiel

British Library Cataloguing in Publication Data

Leonard, Dick
   World atlas of elections.
   1. Elections—Maps
   I. Title   II. Natkiel, Richard
   912'.13246   G1046.F9

   ISBN 0-85058-089-7

Jacket by Rufus Segar
Text design by Susie Home
House editor: Penny Butler

Acknowledgements
The authors' thanks are due to Graham Douglas for his
invaluable assistance with the maps and charts.

Photoset by Paston Press, Norwich
Printed by Hollen St. Press, Slough

Contents

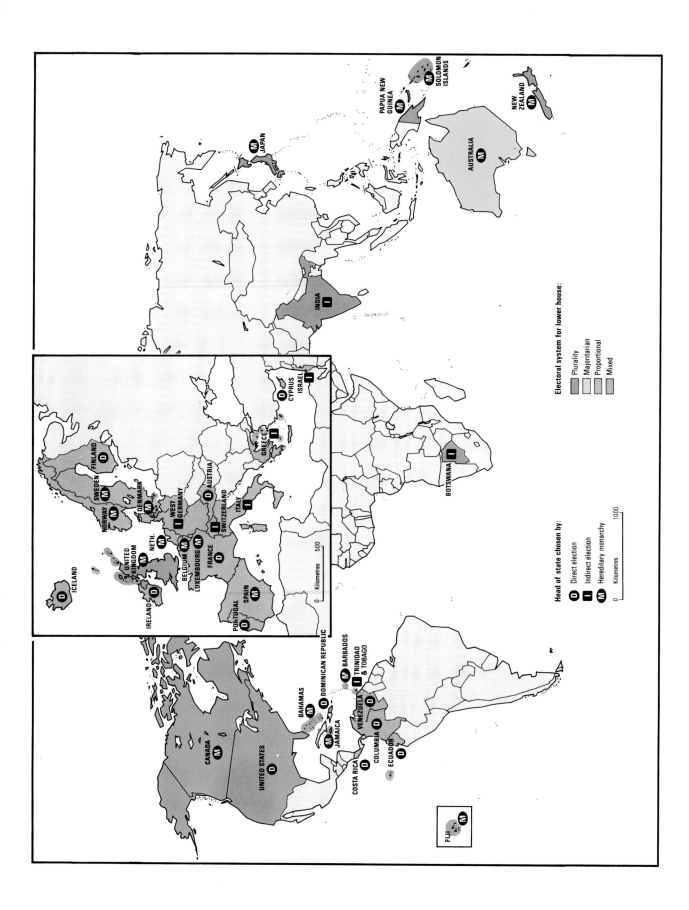

Electoral system for lower house:

- ▨ Plurality
- ▨ Majoritarian
- ▨ Proportional
- ▨ Mixed

Head of state chosen by:

- **D** Direct election
- **I** Indirect election
- **M** Hereditary monarchy

ICELAND **D**

IRELAND **D**

UNITED KINGDOM **M**

NETH. **M**

BELGIUM **M**

LUXEMBOURG **M**

FRANCE **D**

PORTUGAL **D**

SPAIN **M**

NORWAY **M**

SWEDEN **M**

DENMARK **M**

FINLAND **D**

WEST GERMANY **I**

AUSTRIA **D**

SWITZERLAND **I**

ITALY **I**

GREECE **I**

CYPRUS **D**

ISRAEL **I**

Kilometres
0   500

Kilometres
0   1000

JAPAN **M**

INDIA **I**

BOTSWANA **I**

PAPUA NEW GUINEA **M**

SOLOMON ISLANDS **M**

AUSTRALIA **M**

NEW ZEALAND **M**

CANADA **M**

UNITED STATES **D**

BAHAMAS **M**

DOMINICAN REPUBLIC **D**

BARBADOS **M**

TRINIDAD & TOBAGO **I**

JAMAICA **M**

COSTA RICA

VENEZUELA **D**

COLUMBIA **D**

ECUADOR **D**

FIJI **M**

Introduction

The purpose of the *World Atlas of Elections* is to enable the reader to obtain, at a glance, details of the most recent parliamentary and presidential elections in each of 39 democratic countries. For each of these countries a map is provided showing the actual electoral areas, or constituencies, from which its parliamentarians or congressmen are elected, the winning party being shown for each seat.

In the case of countries with two-chamber parliaments, it is the result for the lower house which is shown. The United States of America is perhaps unique in having an upper house, the Senate, which is at least as powerful as the lower house of its Congress. So for the USA only, maps are included illustrating results for both chambers.

The other maps in each country section show the spread of support for each of the main political parties and the support for the president, where he is chosen by popular vote, and his defeated rivals. Each country section also contains text giving details of the electoral system, or systems, in use and tabulated results for earlier elections for many of the countries.

Why 39?

Because that is the number of countries which fulfil the criteria which were established at the outset of the work. These were three in number.

1. Size

A minimum population of 200,000. This was, largely, a practical consideration. All the main democratic countries easily surmount this threshold, and it is likely that disproportionate difficulty would have been experienced in collecting the data from many of the mini-states that might otherwise have qualified.

2. Independence

All the countries included are sovereign states. Only those which had been independent in 1985 for at least five years and had had at least two contested parliamentary elections in that period have been included.

3. Freedom

A more subjective measure. For the purposes of this book, the authors have been guided by the surveys published by the Freedom House organisation of New York.[1] Freedom House every year invites a distinguished panel of political scientists to rank every country in the world on two seven-point scales, one measuring political rights and the other civil liberties. On the basis of these scales the countries of the world are categorised as 'free', 'partly free' and 'not free'. Broadly speaking, countries which are ranked 1 and 2 in the scales, on average, appear in the first category, those ranked 3–5 in the second, and those ranked 6 and 7 in the third. No country which does not provide for regular, freely contested and competitive elections would qualify for the first category.

The minimum qualification for inclusion in this book has been that a country must have figured for at least the most recent five consecutive years in the 'free' category. This is a high threshold: it has meant, for example, that in the whole of Africa only Botswana has qualified; in Asia only India, Israel and Japan.

There are good reasons for this exclusivity. It is not a purpose of the authors to lend a spurious respectability to regimes whose concept of freedom of choice for their fellow citizens does not extend to the right to give marching orders to their rulers. Moreover, it is hoped that this book will establish itself as a standard work of reference. This dictates a certain measure of consistency, and it would not be helpful to include a lot of countries that drop in and out of successive editions.

This does not mean that the threshold has been set so high as to be virtually unattainable. A number of countries which have regained their freedom in recent years – to name, in South America alone, Peru, Brazil, Argentina and Uruguay – may well qualify for inclusion in the future if their democratic transition is sustained. Similarly, Spain, Portugal and Greece would not have been included a dozen years ago, but each of them appears now to be a secure member of the democratic club.

Conversely, The Gambia, Malta, Mauritius and Sri Lanka have been excluded, whereas a few years back they would have qualified. Mauritius, in fact, is the most borderline case. Had the authors wanted to bend the rules ever so slightly, to reach a round number of 40, Mauritius would have been included.

As it is, while there may be some argument about the exclusions, there cannot seriously be any about those countries which do appear in this book. Each of them has demonstrated its democratic credentials, and has done so over a reasonably lengthy period.

What's left?

After applying this rigorous selection process, we are left with 19 countries in Western Europe, two in North America, nine in Latin America and the Caribbean, three in Asia, one in Africa and five in the South Pacific. They may be classified in several ways. Thirteen of them elect

---

[1] See most recently, Raymond D. Gastil, *Freedom in the World 1983–84* (Westport, Connecticut, Greenwood Press, 1984).

their presidents by popular vote, and details of all these elections are included, even in those cases (five in number) where the presidents do not have executive powers. Another nine countries have presidents who are elected indirectly, while the remaining 17 countries are constitutional monarchies. In nine of these the monarch is the British Queen, but her duties are carried out by an appointed governor-general in all of these except the United Kingdom itself.

Electoral systems

A crucial variable is the type of electoral system used. There are three broad categories: plurality, majoritarian and proportional representation (PR). For the convenience of the reader, definitions are given here, and cross-referenced in the country sections, to avoid a great deal of unnecessary repetition.

The plurality system

This system awards seat(s) to the candidate(s) who get the most votes even if this is less than an absolute majority. This is often known, particularly in the United Kingdom, as the 'first past the post' system.

Most frequently it is used in single-member constituencies, but it may equally be applied to multi-member constituencies where the voter normally has as many votes as there are seats to be filled (for example, in some local government elections in the UK). A unique example of the use of multi-member constituencies, where the elector has only one vote, is in Japan, whose electoral system is known as the *single non-transferable vote*.

Plurality systems are very widely used for parliamentary elections, though they are nowadays mostly restricted to countries (including the USA) which were once under British rule. For presidential elections, however, where, by definition, only one person is to be elected, the plurality system is more widely employed. Of the 13 countries directly electing their president, six use plurality voting.

The majoritarian system

This means that only candidates winning more than 50 per cent of the votes cast may be elected. The system has two sub-categories: the *two-ballot* system and the *alternative vote*.

In the two-ballot system, which is normally restricted to single-member constituencies, a second round of voting is held if no candidate gains more than 50 per cent of the votes cast in the first ballot. The second ballot is often legally limited to the two leading candidates in the first round. Historically, it has been the system used most frequently in France in parliamentary elections, but it was replaced by a proportional system in 1986. It is widely used, however, in presidential elections. Seven out of the countries directly electing their presidents, including France, use the two-ballot system.

The alternative vote is used for the election of the Australian House of Representatives. Voters number the candidates in the order of their choice, and if no candidate wins more than 50 per cent of the votes cast the bottom candidate is eliminated and his votes are redistributed to their second choices. Further candidates may be eliminated until one candidate achieves an absolute majority. The alternative vote is also used in the Republic of Ireland in the event of parliamentary by-elections and for the election of the president.

Proportional representation

This is the final broad category of election systems. As its name implies, it attempts to relate the allocation of seats as closely as possible to the distribution of votes. By definition, this requires more than one vacancy, so multi-member constituencies are necessary.

This system is divided between two main sub-categories and a number of sub-sub-categories. The sub-categories are: *largest remainder* and *highest average*. These refer to the mathematical formulae by which the seats are allocated, as there is no way of ensuring 100 per cent proportionality.

The largest remainder method is the simplest means of allocation. It involves setting a quota of votes which party lists of candidates must achieve in order to be guaranteed a seat. The most common quota is the *Hare quota*, named after Thomas Hare, a Victorian lawyer and associate of John Stuart Mill. This is derived by dividing the number of votes cast by the number of seats to fill. For example, in a four-member constituency where 20,000 votes have been cast the quota will be 5,000.

Table 1

Four-member constituency. 20,000 votes cast.
Hare quota: 5,000

Party	Votes	Quota	Seats	Remainder	Seats	Total seats
A	8,200	5,000	1	3,200	1	2
B	6,100	5,000	1	1,100	0	1
C	3,000	–	0	3,000	1	1
D	2,700	–	0	2,700	0	0
TOTAL	20,000		2		2	4

In the example shown in Table 1 only two of the four parties achieve an electoral quota. So only two of the four seats can be directly allocated: one each to parties A and B. But under the *largest remainder* system the third seat also goes to party A and the fourth seat to party C. The *largest remainder* system is regarded as being favourable to smaller parties, and it is noteworthy in the above example that party C gets as many seats as party B while getting less than half the number of votes.

The *highest average* system was devised by another nineteenth-century lawyer, the Belgian Victor D'Hondt, after whom it is named. Its central idea is to divide each party's votes by successive divisors, and then allocate the

Table 2

Four-member constituency. 20,000 votes cast.
Division by D'Hondt divisors

Party	Votes	Divisor: 1	Divisor: 2	Divisor: 3	Total seats
A	8,200	8,200 (1)	4,100 (3)	2,733	2
B	6,100	6,100 (2)	3,050 (4)	2,033	2
C	3,000	3,000	1,500	1,000	0
D	2,700	2,700	1,350	900	0
TOTAL	20,000				4

seats to the parties in descending order of quotients.
Table 2 shows the same results in votes as Table 1, but
under the *D'Hondt* system the allocation of seats is
different.

In the example in Table 2 the first seat will go to party
A, the second to party B, the third to party A and the
fourth to party B whose second quotient is 50 more than
the first quotient of party C. Party C is left without a seat,
which suggests that the D'Hondt system is less
favourable to smaller parties than the Hare quota.

It is possible to combine both methods by first applying
the Hare quota and then allocating the remaining seats by
D'Hondt divisors. Different quotas and divisors have also
been devised, with the objective of giving greater or lesser
advantages to large, small or medium-sized parties.

Two different quotas, whose practical effect is to
allocate more seats by quota, leaving fewer to the
remainders, are the *Hagenbach-Bischoff quota* and the
Imperiali quota. The Hagenbach-Bischoff quota involves
dividing the total votes cast by the number of seats plus
one, and the Imperiali quota by the number of seats plus
two.

Alternative divisors to those used in the D'Hondt
system are the *Sainte-Laguë* and the *Sainte-Laguë modified
divisors*. The first of these involves dividing each party's
votes by 1, 3, 5, 7, etc, instead of by 1, 2, 3, 4, etc. The
second, which has been adopted in several Scandinavian
countries, involves setting the first divisor at 1.4 instead
of 1 (1.4, 3, 5, 7, etc). This has the effect of strengthening
medium-sized parties in a multi-party system.

Several countries practise a double allocation of seats,
in so far as remainders are transferred to a regional or
national pool before the remaining seats are allocated.
The effect is usually to make the overall result more
proportional, except in Greece and Cyprus, where a high
threshold has been set for pool seats with the deliberate
intention of discriminating against smaller parties.

Many countries apply a threshold, in any event, before
parties can qualify for seats, either at a constituency or at
national level. The size of the threshold varies from
country to country, but the most common figure is 5 per
cent. Other things being equal, the larger the number of
seats in each constituency the more proportional a system
will be. The extreme examples are Israel and the
Netherlands, in each of which the entire country forms
one constituency.

A particular form of proportional representation is the
single transferable vote (STV), which is used for
parliamentary elections in the Republic of Ireland. Under
this system the voter may list all the candidates on a ballot
paper in his order of preference. The total number of votes
cast is divided by the number of seats plus one, and one
is added to the quotient. This is known as the *Droop* quota.
Candidates exceeding the Droop quota are allocated
seats, and their excess votes are transferred to their
second preferences. The process is repeated until all the
seats have been filled, if necessary eliminating the bottom
candidates and transferring their votes in the same way.

The STV system, as used in the Republic of Ireland, is
less proportional than most party list systems, mainly
because the constituencies are relatively small (3–5
members), but it gives a much larger choice of individual
candidates to the voter.

Table 3

Quotas and Divisors: the Formulae

1. Hare quota $= \dfrac{\text{Votes}}{\text{Seats}}$

2. Hagenbach-Bischoff quota $= \dfrac{\text{Votes}}{\text{Seats} + 1}$

3. Imperiali quota $= \dfrac{\text{Votes}}{\text{Seats} + 2}$

4. Droop quota $= \dfrac{\text{Votes}}{\text{Seats} + 1} + 1$

5. D'Hondt divisors: 1, 2, 3, 4, 5, etc

6. Sainte-Laguë divisors: 1, 3, 5, 7, 9, etc

7. Sainte-Laguë modified divisors: 1.4, 3, 5, 7, 9, etc

One other device, which also produces this effect, is
panachage, as practised in Switzerland and Luxembourg.
These countries employ party list systems, but the voter
has as many votes as there are seats to be filled and may,
if he chooses, distribute his choices between candidates
on several different lists.

West Germany employs a hybrid system, in that one
half of the parliamentary seats are filled by plurality,
using single-member constituencies, while the other half
are filled by party lists, using the D'Hondt system. The
objective is to achieve overall proportionality, while
preserving the advantages of single-member
constituencies (see page 58).[2]

---

[2] For a more detailed, but still succinct, description of electoral
systems see Thomas T. Mackie and Richard Rose, *The International
Almanac of Electoral History* (London, Macmillan, 1982, 2nd edn),
pages 406–12.

The maps

Although there are some variations, the format is that each country section contains a detailed constituency map, showing which party has won each parliamentary seat in the most recent election. The names of each constituency are given, using the spelling used in the country concerned rather than anglicised versions (for example, Lisboa *not* Lisbon).

There follows a series of maps showing the relative strengths of the main political parties throughout the country. Where the number of electoral divisions is fairly small these maps are identical in outline to the constituency map. Otherwise, for the sake of clarity, they are subdivided on a provincial or regional basis. Finally, where the head of state is elected by direct popular vote, including through an electoral college, a further map shows the result of the last presidential election.

In the constituency maps it is often necessary to include insets for the more populous areas in order to provide sufficient detail. Normally the area inset is left white in the main map. Any other white patches, where no inset is indicated, are lakes or inland seas.

The European Parliament

A special section of the book, beginning on page 149, is devoted to elections to the European Parliament. Maps of each member state of the European Community are included, with detailed results of the 1979 and 1984 elections, when voters from all the countries concerned went to the polls within a four-day period.

The text

Each country section contains a brief description of the features of the electoral system, with a list of the main political parties, the dates and result of the most recent election and the latest date by which the next election should be held.

For many of the longer established democracies, particularly those in Western Europe, tabulated results of earlier elections are given, as well as a chart showing the rise and fall of party strengths. Such data are unfortunately not readily available for most of the other countries, so they are provided in only 25 of the 39 country sections.

In addition, a pie chart has been drawn for each country showing the parties in Parliament at the last election and the present government.

An attempt has been made to present the information in as consistent a way as possible amongst the various countries. Thus, for example, the main political parties are always listed in a left–right rank order, wherever such a classification is valid. Parties which defy such ideological differentiation are normally placed at the end of the list. English translations of party names are used in most cases, though the abbreviations shown in brackets usually refer to the indigenous language.

Statistical note

Despite the attempt to present election results and other data in a consistent way, there are some inevitable differences. Where data are missing, the usual explanation is that they are not available, or were not available in time for inclusion in the book. Official figures have been obtained wherever possible, and not all governments provide information in the same form. Unofficial figures, from newspapers or otherwise, vary even more in their presentation, if not in their reliability.

The *electorate* figure normally refers to the number of citizens registered as eligible to vote.

Valid votes are those which are attributed to a party or candidate.

Invalid votes are votes not attributed because they are blank, unclear in their intention, or because they infringe some legal requirement.

The *turnout* figure is normally the proportion of the electorate which cast valid votes.

Where percentages do not add up to 100, it is because of rounding to the nearest decimal point.

Sources

A major debt should be acknowledged at the outset to *The International Almanac of Electoral History* by Thomas T. Mackie and Richard Rose (London, Macmillan, 1982, 2nd edn), which contains comprehensive historical, descriptive and tabulated data on 24 countries. Even when this has not been used as a source for election results, an attempt has been made to present the data in a manner as consistent as possible with Mackie and Rose, and it is hoped that this volume and *The International Almanac* will act as complementary sources in the future.

For the period since 1982, reference has been made to two political science journals, *The European Journal of Political Research* (Elsevier), to which Mackie and Rose contribute an annual report of election results in advanced industrial countries, and *Electoral Studies* (published by Butterworth).

General

Vernon Bogdanor and David Butler (eds), *Democracy and Elections: Electoral Systems and Their Political Consequences* (Cambridge University Press, 1983).

David Butler, Howard R. Penniman and Austin Ranney (eds), *Democracy at the Polls: A Comparative Study of Competitive National Elections* (Washington DC, American Enterprise Institute, 1981).

Chris Cook and John Paxton, *European Political Facts 1918–73* (London, Macmillan, 1975).

Alan J. Day and Henry W. Degenhardt, *Political Parties of the World* (London, Longman, 1984, 2nd edn).

George W. Delury (ed.), *World Encyclopaedia of Political Systems* (2 vols) (London, Longman, 1983).

Europa Year Book 1985: A World Survey (2 vols) (London, Europa Publications, 1985).

Geoffrey Hand, Jacques Georgel and Christoph Sasse (eds), *European Electoral Systems Handbook* (London, Butterworth, 1979).

George Thomas Kurian, *Encyclopaedia of the Third World* (3 vols) (London, Mansell Publishing Ltd, 1982).

Enid Lakeman, *How Democracies Vote: A Study of Majority and Proportional Electoral Systems* (London, Faber and Faber, 1970, 3rd edn).

Robert A. Newland, *Comparative Electoral Systems* (London, Arthur McDougall Fund, 1982).

Richard Rose (ed.), *Electoral Behavior: A Comparative Handbook* (New York, The Free Press, 1974).

John Sallnow and Anna John, *An Electoral Atlas of Europe 1968–1981* (London, Butterworth, 1982).

Jean Vanlaer, *200 Millions de Voix* (Brussels, Royal Belgian Geographical Society, 1984).

Inter-Parliamentary Union (prepared by Valentine Herman and Françoise Mendel), *Parliaments of the World: A Reference Compendium* (London, Macmillan, 1976).

Sources for the countries and for the European Parliament

Australia
Australian Electoral Commission, 'Commonwealth Electoral Procedures' (Canberra, 1985).
Australian Electoral Commission, 'Election Statistics 1984 – House of Representatives' (Canberra, 1985).
Australian Electoral Commission, 'Result of Count of First Preference Votes etc (House of Representatives, 1984 election)' (Canberra, 1985).
Australian Electoral Commission, Redistribution Proposals for New South Wales (2 vols), Victoria (2 vols), Queensland (2 vols), South Australia (2 vols), West Australia (2 vols), Tasmania and the Australian Capital Territory (Canberra, 1984).
Howard R. Penniman (ed.), *Australia at the Polls: National Elections of 1975* (Washington DC, American Enterprise Institute, 1977).

Information supplied by the Australian Embassy to the European Community in Brussels.

Austria
Federal Press Service, 'The Nationalrat Election in Austria, April 24 1983' (Vienna, 1983).
Federal Press Service, 'Le Système Politique en Autriche' (Vienna, 1982).
Peter Pulzer, 'The Austrian General Election of 1983', *Electoral Studies*, Vol. 2, No. 3, 1983, pages 275–80.

Information supplied by the Bundeskanzleramt, Vienna.

Bahamas
Department of Lands and Surveys, Map of Commonwealth of Bahamas (Nassau, 1978).
Nassau Guardian, June 15 1982.
The Tribune, June 16 1982.

Barbados
Information supplied by the Barbados Embassy in Brussels and the Barbados High Commission in London.

Belgium
Inbel, 'Les Elections Législatives en 1985' (Brussels, 1985).
Le Soir, October 15 1985.
Clair Ysebaert, *Memento Politique 1985* (Antwerp, Kluwer, 1985).

Information supplied by the Ministère de l'Intérieur.

Botswana
Information supplied by the Department of External Affairs.

Sources

Canada
Howard R. Penniman (ed.), *Canada at the Polls, 1979 and 1980* (Washington DC, American Enterprise Institute, 1981).

Information supplied by the Ministry of External Affairs and by the Canadian Embassy to the European Community in Brussels.

Colombia
Registraduria Nacional del Estado Civil, 'Estadisticas Electorales: Presidente de la Republica, 30 Mayo de 1982' (Bogota, undated).
Registraduria Nacional del Estado Civil, 'Estadisticas Electorales: Corporaciones Publicas Marzo 14 de 1982' (Bogota, undated).

Information supplied by the Colombian Embassy in Brussels.

Costa Rica
Tribunal Supremo de Elecciones, 'Computo de Votos y Declaratorias de Eleccion 1982 (San José, undated).

Information supplied by the Costa Rican Embassy in Brussels.

Cyprus
Department of Land and Surveys, Electoral Map of Cyprus (1971).

Information supplied by the Cyprus Embassy in Brussels.

Denmark
Karl H. Cerny (ed.), *Scandinavia at the Polls* (Washington DC, American Enterprise Institute, 1977).

Information supplied by the Folketingets Bureau, Copenhagen.

Dominican Republic
Gaceta Oficial, May 16 1983, 'Junta Central Electoral: Relacion General del resultado de las elecciones celebrados el dia 16 de mayo de 1982, etc.'

Information supplied by the Embassy of the Dominican Republic in Washington DC.

Ecuador
Information supplied by the Tribunal Supremo Electoral, Quito, and by the Ecuadorean Embassy in Brussels.

Fiji
Government of Fiji, 'The Parliament of Fiji' (Suva, 1983).
Government of Fiji, 'Fiji Today 1983–84' (Suva, 1983).
Fiji Royal Gazette, August 4 1982, 'Results of General Election to the House of Representatives'.
Department of Lands and Surveys, constituency boundary maps (1981).

Information supplied by the Fiji Embassy in Brussels.

Finland
Statistical Yearbook of Finland 1982 (Helsinki, 1983).

Information supplied by the Finnish Embassy in Brussels.

France
Le Figaro, March 18 1986.
Le Monde, March 18 and 19 1986.
Le Monde Dossiers et Documents, *L'Election Présidentielle 26 avril–10 mai 1981* (Paris, 1981).
Andrew F. Knapp, 'Orderly Retreat: Mitterrand Chooses PR', *Electoral Studies*, Vol. 4, No. 3, 1985, pages 255–60.

West Germany
Statistisches Bundesamt, Wiesbaden, 'Wahl zum 10-Deutschen Bundestag am 6 März 1983', Volume 3.
Statistisches Bundesamt, Wiesbaden, 'Endgültiges Ergebnis der Wahl zum 10-Deutschen Bundestag am 6 März 1983'.
Internationes, 'Procedures, Programmes, Profiles: The Federal Republic of Germany elects the German Bundestag on 5 October 1980' (Bonn, 1980).

Information supplied by the West German delegation to the European Community, Brussels.

Greece
Jean Catsiapis, *La Grèce: dixième membre des Communautés européennes* (Paris, La Documentation Française, 1980).
Howard R. Penniman (ed.), *Greece at the Polls: The National Elections of 1974 and 1977* (Washington DC, American Enterprise Institute, 1981).

Information supplied by the Greek Embassy in Brussels.

Iceland
Information supplied by the Icelandic Embassy in Brussels.

India
Myron Weiner, *India at the Polls 1980* (Washington DC, American Enterprise Institute, 1983).

Information supplied by the Election Commission of India, the Indian Embassy in Brussels and the Indian High Commission in London.

Republic of Ireland
Department of Foreign Affairs, 'Results of General Election 24 November 1982', *Bulletin*, No. 994, January 1983.
Nealon's Guide to the 24th Dail and Seanad (Dublin, 1983).

Italy
Howard R. Penniman (ed.), *Italy at the Polls, 1979* (Washington DC, American Enterprise Institute, 1981).

Information supplied by the Italian Delegation to the European Community, Brussels.

Jamaica
Information supplied by the Jamaican Embassy in Brussels and High Commission in London.

Japan
Michael K. Blaker, *Japan at the Polls: The House of Councillors Election 1974* (Washington DC, American Enterprise Institute, 1976).

The data for Japan were mostly collected in Tokyo by the former correspondent of *The Economist*, Bill Emmott, from a variety of official and non-official sources.

Luxembourg
George Als, *Le Luxembourg* (Paris, La Documentation Française, 1982).
Annuaire Statistique du Luxembourg (Luxembourg, Statec, annually).
Le Républicain Lorrain, June 18 and 19 1984.
Tageblatt, June 19 1984.

Information supplied by the Luxembourg Delegation to the European Community, Brussels.

Netherlands
Ministry of Foreign Affairs, 'The Kingdom of the Netherlands: Elections, The Party System' (The Hague, 1979).
Nederlandse Staatscourant, September 9 1982.
NRC Handelsblad, September 9 1982.

Information supplied by the Dutch Embassy in Brussels.

New Zealand
House of Representatives: 'The General Election 1984: Enrolment and Voting Statistics from the General Election held on 14 July 1984' (Wellington, 1984).
National Business Review, July 9 1984.
Howard R. Penniman (ed.), *New Zealand at the Polls: The General Election of 1978* (Washington DC, American Enterprise Institute, 1980).

Information supplied by the New Zealand Embassy in Brussels.

Norway
Karl H. Cerny (ed.), *Scandinavia at the Polls* (Washington DC, American Enterprise Institute, 1977).

Information supplied by the Norwegian Embassy in Brussels.

Papua New Guinea
The Times (Port Moresby), July 2 1982.
Papua New Guinea Foreign Affairs Review, 'PNG goes to the polls', Vol. 2, No. 2, 1982.

Information supplied by the Papua New Guinea Embassy in Brussels.

Portugal
Diario de Noticias, October 8 1985 and February 17 1986.

Information supplied by the Portuguese Embassy in Brussels.

Solomon Islands
Solomon Star, September 21 1984.

Information supplied by the Government of the Solomon Islands.

Spain
ABC, October 30 1982.
El Pais, October 30 1982.

Information supplied by the Spanish Mission to the European Community, Brussels.

Sweden
Joint publication of five leading Swedish political parties, *Swedish Election Guide 1985* (Stockholm, 1985).
Rikskatteverkerhet, 'The Electoral System in Sweden: a Summary' (Stockholm, 1983).
Swedish Institute, Fact Sheets on Sweden, 'The Swedish Political Parties', February 1985.
Karl H. Cerny (ed.), *Scandinavia at the Polls* (Washington DC, American Enterprise Institute, 1977).

Information supplied by the Swedish Mission to the European Community, Brussels.

Switzerland
Neue Züricher Zeitung, October 26 and 27 1983.
Norbert Hochreutener, 'Le Citoyen et L'Etat' (Berne, Banque Populaire Suisse, 1983).
Howard R. Penniman (ed.), *Switzerland at the Polls: The National Election of 1979* (Washington DC, American Enterprise Institute, 1983).

Information supplied by the Swiss Embassy in Brussels.

Trinidad and Tobago
Lands and Surveys Department, Trinidad, Map of Recommended Electoral Boundaries of Trinidad and Tobago (1981).

Information provided by the Government of Trinidad and Tobago.

United Kingdom
BBC/ITN Guide to the New Parliamentary Constituencies (Chichester, Parliamentary Research Services, 1983).
David Butler and Dennis Kavanagh, *The British General Election of 1983* (London, Macmillan, 1984).
Reports to Parliament of the Parliamentary Boundary Commissions for England, Scotland, Wales and Northern Ireland (London, 1982 and 1983).
The Times Guide to the House of Commons 1983 (London, 1983).
Robert Waller, *The Almanac of British Politics* (London, Croom Helm, 1983).

Sources

United States of America

Congressional Quarterly, *Almanac*, 1980, 1982, 1984.
Congressional Quarterly, *Weekly Report*, 1984 and 1985.

Information supplied by the Republican National Committee and the United States Information Service.

Venezuela

Consejo Supremo Electoral: 'Elecciones 1983' (Caracas, 1984).
Howard R. Penniman (ed.), *Venezuela at the Polls: The National Elections of 1978* (Washington DC, American Enterprise Institute 1980).

European Parliament

European Parliament, *Official Handbook of the European Parliament 1984* (Luxembourg, 1985).
European Parliament, *Forging Ahead: Thirty years of the European Parliament 1952–1982* (Luxembourg, 1982).
The Times Guide to the European Parliament June 1984 (London, 1984).

39 Countries at a glance

	A	B	C	D	E	F	G	H	I	J	K
Australia	M		2	M		148	148	Y 3	Y	18	Y
Austria	P	M 6	2	PR	HA	183	9	Y 4	N	18	Y
Bahamas	M		2	PL		43	43	Y 5	Y	18	N
Barbados	M		2	PL		27	27	Y 5	Y	18	N
Belgium	M		2	PR	HA	212	30	Y 4	N	18	Y
Botswana	pE		2	PL		34	34	Y 5	Y	21	N
Canada	M		2	PL		282	282	Y 5	Y	18	Y
Colombia	PE	PL 4	2	PR	LR	199	23	N 4	N	18	N
Costa Rica	PE	PL 4	1	PR	LR	57	7	N 4	N	18	N
Cyprus	PE	M 5	1	PR	LR	56[b]	6	N 5	Y	21	N
Denmark	M		1	PR	LR	179	19	Y 4	N	18	Y
Dominican Republic	PE	PL 4	2	PR	LR	120	27	N 4	N	18	N
Ecuador	PE	M 5	1	PR	LR	71	12	N 5	N	18	N
Fiji	M		2	PL		52	52	Y 5	Y	21	N
Finland	P	M[a] 6	1	PR	HA	200	15	Y 4	N	18	Y
France	P	M 7	2	PR	HA	577	104	Y 5	N	18	Y
West Germany	p		2	MX	HA	496[c]	248	Y 4	N	18	Y
Greece	p		1	PR	LR	300	56	Y 4	N	18	Y
Iceland	P	PL 4	1[d]	PR	HA	60	8	Y 4	Y	20	Y
India	p		2	PL		542	542	Y 5	Y	21	Y
Republic of Ireland	P	M 7	2	PR	STV	166	41	Y 5	Y	18	Y
Israel	p		1	PR	HA	120	1	Y 4	N	18	Y
Italy	p		2	PR	LR	630	32	Y 5	N	18	Y
Jamaica	M		2	PL		60	60	Y 5	Y	18	N
Japan	M		2	PL		511	130	Y 4	Y	20	Y
Luxembourg	M		1	PR	HA	64	4	Y 5	N	18	Y
Netherlands	M		2	PR	HA	150	1	Y 4	N	18	Y
New Zealand	M		1	PL		95	95	Y 3	Y	18	Y
Norway	M		1[d]	PR	HA	157	19	N 4	N	18	Y
Papua New Guinea	M		1	PL		109	109	Y 5	Y	18	N
Portugal	P	M 5	1	PR	HA	250	20	Y 4	N	18	Y
Solomon Islands	M		1	PL		38	38	Y 4	Y	18	N
Spain	M		2	PR	HA	350	52	Y 4	N	18	Y
Sweden	M		1	PR	LR	349	28	Y 3	N	18	Y
Switzerland	p		2	PR	HA	200	26	N 4	N	18	Y
Trinidad	p		2	PL		36	36	Y 5	Y	18	N
United Kingdom	M		2	PL		650	650	Y 5	Y	18	Y
United States of America	PE	PL 4	2	PL		435	435	N 4	Y	18	Y
Venezuela	PE	PL 5	2	PR	LR	200	23	N 5	N	18	N

Key

A Head of state: M = monarch; P = directly elected president; p = indirectly elected president; E = president has executive powers.

B How president is elected: M = majoritarian; PL = plurality; term of office in years.

C Number of chambers in parliament or congress.

D How parliament or lower chamber is elected: M = majoritarian; PL = plurality; PR = proportional representation; MX = mixed system.

E What type of PR is used: LR = largest remainder; HA = highest average; STV = single transferable vote.

F Number of elected members.

G Number of constituencies.

H Is dissolution possible? Y = Yes; N = No; term of office in years.

I Are by-elections possible? Y = Yes; N = No.

J Minimum voting age.

K Are a voting flow chart and tabulated data on past elections included? Y = Yes; N = No.

[a] In Finland an electoral college, which is elected by proportional representation, chooses the president by majoritarian vote.
[b] The number of Greek Cypriot MPs. Provision is made for the election of 24 Turkish Cypriot members, but these seats have remained vacant.
[c] The number of West German MPs is, on occasion, rather higher (see page 58).
[d] In Iceland and Norway the Parliament, elected as a single chamber, is divided into two for certain purposes.

Australia

A constitutional monarchy, the role of the British monarch being filled by a governor-general, appointed on the advice of the Australian government. Australia is a federal state, with a two-chamber federal parliament and separate parliaments (also two-chamber except for Queensland) for the six states. There are also two territories, the Northern Territory and the Capital Territory, each of which is represented in both houses of parliament.

The federal government is responsible to the lower house of the federal parliament, the House of Representatives, with 148 members. Its term of office is three years, with the possibility of early dissolution. The 76 members of the upper house, the Senate, serve for a six-year term. Normally half of them are elected at the same time as the House of Representatives. In certain circumstances the government may declare a 'double dissolution', under which the whole Senate is subject to re-election at the same time as the House.

Result of election of December 1 1984

Electorate: 9,866,266   Valid votes: 8,665,240 (87.8%)
Invalid votes: 626,125 (6.3%)

	Votes	%	Seats	%
Australian Labor Party	4,120,304	47.5	82	55.4
Liberal Party	2,979,007	34.4	45	30.4
National Party	921,150	10.6	21	14.2
Australian Democrats Party	472,246	5.4	0	0.0
Democratic Labor Party	49,121	0.6	0	0.0
Others	123,412	1.4	0	0.0
TOTAL	8,665,240		148	

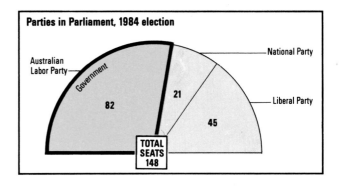

Parties in Parliament, 1984 election

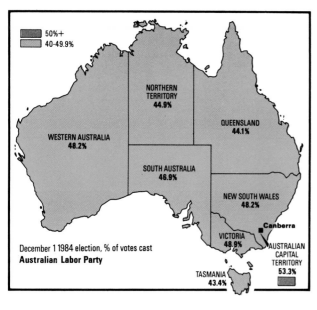

December 1 1984 election, % of votes cast
Australian Labor Party

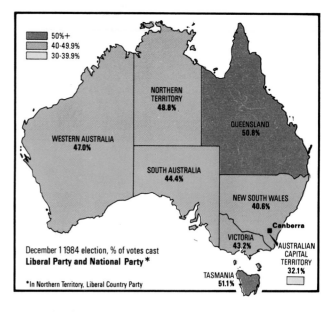

December 1 1984 election, % of votes cast
Liberal Party and National Party *

*In Northern Territory, Liberal Country Party

Election results: percentage votes and seats gained since 1946

Election year	1946		1949		1951		1954		1955		1958		1961		1963		1966	
Electorate	4,739,853		4,895,227		4,962,675		5,096,468		5,172,443		5,384,624		5,651,561		5,824,917		6,193,881	
Turnout %[a]	91.7		94.1		92.0		89.4		85.0		92.7		92.8		93.9		92.2	
	V[b] %	S[b]	V %	S	V %	S	V %	S	V %	S	V %	S	V %	S	V %	S	V %	S
Australian Labor Party	49.7	43	46.0	47	40.6	52	50.0	57	44.6	47	42.8	45	47.9	60	45.5	50	40.0	41
Australian Democrats Party																		
Democratic Labor Party									5.2	0	7.8	0	7.6	0	7.4	0	7.3	0
National Party	11.4	12	10.8	19	9.7	17	8.5	17	7.9	18	9.3	19	8.5	17	8.9	20	9.8	21
Liberal Party	32.3	17	39.4	55	47.6	52	38.6	47	39.7	57	37.2	58	33.6	45	37.1	52	40.1	61
Others	6.6	2	3.8	1	2.1	0	2.9	0	2.6	0	2.9	0	2.4	0	1.1	0	2.8	1
TOTAL SEATS		74		122		121		121		122		122		122		122		124

Election year	1969		1972		1974		1975		1977		1980		1983		1984	
Electorate	6,606,873		7,074,070		7,898,922		8,262,413		8,553,780		9,014,920		9,373,580		9,866,266	
Turnout %	92.6		93.3		93.6		93.6		92.6		92.1		92.7		87.8	
	V %	S	V %	S	V %	S	V %	S	V %	S	V %	S	V %	S	V %	S
Australian Labor Party	47.0	59	49.6	67	49.3	66	42.8	36	39.6	38	45.1	51	49.5	75	47.5	82
Australian Democrats Party									9.4	0	6.6	0	5.0	0	5.4	0
Democratic Labor Party	6.0	0	5.3	0	1.4	0	1.3	0	1.4	0	0.3	0	0.2	0	0.6	0
National Party	8.6	20	9.4	20	10.0	21	11.3	23	10.0	19	8.9	20	9.2	17	10.6	21
Liberal Party	34.8	46	32.0	38	35.0	40	41.8	68	38.1	67	37.4	54	34.4	33	34.4	45
Others	3.6	0	3.7	0	4.3	0	2.8	0	1.5	0	1.7	0	1.7	0	1.4	0
TOTAL SEATS		125		125		127		127		125		125		125		148

[a] The percentage figures relate to first preference votes.
[b] In these and all subsequent similar tables, V = Votes, S = Seats.

Voting is compulsory, and the minimum voting age is 18. Lower-house elections are held in single-member constituencies, on a majoritarian basis, using the alternative vote (see page 2). Senate elections are held on a state-wide basis, using the single transferable vote (see page 2) system of proportional representation. Casual vacancies in the House are filled by by-elections, in the Senate through indirect election.

Last election: December 1 1984.

Next election due: December 1987.

Main political parties

1. Australian Labor Party (ALP)
2. Australian Democrats Party (ADP)
3. Democratic Labor Party (ADLP), right-wing breakaway from Labor
4. National Party, formerly National Country Party
5. Liberal Party

The National Party and the Liberal Party are in permanent alliance.

Government

The present government, re-formed in December 1984, is a Labor government, with Robert Hawke as prime minister.

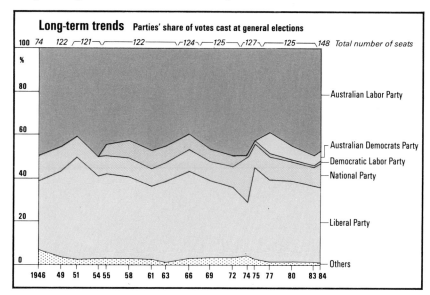

Long-term trends Parties' share of votes cast at general elections

Australia

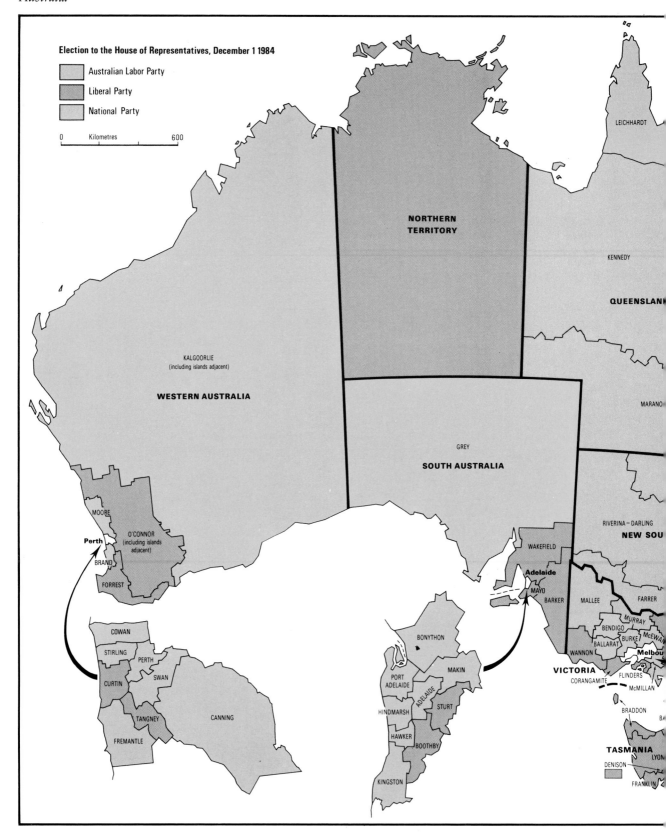

Election to the House of Representatives, December 1 1984

Australian Labor Party

Liberal Party

National Party

0   Kilometres   600

NORTHERN
TERRITORY

LEICHHARDT

KENNEDY

QUEENSLAND

KALGOORLIE
(including islands adjacent)

WESTERN AUSTRALIA

MARANO

GREY

SOUTH AUSTRALIA

MOORE

O'CONNOR
(including islands
adjacent)

Perth

BRAND

FORREST

RIVERINA—DARLING

NEW SOU

WAKEFIELD

Adelaide

MAYO

BARKER

MALLEE

FARRER

COWAN

BONYTHON

MURRAY

STIRLING

PERTH

SWAN

PORT
ADELAIDE

MAKIN

BENDIGO

BURKE

McEWA

BALLARAT

CURTIN

WANNON

Melbou

TANGNEY

CANNING

HINDMARSH

ADELAIDE

STURT

VICTORIA

FLINDERS

CORANGAMITE

McMILLAN

FREMANTLE

HAWKER

BOOTHBY

BRADDON

BA

KINGSTON

TASMANIA

LYON

DENISON

FRANKLIN

12

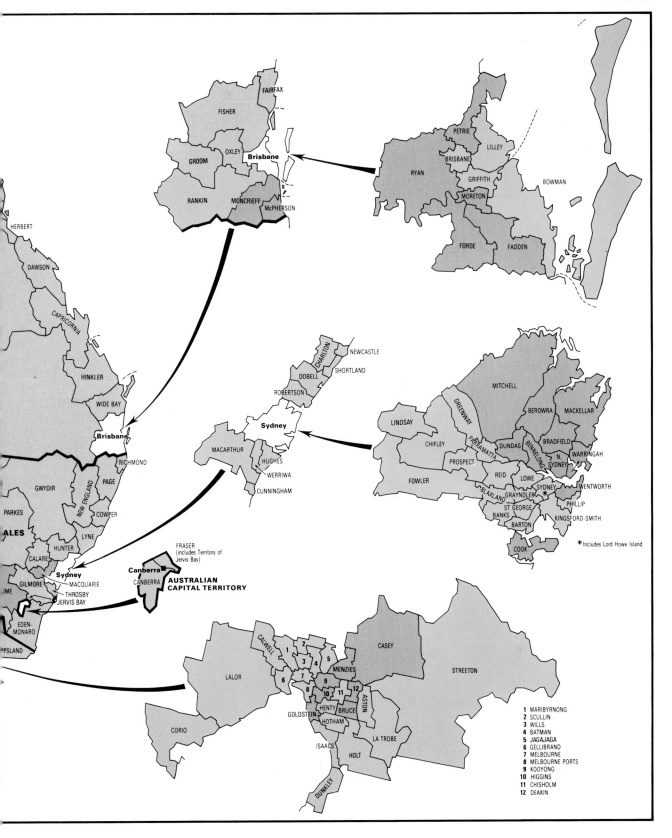

1 MARIBYRNONG
2 SCULLIN
3 WILLS
4 BATMAN
5 JAGAJAGA
6 GELLIBRAND
7 MELBOURNE
8 MELBOURNE PORTS
9 KOOYONG
10 HIGGINS
11 CHISHOLM
12 DEAKIN

Austria

A republic, with a directly elected president, without executive powers. The president is elected on a majoritarian basis (see page 2) for a six-year term, and may not serve for more than two terms. If no candidate polls more than 50 per cent of the votes there is a second, run-off ballot between the two leading contenders.

A federal state, with nine provinces (*Bundesländer*). The government is responsible to the lower house (*Nationalrat*) of a two-chamber federal parliament. This has had 183 members since 1970, when the number was increased from 165. The Nationalrat is elected for a four-year term, with the possibility of early dissolution. The indirectly elected upper house (*Bundesrat*), with 58 members, has very limited powers.

The minimum voting age is 18. Voting is compulsory in three provinces, but not in the remaining six, except in presidential elections. For the Nationalrat a system of proportional representation is employed, with a two-stage distribution of seats. The first stage, based on the Hare quota (see page 2) takes place on a provincial level. The second stage, using the D'Hondt system (see page 2), allocates any remaining seats on the basis of two national constituencies, one grouping the three eastern provinces, the other the remaining six. The voters choose between rival party lists with a limited right to vary the order of candidates. Casual vacancies are filled by co-opting the runner-up in the relevant party list. See also Stop Press, page 158.

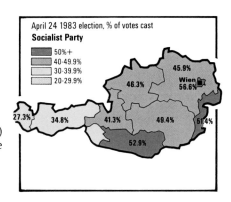

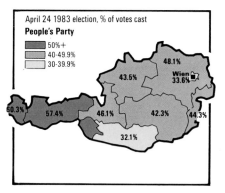

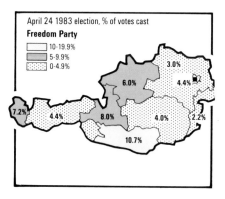

Result of Presidential election of May 18 1980

Electorate: 5,215,875   Valid votes: 4,430,889 (85.0%)
Invalid votes: 348,165 (6.7%)

	Votes	%
Rudolph Kirschläger (Socialist Party)	3,538,748	79.9
Willfried Gredler (Freedom Party)	751,400	16.9
Norbert Burger (National Democratic Party)	140,741	3.2

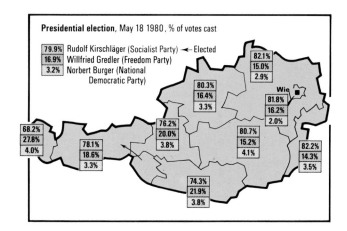

Last parliamentary election: April 24 1983.

Next election due: April 1987.

Last Presidential election: May 18 1980.

Next election: May 1986 (see Stop Press, page 158).

Main political parties

1. Communist Party (KPÖ)
2. Socialist Party (SPÖ)
3. People's Party (ÖVP)
4. Freedom Party (FPÖ)

Government

The present government, formed in May 1983, is a coalition between the Socialist Party and the Freedom Party. The chancellor is Fred Sinowatz (Socialist).

The president is Rudolf Kirschläger (Socialist), elected in 1974 and re-elected in 1980.

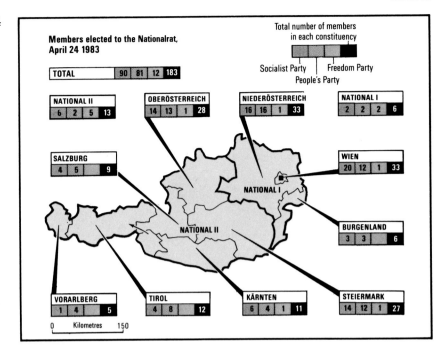

Members elected to the Nationalrat, April 24 1983

Result of election to the Nationalrat of April 24 1983

Electorate: 5,316,436   Valid votes: 4,853,417 (91.3%)
Invalid votes: 69,037 (1.3%)

	Votes	%	Seats	%
Socialist Party	2,312,529	47.7	90	49.2
People's Party	2,097,808	43.0	81	44.3
Freedom Party	241,789	5.0	12	6.6
Communist Party	31,912	0.7	0	0.0
Others	169,379	3.5	0	0.0
TOTAL	4,853,417		183	

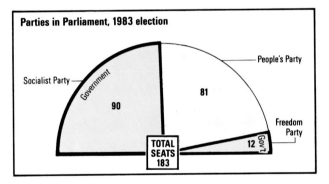

Parties in Parliament, 1983 election

Austria

Election results: percentage votes and seats gained since 1946

Election year	1945		1949		1953		1956		1959		1962		1966		1970		1971		1975		1979		1983	
Electorate	3,449,605		4,391,815		4,586,870		4,614,464		4,696,603		4,805,351		4,886,818		5,045,841		4,984,448		5,019,277		5,186,735		5,316,436	
Turnout %	93.3		95.5		94.2		94.3		92.9		92.7		92.7		90.9		91.4		91.9		91.2		91.3	
	V %	S	V %	S	V %	S	V %	S	V %	S	V %	S	V %	S	V %	S	V %	S	V %	S	V %	S	V %	S
Communist Party	5.4	4	5.1	5	5.3	4	4.4	3	3.3	0	3.0	0	0.4	0	1.0	0	1.4	0	1.2	0	1.0	0	0.7	0
Socialist Party	44.6	76	38.7	67	42.1	73	43.0	74	44.8	78	44.0	76	42.6	74	48.4	81	50.0	93	50.4	93	51.0	95	47.7	90
People's Party	49.8	85	44.0	77	41.3	74	46.0	82	44.2	79	45.4	81	48.3	85	44.7	79	43.1	80	42.9	80	41.9	77	43.0	81
Freedom Party			11.7	16	10.9	14	6.5	6	7.7	8	7.0	8	5.4	6	5.5	5	5.5	10	5.4	10	6.1	11	5.0	12
Others	0.2	0	0.5	0	0.4	0	0.1	0	0.1	0	0.5	0	3.3	0	0.4	0	0.0	0	0.0	0	0.0	0	3.5	0
TOTAL SEATS		165		165		165		165		165		165		165		165		183		183		183		183

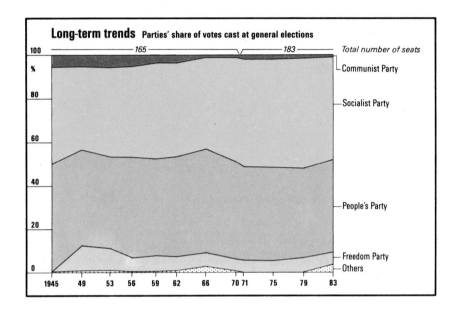

Long-term trends Parties' share of votes cast at general elections

Total number of seats
- Communist Party
- Socialist Party
- People's Party
- Freedom Party
- Others

Bahamas

A constitutional monarchy, which became independent in 1973. The role of the British monarch is now played by a governor-general appointed on the advice of the Bahamian government.

Result of election of June 10 1982

Electorate: 84,158   Votes cast: 75,604 (89.8%)

	Votes	%	Seats	%
Progressive Liberal Party	42,995	56.9	32	74.4
Free National Movement	31,092	41.1	11	25.6
Others	1,517	2.0	0	0.0
TOTAL	75,604		43	

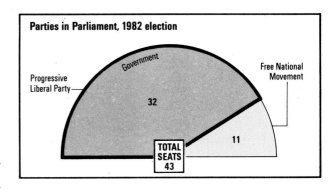

Parties in Parliament, 1982 election

Progressive Liberal Party — Government — 32

Free National Movement — 11

TOTAL SEATS 43

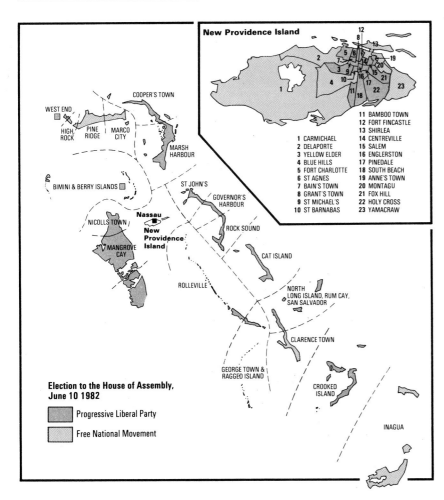

New Providence Island

1 CARMICHAEL
2 DELAPORTE
3 YELLOW ELDER
4 BLUE HILLS
5 FORT CHARLOTTE
6 ST AGNES
7 BAIN'S TOWN
8 GRANT'S TOWN
9 ST MICHAEL'S
10 ST BARNABAS
11 BAMBOO TOWN
12 FORT FINCASTLE
13 SHIRLEA
14 CENTREVILLE
15 SALEM
16 ENGLERSTON
17 PINEDALE
18 SOUTH BEACH
19 ANNE'S TOWN
20 MONTAGU
21 FOX HILL
22 HOLY CROSS
23 YAMACRAW

COOPER'S TOWN
WEST END
HIGH ROCK   PINE RIDGE   MARCO CITY
MARSH HARBOUR
BIMINI & BERRY ISLANDS
ST JOHN'S
GOVERNOR'S HARBOUR
NICOLLS TOWN
Nassau
New Providence Island
ROCK SOUND
MANGROVE CAY
CAT ISLAND
ROLLEVILLE
NORTH LONG ISLAND, RUM CAY, SAN SALVADOR
CLARENCE TOWN
GEORGE TOWN & RAGGED ISLAND
CROOKED ISLAND
INAGUA

Election to the House of Assembly, June 10 1982

Progressive Liberal Party

Free National Movement

The Parliament, to which the government is responsible, is divided into two houses: a wholly nominated Senate, of 16 members, and the elected House of Assembly, with 43. The prime minister is the leader of the majority party in the House.

The House serves a five-year term, but may be dissolved at any time on the advice of the prime minister. It is elected on a plurality basis (see page 2) in single-member constituencies. The minimum voting age is 18. Casual vacancies are filled by by-elections.

Last election: June 10 1982.

Next election due: June 1987.

Main political parties

1. Progressive Liberal Party (PLP)
2. Free National Movement (FNM)

Government

The present government, reconstituted after the June 1982 election, is formed by the Progressive Liberal Party. The prime minister is Lynden O. Pindling.

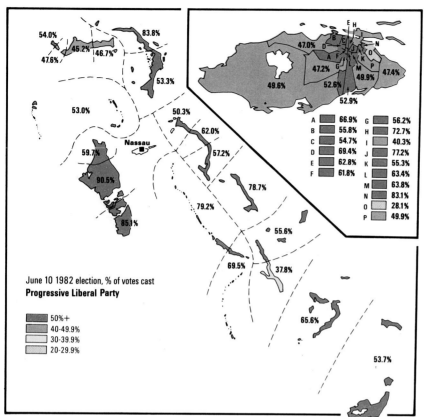

54.0%
45.2% 46.7%
83.8%
47.6%
53.3%

53.0%
50.3%
62.0%
59.7%
Nassau
57.2%
90.5%
78.7%
85.1%
79.2%
55.6%
69.5% 37.8%

65.6%

53.7%

47.0%
B C
D
H
E
N
A F
G
K O
49.6%
47.2%
52.6%
M P
49.9% 47.4%
52.9%

A	66.9%	G	56.2%
B	55.8%	H	72.7%
C	54.7%	I	40.3%
D	69.4%	J	77.2%
E	62.8%	K	55.3%
F	61.8%	L	63.4%
		M	63.8%
		N	83.1%
		O	28.1%
		P	49.9%

June 10 1982 election, % of votes cast
Progressive Liberal Party

- 50%+
- 40-49.9%
- 30-39.9%
- 20-29.9%

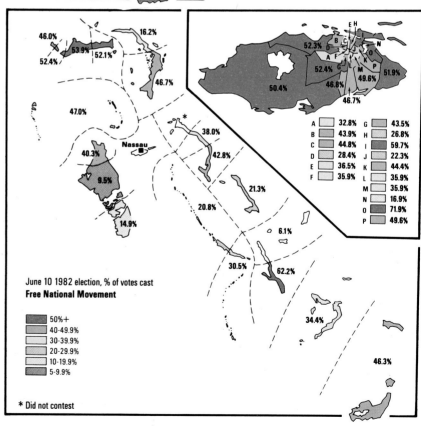

46.0%
53.9% 52.1%
16.2%
52.4%
46.7%

47.0%
*
38.0%
40.3%
Nassau
42.8%
9.5%
21.3%
14.9%
20.8%
6.1%
30.5%
62.2%

34.4%

46.3%

52.3%
B C
D
H
E
N
A F
C
L K O
52.4%
M P
46.8%
49.6% 51.9%
46.7%
50.4%

A	32.8%	G	43.5%
B	43.9%	H	26.8%
C	44.8%	I	59.7%
D	28.4%	J	22.3%
E	36.5%	K	44.4%
F	35.9%	L	35.9%
		M	35.9%
		N	16.9%
		O	71.9%
		P	49.6%

June 10 1982 election, % of votes cast
Free National Movement

- 50%+
- 40-49.9%
- 30-39.9%
- 20-29.9%
- 10-19.9%
- 5-9.9%

* Did not contest

18

Barbados

A constitutional monarchy, which became independent in 1966. The role of the British monarch is played by the governor-general, appointed on the advice of the Barbadian government.

The government is responsible to a two-chamber Parliament. The upper house, or Senate, is a purely nominated body, with 21 members. The lower house, or House of Assembly, has 27 members, elected on a plurality basis (see page 2) in single-member constituencies. The House serves a five-year term with the possibility of early dissolution. Casual vacancies are filled by by-elections. The minimum voting age is 18.

Further maps showing the relative strengths of the Barbados Labour Party and of the Democratic Labour Party, and illustrating the constituency results in the election of May 28 1986, are shown on page 158.

Last election: June 18 1981.

Next election due: June 1986 (see Stop Press, page 158).

Main political parties

1. Barbados Labour Party (BLP)
2. Democratic Labour Party (DLP)

Government

The present government, formed by the Barbados Labour Party, was reconstituted in March 1985, when H. Bernard St John became prime minister.

Result of election of June 18 1981

	Votes	%	Seats	%
Barbados Labour Party	61,844	52.5	17	63.0
Democratic Labour Party	55,214	46.9	10	37.0
Independents	739	0.6	0	0.0
TOTAL	117,797		27	

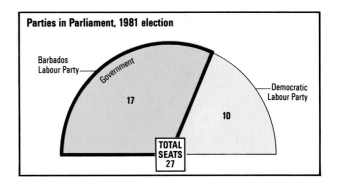

Parties in Parliament, 1981 election

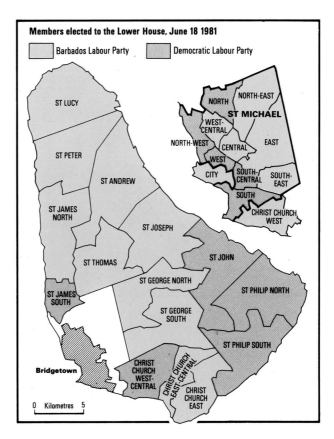

Members elected to the Lower House, June 18 1981

Belgium

A constitutional monarchy. Though traditionally a unitary state, a strong element of federalism was introduced into the constitution in 1981. The national government is responsible to a two-chamber parliament. The Chamber of Representatives has 212 members and the Senate 181 (only 106 of whom are directly elected). The Parliament serves a four-year term, with the possibility of early dissolution.

The minimum voting age is 18, and voting is compulsory. Both the Chamber and the elected part of the Senate are elected by a system of proportional representation, with a two-stage distribution of seats. The first stage, using the Hare quota (see page 2), is based on multi-member constituencies, or *arrondissements*. The second stage, using the D'Hondt system (page 2) allocates residual seats on a provincial basis. The voters choose between rival party lists, with a limited right to vary the order of candidates.

Last parliamentary election: October 13 1985.

Next election due: October 1989.

Main political parties

The three main parties have been divided on a linguistic basis since the 1970s, with distinct parties for French-speakers and Dutch-speakers, which do not normally compete with each other.
1. Communist Party (PCB/KPB)
2a. French-speaking Socialist Party (PS)
2b. Flemish Socialist Party (SP)
   Nos. 2a and 2b were divided in 1978.
3a. Social Christian Party (PSC)
3b. Christian Democratic Party (CVP)
   Nos. 3a and 3b were divided in 1971.
4a. French-speaking Liberal Party (PRL)

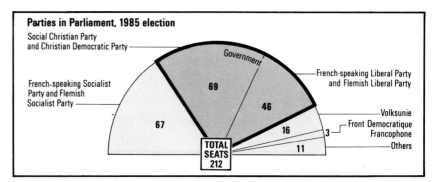

Parties in Parliament, 1985 election

Social Christian Party and Christian Democratic Party — 69 (Government)
French-speaking Liberal Party and Flemish Liberal Party — 46
French-speaking Socialist Party and Flemish Socialist Party — 67
Volksunie — 16
Front Democratique Francophone — 3
Others — 11
TOTAL SEATS 212

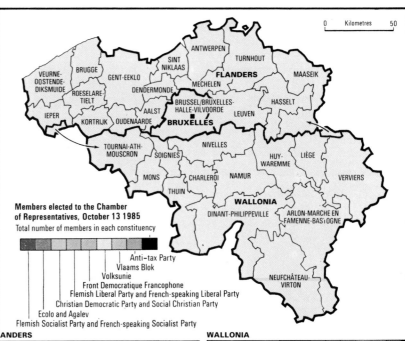

Members elected to the Chamber of Representatives, October 13 1985

Total number of members in each constituency

Legend:
Flemish Socialist Party and French-speaking Socialist Party
Ecolo and Agalev
Christian Democratic Party and Social Christian Party
Flemish Liberal Party and French-speaking Liberal Party
Front Democratique Francophone
Volksunie
Vlaams Blok
Anti-tax Party

FLANDERS

Constituency	Soc	Eco	CD	Lib	FDF	VU	VB	AT	Total
AALST	2		2	1		1			6
ANTWERPEN	5	2	6	3		3	1		20
BRUGGE	2		2	1					5
DENDERMONDE	1		2	1					4
GENT-EEKLO	3	1	4	3		1			12
HASSELT	3		3	1		1			8
IEPER			2						2
KORTRIJK	2		2	1		1			6
LEUVEN	3		3	2		1			9
MAASEIK	2		3	1		2			8
MECHELEN	1	1	3	1					6
OUDENAARDE			1	1					2
ROESELARE-TIELT	1		2	1		1			5
SINT NIKLAAS	1		2			1			4
TURNHOUT	2		4	1		1			8
VEURNE-OOSTENDE-DIKSMUIDE	1		2	1		1			5

BRUXELLES

Constituency	Soc	Eco	CD	Lib	FDF	VU	VB	AT	Total
BRUSSEL/BRUXELLES-HALLE-VILVOORDE	7	2	8	10	3	2		1	33

WALLONIA

Constituency	Soc	Eco	CD	Lib	FDF	VU	VB	AT	Total
ARLON-MARCHE EN FAMENNE-BASTOGNE	1		1	1					3
CHARLEROI	5	1	2	2					10
DINANT-PHILIPPEVILLE	1		1	1					3
HUY-WAREMME	2		1						3
LIÈGE	6	1	2	4					13
MONS	3		1	1					5
NAMUR	3		2	1					6
NEUFCHÂTEAU-VIRTON			1	1					2
NIVELLES	2		2	2					6
SOIGNIES	2	1	1						4
THUIN	2			1					3
TOURNAI-ATH-MOUSCRON	2		2	2					6
VERVIERS	2		2	1					5
TOTAL	**67**	**9**	**69**	**46**	**3**	**16**	**1**	**1**	**212**

4b. Flemish Liberal Party (PVV)
   Nos. 4a and 4b were divided in
1974.
5a. Ecolo, French-speaking ecologist
   party
5b. Agalev, Flemish ecologist party
6. Volksunie, moderate Flemish
   Nationalist party
7. Vlaams Blok, extreme Flemish
   Nationalist Party
8. Front Démocratique
   Francophone (FDF)
9. Rassemblement Wallon (RW)
   Nos. 8 and 9 are French linguistic
parties.
10. Union Démocratique pour le
   Respect du Travail (UDRT), anti-
   tax party

Government

The present government, formed in
November 1985, is a coalition
between the two Social Christian/
Christian Democratic parties and the
two Liberal parties. The prime
minister is Wilfried Martens
(Christian Democrat).

Result of election of October 13 1985

Electorate: 7,001,203   Valid votes: 6,064,260 (86.6%)
Invalid votes: 487,974 (7.0%)

	Votes	%	Seats	%
Christian Democratic Party/Social Christian Party	1,773,498	29.2	69	32.5
Socialist parties	1,716,688	28.3	67	31.6
Liberal parties	1,271,196	21.0	46	21.7
Volksunie	477,755	7.9	16	7.5
Ecology parties	379,241	6.2	9	4.2
Vlaams Blok	85,391	1.4	1	0.5
Front Démocratique Francophone	72,361	1.2	3	1.4
Communist Party	71,695	1.2	0	0.0
UDRT	69,707	1.1	1	0.5
Others	146,728	2.4	0	0.0
TOTAL	6,064,260		212	

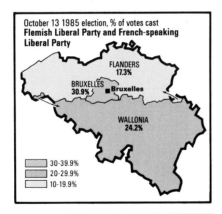
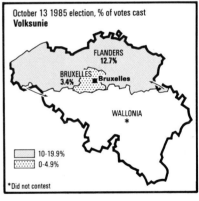
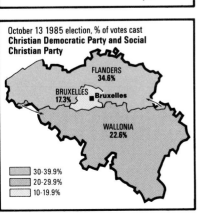

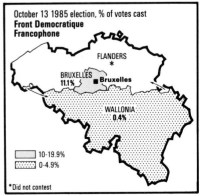

Election results: percentage votes and seats gained since 1946

Election year	1946		1949		1950		1954		1958		1961		1965	
Electorate	2,724,796		5,635,452		5,635,452		5,863,092		5,954,858		6,036,165		6,091,534	
Turnout %	86.8		89.3		87.7		88.0		89.0		87.2		85.1	
	V %	S	V %	S	V %	S	V %	S	V %	S	V %	S	V %	S
Communist Party	12.7	23	7.5	12	4.7	7	3.6	4	1.9	2	3.1	5	4.6	6
Socialist parties	31.6	69	29.7	66	34.5	77	37.3	86	35.8	84	36.7	84	28.2	64
Social Christians/Christian Democrats	42.5	92	43.5	105	47.7	108	41.1	95	46.5	104	41.5	96	34.4	77
Liberal parties	8.9	17	15.2	29	11.3	20	12.1	25	11.1	21	12.3	20	21.6	48
Flemish Nationalists			2.1	0			2.1	1	2.0	1	3.5	5	6.4	12
French linguistic parties													2.4	5
Others	4.3	1	1.9	0	1.8	0	3.6	1	2.8	0	2.9	2	2.4	0
TOTAL SEATS		202		212		212		212		212		212		212

Election year	1968		1971		1974		1977		1978		1981		1985	
Electorate	6,170,167		6,271,240		6,322,227		6,316,292		6,366,652		6,878,141		7,001,203	
Turnout %	83.9		84.2		83.2		88.3		87.0		86.1		86.6	
	V %	S	V %	S	V %	S	V %	S	V %	S	V %	S	V %	S
Communist Party	3.3	5	3.1	5	3.2	4	2.1	2	3.3	4	2.3	2	1.2	0
Socialist parties	28.0	59	27.2	61	26.7	59	26.5	61	25.4	58	25.1	61	28.3	67
Social Christians/Christian Democrats	31.8	69	30.1	67	32.3	72	36.0	80	36.1	82	26.4	61	29.2	69
Liberal parties	20.9	47	16.4	34	15.2	30	15.5	33	16.4	37	21.5	52	21.0	46
Flemish Nationalists	9.8	20	11.1	21	10.2	22	10.0	20	8.4	15	10.9	21	9.3	17
French linguistic parties	5.9	12	11.3	24	10.9	25	7.7	16	7.2	15	4.2	8	1.2	3
Others	0.3	0	0.9	0	1.5	0	2.2	0	3.3	1	9.6	7	9.6	10
TOTAL SEATS		212		212		212		212		212		212		212

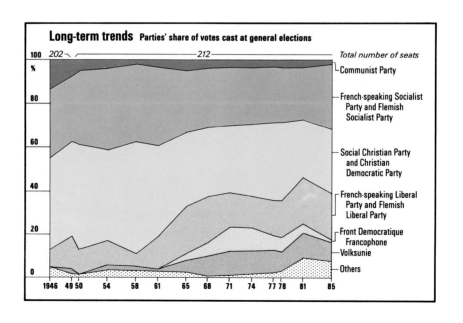

Long-term trends Parties' share of votes cast at general elections

Total number of seats
Communist Party
French-speaking Socialist Party and Flemish Socialist Party
Social Christian Party and Christian Democratic Party
French-speaking Liberal Party and Flemish Liberal Party
Front Democratique Francophone
Volksunie
Others

Botswana

A republic, which became independent in 1966, formerly the British Protectorate of Bechuanaland. The president, who has executive powers, is indirectly elected, though the choice is derived from the result of the parliamentary election. There is a two-chamber Parliament, but the 15-member House of Chiefs has only advisory powers.

The National Assembly has 40 members, 34 of whom are directly elected, on a plurality basis (see page 2) in single-member constituencies. Elections take place every five years, and each candidate is required to specify his choice for the presidency. Whichever presidential candidate has majority support in the Assembly after the election becomes president for the next five years (or until the next election if the assembly is dissolved prematurely by the president). The six non-elected members consist of the Attorney-General, the Speaker and four members nominated by the president and approved by the Assembly. The president is an ex-officio member. The minimum age for voting is 21. Casual vacancies are filled by by-elections.

Last election: September 8 1984.

Next election due: September 1989.

President
The president is Quett Masire (BDP) who was re-elected in September 1984.

Main political parties
1. Democratic Party (BDP)
2. National Front (BNF)
3. People's Party (BPP)

Result of election of September 8 1984

Turnout: 76%

	Votes	%	Seats	%
Democratic Party	154,863	68.0	29	85.3
National Front	46,550	20.4	4	11.8
People's Party	14,961	6.6	1	3.0
Others	11,482	5.0	0	0.0
TOTAL	227,856		34	

Election to the National Parliament, September 8 1984

- Democratic Party
- National Front
- People's Party

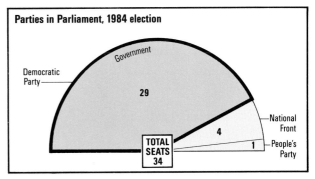

Parties in Parliament, 1984 election

Democratic Party — Government — 29
National Front — 4
People's Party — 1
TOTAL SEATS 34

Botswana

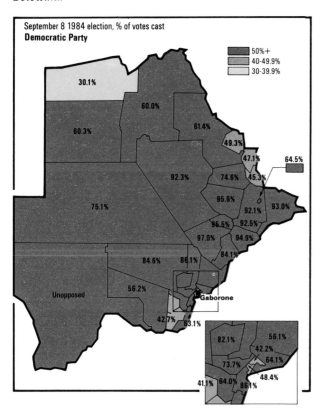

September 8 1984 election, % of votes cast
Democratic Party

	50%+
	40-49.9%
	30-39.9%

30.1%
60.0%
60.3%
61.4%
49.3%
47.1%
64.5%
92.3%
74.6%
45.3%
95.6%
O
93.0%
75.1%
92.1%
96.5%
92.5%
97.0%
94.9%
84.1%
84.6%
86.1%
Unopposed
56.2%
Gaborone
42.7%
63.1%

82.1%
56.1%
42.2%
73.7%
64.1%
48.4%
41.1%
64.0%
86.1%

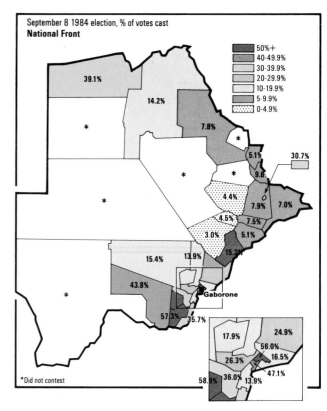

September 8 1984 election, % of votes cast
National Front

	50%+
	40-49.9%
	30-39.9%
	20-29.9%
	10-19.9%
	5-9.9%
	0-4.9%

39.1%
14.2%
*
7.8%
*
5.1%
9.8
*
*
4.4%
7.0%
*
7.9%
4.5%
7.5%
3.0%
5.1%
15.4%
13.9%
15.2%
43.8%
*
Gaborone
57.3%
35.7%

17.9%
24.9%
56.0%
26.3%
16.5%
47.1%
58.9%
36.0%
13.9%

*Did not contest

24

Canada

A constitutional monarchy, the role of the British monarch being played by a governor-general, appointed on the advice of the Canadian prime minister. Canada is a federal state, with ten provinces and two territories. The federal Parliament has two chambers, a wholly nominated Senate, with 104 members, and the House of Commons with 282.

The government is responsible to the House, which is elected for a five-year term, which may be prematurely terminated at the will of the government. Casual vacancies are filled by by-elections.

The House is elected on a plurality basis (see page 2) in single-member constituencies. The minimum voting age is 18.

Last election: September 4 1984.

Next election due: September 1989.

Main political parties

1. New Democratic Party (NDP), formerly Co-operative Commonwealth Federation (CCF)
2. Liberal Party
3. Social Credit Party
4. Progressive Conservative Party
5. Parti Québécois (PQ)
6. L'Union Nationale (UN)
   Nos. 5 and 6 are regional parties in Quebec.

Government

The present government, elected in September 1984, is formed by the Progressive Conservative Party. The prime minister is Brian Mulroney.

Result of election of September 4 1984

Electorate: 16,700,565   Valid votes: 12,545,973 (75.1%)

	Votes	%	Seats	%
Progressive Conservative Party	6,276,530	50.0	211	74.8
Liberal Party	3,516,173	28.0	40	14.2
New Democratic Party	2,358,676	18.8	30	10.6
Others	394,594	3.1	1	0.4
TOTAL	12,545,973		282	

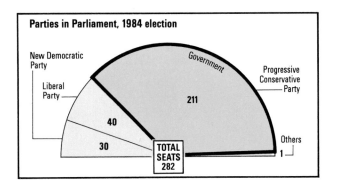

Parties in Parliament, 1984 election

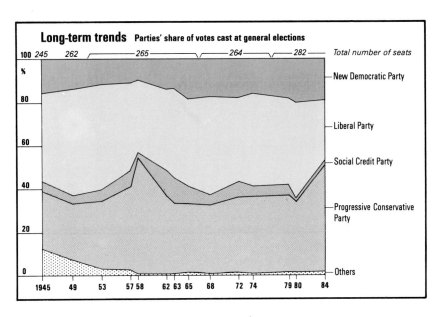

Long-term trends Parties' share of votes cast at general elections

Election results: percentage votes and seats gained since 1945

Election year	1945		1949		1953		1957		1958		1962		1963	
Electorate	6,952,445		7,893,629		8,401,691		8,902,125		9,131,200		9,700,325		9,910,757	
Turnout %	75.5		74.1		67.1		74.2		79.8		79.3		79.7	
	V %	S	V %	S	V %	S	V %	S	V %	S	V %	S	V %	S
CCF/NDP	15.6	28	13.4	13	11.3	23	10.7	25	9.5	8	13.5	9	13.1	17
Liberal Party	40.9	125	49.5	193	48.8	171	40.9	105	33.6	49	37.2	100	41.7	129
Social Credit parties	4.1	13	3.8	10	5.4	15	6.6	19	2.6	0	11.7	30	11.9	24
Progressive Conservative Party	27.4	67	29.7	41	31.0	51	38.9	112	53.6	208	37.3	116	32.8	95
Others	12.0	12	3.6	5	3.5	5	2.9	4	0.7	0	0.3	0	0.5	0
TOTAL SEATS		245		262		265		265		265		265		265

Election year	1965		1968		1972		1974		1979		1980		1984	
Electorate	10,274,904		10,860,888		12,909,179		13,620,553		15,234,997		15,890,416		16,700,565	
Turnout %	75.1		74.8		74.9		68.9		75.1		68.9		75.1	
	V %	S	V %	S	V %	S	V %	S	V %	S	V %	S	V %	S
CCF/NDP	17.9	21	17.0	22	17.7	31	15.4	16	17.9	26	19.8	32	18.8	30
Liberal Party	40.2	131	45.5	155	38.5	109	43.2	141	40.1	114	44.3	147	28.0	40
Social Credit parties	8.4	14	5.2	14	7.6	15	5.1	11	4.6	6	1.7	0	1.3	0
Progressive Conservative Party	32.4	97	31.4	72	35.0	107	35.4	95	35.9	136	32.5	103	50.0	211
Others	1.1	2	0.9	1	1.2	2	0.9	1	1.5	0	1.7	0	1.9	1
TOTAL SEATS		265		264		264		264		282		282		282

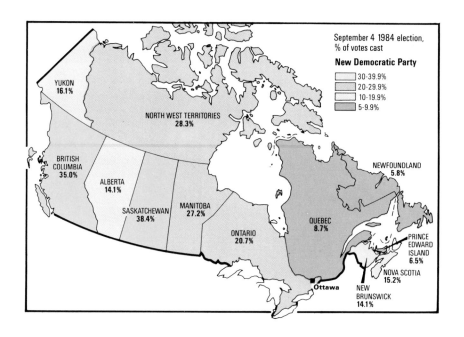

September 4 1984 election, % of votes cast

New Democratic Party
- 30-39.9%
- 20-29.9%
- 10-19.9%
- 5-9.9%

YUKON 16.1%
NORTH WEST TERRITORIES 28.3%
BRITISH COLUMBIA 35.0%
ALBERTA 14.1%
SASKATCHEWAN 38.4%
MANITOBA 27.2%
ONTARIO 20.7%
QUEBEC 8.7%
NEWFOUNDLAND 5.8%
PRINCE EDWARD ISLAND 6.5%
NOVA SCOTIA 15.2%
NEW BRUNSWICK 14.1%
Ottawa

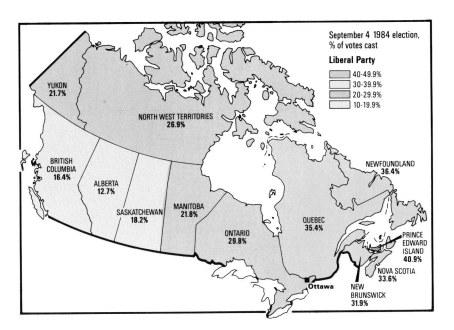

September 4 1984 election,
% of votes cast
Liberal Party

	40-49.9%
	30-39.9%
	20-29.9%
	10-19.9%

YUKON
21.7%

NORTH WEST TERRITORIES
26.9%

BRITISH COLUMBIA
16.4%

ALBERTA
12.7%

SASKATCHEWAN
18.2%

MANITOBA
21.8%

ONTARIO
29.8%

QUEBEC
35.4%

NEWFOUNDLAND
36.4%

PRINCE EDWARD ISLAND
40.9%

NOVA SCOTIA
33.6%

Ottawa

NEW BRUNSWICK
31.9%

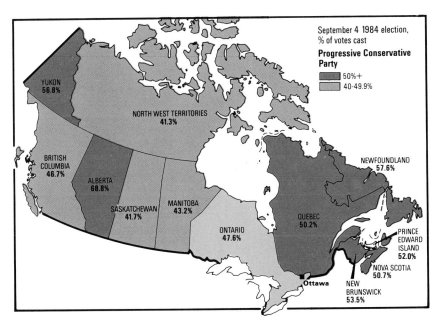

September 4 1984 election,
% of votes cast
Progressive Conservative Party

	50%+
	40-49.9%

YUKON
56.8%

NORTH WEST TERRITORIES
41.3%

BRITISH COLUMBIA
46.7%

ALBERTA
68.8%

SASKATCHEWAN
41.7%

MANITOBA
43.2%

ONTARIO
47.6%

QUEBEC
50.2%

NEWFOUNDLAND
57.6%

PRINCE EDWARD ISLAND
52.0%

NOVA SCOTIA
50.7%

Ottawa

NEW BRUNSWICK
53.5%

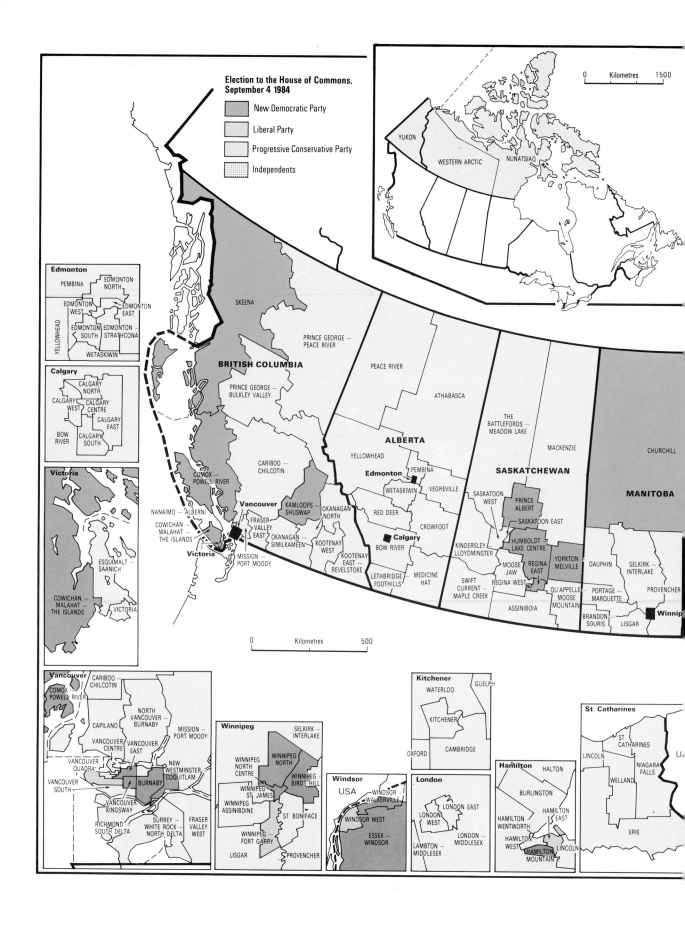

Election to the House of Commons, September 4 1984

- New Democratic Party
- Liberal Party
- Progressive Conservative Party
- Independents

Edmonton

PEMBINA | EDMONTON NORTH
EDMONTON WEST | EDMONTON EAST
YELLOWHEAD | EDMONTON SOUTH | EDMONTON STRATHCONA
WETASKIWIN

Calgary

CALGARY NORTH
CALGARY WEST | CALGARY CENTRE
CALGARY EAST
BOW RIVER | CALGARY SOUTH

Victoria

ESQUIMALT — SAANICH
COWICHAN — MALAHAT — THE ISLANDS
VICTORIA

Vancouver

COMOX — POWELL RIVER | CARIBOO — CHILCOTIN
CAPILANO | NORTH VANCOUVER BURNABY | MISSION — PORT MOODY
VANCOUVER CENTRE | VANCOUVER EAST
VANCOUVER QUADRA | NEW WESTMINSTER COQUITLAM
VANCOUVER SOUTH | BURNABY
VANCOUVER KINGSWAY
RICHMOND SOUTH DELTA | SURREY — WHITE ROCK — NORTH DELTA | FRASER VALLEY WEST

Winnipeg

SELKIRK — INTERLAKE
WINNIPEG NORTH CENTRE | WINNIPEG NORTH
WINNIPEG ST. JAMES | WINNIPEG BIRDS HILL
WINNIPEG ASSINIBOINE | ST. BONIFACE
WINNIPEG FORT GARRY
LISGAR | PROVENCHER

Kitchener

WATERLOO | GUELPH
KITCHENER
OXFORD | CAMBRIDGE

Windsor

USA | WINDSOR — WALKERVILLE
WINDSOR WEST
ESSEX — WINDSOR

London

LONDON EAST
LONDON WEST
LAMBTON — MIDDLESEX | LONDON — MIDDLESEX

Hamilton

HALTON
BURLINGTON
HAMILTON WENTWORTH | HAMILTON EAST
HAMILTON WEST
HAMILTON MOUNTAIN | LINCOLN

St Catharines

ST CATHARINES
LINCOLN | NIAGARA FALLS
WELLAND
ERIE

YUKON
WESTERN ARCTIC | NUNATSIAQ

0 Kilometres 1500

BRITISH COLUMBIA

SKEENA
PRINCE GEORGE — PEACE RIVER
PRINCE GEORGE — BULKLEY VALLEY
CARIBOO — CHILCOTIN
COMOX — POWELL RIVER
NANAIMO — ALBERNI
COWICHAN — MALAHAT — THE ISLANDS
Victoria
Vancouver
FRASER VALLEY EAST
KAMLOOPS SHUSWAP
OKANAGAN NORTH
OKANAGAN — SIMILKAMEEN
KOOTENAY WEST
KOOTENAY EAST — REVELSTOKE
MISSION — PORT MOODY

ALBERTA

PEACE RIVER
ATHABASCA
YELLOWHEAD
Edmonton | PEMBINA
WETASKIWIN | VEGREVILLE
RED DEER
Calgary | CROWFOOT
BOW RIVER
LETHBRIDGE — FOOTHILLS
MEDICINE HAT

SASKATCHEWAN

THE BATTLEFORDS — MEADOW LAKE
MACKENZIE
SASKATOON WEST
PRINCE ALBERT
SASKATOON EAST
HUMBOLDT LAKE CENTRE
KINDERSLEY LLOYDMINSTER
MOOSE JAW
YORKTON MELVILLE
REGINA EAST
REGINA WEST
SWIFT CURRENT — MAPLE CREEK
QU'APPELLE — MOOSE MOUNTAIN
ASSINIBOIA

MANITOBA

CHURCHILL
DAUPHIN
SELKIRK INTERLAKE
PROVENCHER
PORTAGE MARQUETTE
BRANDON SOURIS | LISGAR
Winnip[eg]

0 Kilometres 500

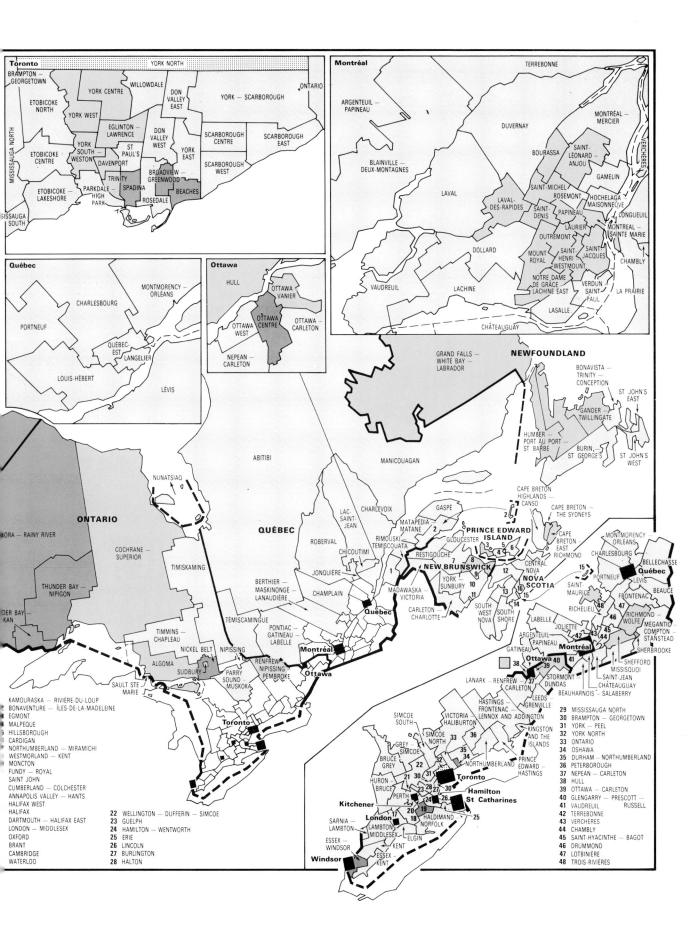

Colombia

A republic, with a directly elected president, with executive powers. Democratic rule was re-established in 1957 after the fall of the Rojas dictatorship. For the next 16 years, however, the Liberal and Conservative Parties agreed to share power, alternating the presidency and splitting evenly the congressional seats. Competitive democracy, consequently, dates only from 1974.

Elections are held every four years for the presidency and the two houses of Congress, the Senate, with 114 members, and the House of Representatives, with 199. The president is elected by plurality (see page 2), the Congress by proportional representation, using the Hare quota (see page 2). The president is limited to serving a single term but may run again after four years or at any subsequent time. There is no limitation on the re-election of congressmen. Both elections take place in the same year, but on different dates.

Voters choose between party lists in multi-member constituencies which coincide with the 23 provinces. Six sparsely populated jungle and mountain territories have no separate congressional representation, their votes being counted in with neighbouring provinces, but they are counted separately in presidential elections. There is no provision for varying the order of candidates, but it is often possible to choose between several rival lists put up by the same party. Each candidate has an alternate who takes over the seat in the event of a casual vacancy, thus avoiding the need for by-elections. The minimum voting age is 18.

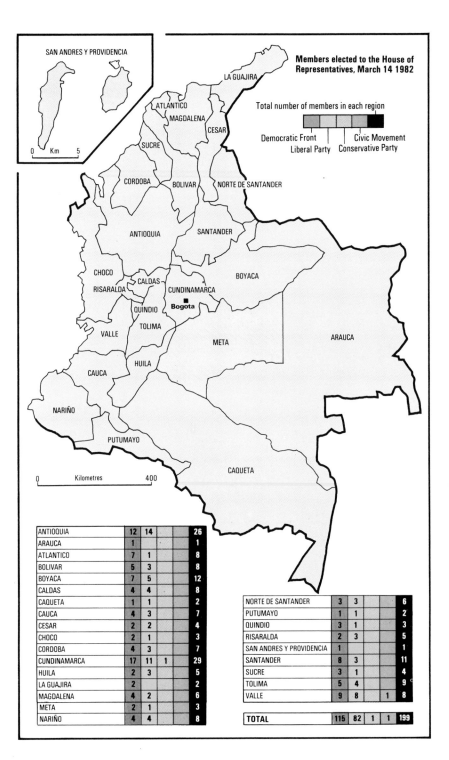

Members elected to the House of Representatives, March 14 1982

Total number of members in each region

Democratic Front | Liberal Party | Civic Movement | Conservative Party

Region					Total
ANTIOQUIA	12	14			26
ARAUCA	1				1
ATLANTICO	7	1			8
BOLIVAR	5	3			8
BOYACA	7	5			12
CALDAS	4	4			8
CAQUETA	1	1			2
CAUCA	4	3			7
CESAR	2	2			4
CHOCO	2	1			3
CORDOBA	4	3			7
CUNDINAMARCA	17	11	1		29
HUILA	2	3			5
LA GUAJIRA	2				2
MAGDALENA	4	2			6
META	2	1			3
NARIÑO	4	4			8
NORTE DE SANTANDER	3	3			6
PUTUMAYO	1	1			2
QUINDIO	3	1			3
RISARALDA	2	3			5
SAN ANDRES Y PROVIDENCIA	1				1
SANTANDER	8	3			11
SUCRE	3	1			4
TOLIMA	5	4			9
VALLE	9	8		1	8
TOTAL	**115**	**82**	**1**	**1**	**199**

SAN ANDRES Y PROVIDENCIA

0 Km 5

LA GUAJIRA
ATLANTICO
MAGDALENA
CESAR
SUCRE
CORDOBA
BOLIVAR
NORTE DE SANTANDER
ANTIOQUIA
SANTANDER
CHOCO
BOYACA
RISARALDA
CALDAS
CUNDINAMARCA
QUINDIO
Bogota
TOLIMA
VALLE
META
ARAUCA
HUILA
CAUCA
NARIÑO
PUTUMAYO
CAQUETA

0 Kilometres 400

Last Presidential election: May 30 1982.

Next election due: May 1986 (see Stop Press, page 159).

Last Congressional election: March 14 1982.

Next election due: March 1986 (see Stop Press, page 159).

Main political parties

1. Democratic Front, Communist-led alliance (now called Patriotic Union)
2. New Liberalism
3. Liberal Party
4. Conservative Party
5. Civic Movement

President

The president is Belisario Betancur, Conservative, elected in 1982.

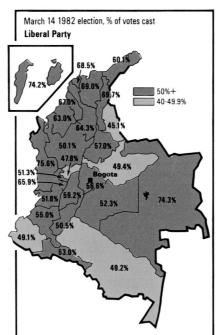

March 14 1982 election, % of votes cast
Liberal Party

50%+
40-49.9%

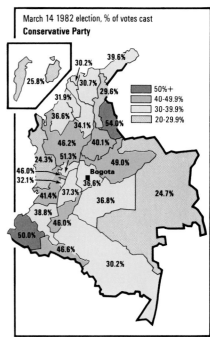

March 14 1982 election, % of votes cast
Conservative Party

50%+
40-49.9%
30-39.9%
20-29.9%

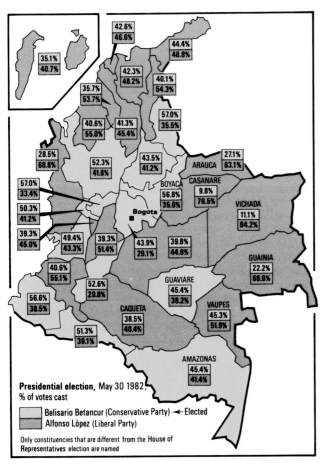

Presidential election, May 30 1982, % of votes cast

Belisario Betancur (Conservative Party) ← Elected
Alfonso López (Liberal Party)

Only constituencies that are different from the House of Representatives election are named

Result of Presidential election of May 30 1982

	Votes	%
Belisario Betancur (Conservative Party)	3,189,278	46.8
Alfonso Lopez (Liberal Party)	2,797,627	41.0
Luis Carlos Galan (New Liberalism)	745,738	11.0
Gerardo Molina (Democratic Front)	82,858	1.2
Florentino Porras	159	0.0
TOTAL valid votes	6,815,660	

Colombia

Result of election to House of Representatives of March 14 1982

Total valid votes: 5,573,469

	Votes	%	Seats	%
Liberal Party	3,141,426	56.4	115	57.8
Conservative Party	2,248,796	40.3	82	41.2
Democratic Front	83,838	1.5	1	0.5
Others (Civic Movement)	99,409	1.8	1	0.5
TOTAL	5,573,469		199	

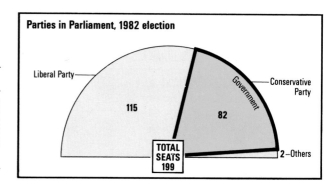

Costa Rica

A republic, with a directly elected president with executive powers. The president is elected, on a plurality basis (see page 2), for a four-year term.

The single-chamber Legislative Assembly is also elected, at the same time, for a four-year term. Its 57 members are elected, on the basis of proportional representation, using the Hare quota (see page 2) in seven multi-member constituencies. Voters choose between rival party lists, with no possibility of varying the rank order. Casual vacancies are filled by co-opting the next-in-line on the relevant party list. The minimum voting age is 18.

Last election: February 1986.

Next election due: February 1990.

Note

The most recent elections were held in February 1986, as this book was going to press (see Stop Press, page 158, for results). The maps shown in this section refer to the previous elections, also won by the PLN, in 1982.

Main political parties

1. United People's Coalition, Communist-led alliance
2. Popular Alliance, left-wing Socialist
3. National Liberation Party (PLN), Social Democrat
4. Social Christian Unity Party (United Coalition), Conservative-led alliance
5. National Movement, right-wing
6. Democratic Action for Alajuela, regional party

President

The president is Oscar Arias of the National Liberation Party. He was elected in February 1986.

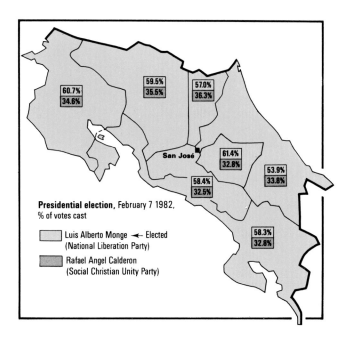

Presidential election, February 7 1982, % of votes cast

Luis Alberto Monge ← Elected (National Liberation Party)

Rafael Angel Calderon (Social Christian Unity Party)

Result of Presidential election of February 7 1982

Electorate: 1,261,127   Valid votes: 991,679 (78.6%)
Invalid votes: 25,103 (2.0%)

	Votes	%
Luis Alberto Monge (National Liberation Party)	568,374	58.8
Rafael Angel Calderon (Social Christian Unity Party)	325,187	33.6
Others	73,015	7.6
TOTAL	966,576	

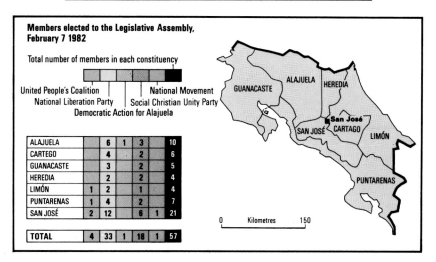

Members elected to the Legislative Assembly, February 7 1982

Total number of members in each constituency

United People's Coalition | National Movement
National Liberation Party | Social Christian Unity Party
Democratic Action for Alajuela

ALAJUELA		6	1	3		10
CARTEGO		4		2		6
GUANACASTE		3		2		5
HEREDIA		2		2		4
LIMÓN	1	2		1		4
PUNTARENAS	1	4		2		7
SAN JOSÉ	2	12		6	1	21
TOTAL	4	33	1	18	1	57

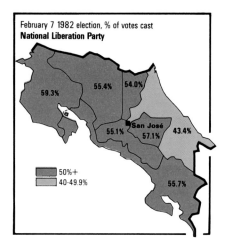

February 7 1982 election, % of votes cast
National Liberation Party

59.3% 55.4% 54.0%
55.1% San José 57.1% 43.4%
55.7%

50%+
40-49.9%

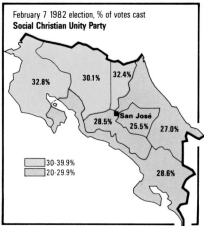

February 7 1982 election, % of votes cast
Social Christian Unity Party

32.8% 30.1% 32.4%
28.5% San José 25.5% 27.0%
28.6%

30-39.9%
20-29.9%

Result of election to Legislative Assembly of February 7 1982

Electorate: 1,261,127   Valid votes: 955,990 (75.8%)
Invalid votes: 35,576 (2.8%)

	Votes	%	Seats	%
National Liberation Party	527,231	55.2	33	57.9
Social Christian Unity Party (United Coalition)	277,998	29.1	18	31.5
United People's Coalition	61,465	6.4	4	7.0
National Movement	34,437	3.6	1	1.8
Democratic Action for Alajuela	12,486	1.3	1	1.8
Others	42,373	4.4	0	0.0
TOTAL	955,990		57	

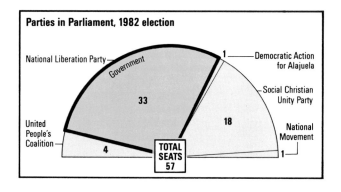

Parties in Parliament, 1982 election

National Liberation Party — Government — 33
1 — Democratic Action for Alajuela
Social Christian Unity Party — 18
National Movement — 1
United People's Coalition — 4
TOTAL SEATS 57

Cyprus

A republic, with a directly elected president with executive powers. The constitution of 1960 provided for the election of a Turkish Cypriot vice-president and for 15 of the 50 members of the single-chamber House of Representatives to be elected by Turks. But the Turks have boycotted the constitution since 1964, and since 1974 Turkish armed forces have occupied the northern third of the island, expelling all its Greek residents and drawing in the Turkish population from the rest of the island.

The Greek Cypriots have subsequently sought to govern the remaining two-thirds of the country under the terms of the original constitution, to the extent that this is possible. The president has been elected only by Greek Cypriot voters, and 35 House seats only have been filled. In 1985 the number of seats was increased to 80, 56 being filled by Greek Cypriots and 24 being left vacant for Turkish Cypriots. Representation has been retained for the constituencies occupied by the Turkish army (Famagusta and Kyrenia), the votes of the displaced Greek Cypriot residents being counted separately for that purpose.

The president is elected on a majoritarian basis (see page 2). If no candidate in the first ballot receives more than 50 per cent of the votes a second round is held between the two leading candidates.

The 56 members of the House are elected by a system of proportional representation, with a two-stage distribution of seats. The first stage uses the Hare quota (see page 2) in six multi-member constituencies. The second stage, from which all parties polling less than 10 per cent (or 8 per cent if they have already secured a seat in the first stage) are eliminated, also uses the Hare quota, with largest remainder (see page 2). Casual vacancies are filled by by-elections.

The minimum voting age is 21. The term of office of the House is five years, with no power of premature dissolution. The president, who is elected at a different time, also serves for five years, with no limit on the number of terms he may serve.

Last Presidential election: February 13 1983.

Next election due: February 1988.

Last parliamentary election: December 8 1985.

Next election due: December 1990.

Main political parties

1. Communist Party (AKEL)
2. Socialist Party (EDEK)
3. Democratic Party (DIKO), Centre Right
4. Democratic Rally (DISY), Conservative

President

The president is Spyros Kyprianou (DIKO), elected in 1978 and again in 1983.

Result of Presidential election of February 13 1983

Electorate: 327,184   Valid votes: 307,392 (93.9%)
Invalid votes: 3,511 (1.1%)

	Votes	%
Spyros Kyprianou	173,791	56.5
Glafkos Clerides	104,294	33.9
Vassos Lyssarides	29,307	9.5
TOTAL	307,392	

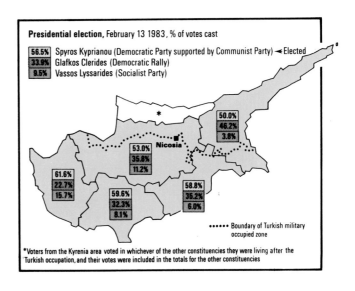

Presidential election, February 13 1983, % of votes cast

56.5% Spyros Kyprianou (Democratic Party supported by Communist Party) ◄ Elected
33.9% Glafkos Clerides (Democratic Rally)
9.5% Vassos Lyssarides (Socialist Party)

•••••• Boundary of Turkish military occupied zone

*Voters from the Kyrenia area voted in whichever of the other constituencies they were living after the Turkish occupation, and their votes were included in the totals for the other constituencies

Cyprus

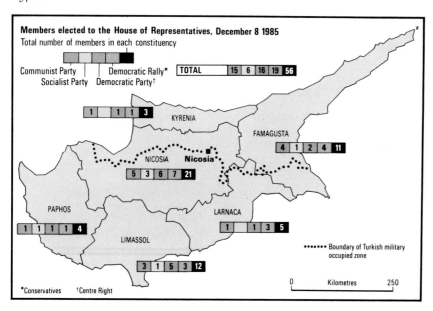

Members elected to the House of Representatives, December 8 1985
Total number of members in each constituency

Communist Party   Democratic Rally*
Socialist Party   Democratic Party†

TOTAL | 15 | 6 | 16 | 19 | 56

KYRENIA | 1 | 1 | 1 | 3
FAMAGUSTA | 4 | 1 | 2 | 4 | 11
NICOSIA Nicosia | 5 | 3 | 6 | 7 | 21
PAPHOS | 1 | 1 | 1 | 1 | 4
LARNACA | 1 | 1 | 3 | 5
LIMASSOL | 3 | 1 | 5 | 3 | 12

•••••• Boundary of Turkish military occupied zone

0   Kilometres   250

*Conservatives   †Centre Right

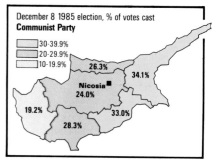

December 8 1985 election, % of votes cast
Communist Party
30-39.9%
20-29.9%
10-19.9%

26.3% / 34.1% / Nicosia 24.0% / 19.2% / 33.0% / 28.3%

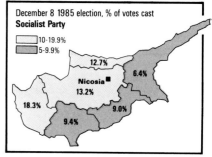

December 8 1985 election, % of votes cast
Socialist Party
10-19.9%
5-9.9%

12.7% / 6.4% / Nicosia 13.2% / 18.3% / 9.0% / 9.4%

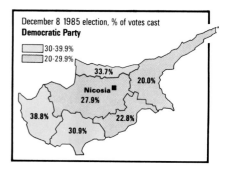

December 8 1985 election, % of votes cast
Democratic Party
30-39.9%
20-29.9%

33.7% / 20.0% / Nicosia 27.9% / 38.8% / 22.8% / 30.9%

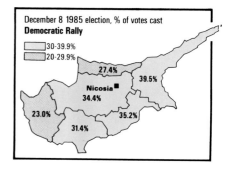

December 8 1985 election, % of votes cast
Democratic Rally
30-39.9%
20-29.9%

27.4% / 39.5% / Nicosia 34.4% / 23.0% / 35.2% / 31.4%

Result of parliamentary election of December 8 1985

Electorate: 346,454   Valid votes: 319,467 (92.2%)
Invalid votes: 8,354 (2.4%)

	Votes	%	Seats	%
Democratic Rally	107,223	33.6	19	33.9
Democratic Party	88,322	27.6	16	28.6
Communist Party	87,628	27.4	15	26.8
Socialist Party	35,371	11.1	6	10.7
Independents	923	0.3	0	0.0
TOTAL	319,467		56	

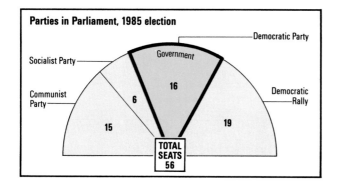

Parties in Parliament, 1985 election

Democratic Party — Government — 16
Socialist Party — 6
Communist Party — 15
Democratic Rally — 19
TOTAL SEATS 56

Denmark

A constitutional monarchy, with a single-chamber parliament, the *Folketing*. There are 179 members, of whom two are elected from the Faeroe islands and two from Greenland. Parliament's term is limited to four years, with the possibility of premature dissolution.

There are no by-elections: vacancies are filled by the next person on the list of a member who dies or resigns. The minimum voting age is 18.

Parliamentary elections for the 175 seats in metropolitan Denmark are held under the St Laguë (modified) system of proportional representation (see page 3). There are two levels of seat allocation: 135 seats are allocated in 17 multi-member constituencies; the remaining 40 seats are allocated nationally (to achieve a more proportional result) and are then reallocated to the constituencies. Voters choose between party lists with an opportunity to express a preference for a particular candidate. The elections in Greenland and the Faeroe Islands are held on the same basis: each consists of a two-seat constituency.

Last election: January 10 1984.

Next election due: January 1988.

Main political parties

1. Left Socialist Party
2. Socialist People's Party
3. Social Democratic Party
4. Radical Liberal Party
5. Christian People's Party
6. Centre Democratic Party
7. Liberal Party
8. Conservative Party
9. Progress Party (anti-tax)

Result of election of January 10 1984

Electorate: 3.8 million (approx.)   Valid votes: 3,386,733 (89.1%)

	Votes	%	Seats	%
Social Democratic Party	1,062,602	31.4	56	31.3
Conservative Party	788,225	23.3	42	23.5
Liberal Party	405,722	12.0	22	12.3
Socialist People's Party	387,115	11.4	21	11.7
Radical Liberal Party	184,634	5.5	10	5.6
Centre Democratic Party	154,557	4.6	8	4.5
Progress Party	120,631	3.6	6	3.4
Christian People's Party	91,633	2.7	5	2.8
Left Socialist Party	89,359	2.6	5	2.8
Others	102,255	3.0	0	0.0
TOTAL (Metropolitan Denmark)			175	

	Votes	%	Seats	%
Faeroe Islands				
Union Party (Liberal)	4,744	25.9	1	0.6
People's Party (Conservative)	4,605	25.1	1	0.6
Social Democratic Party	4,317	23.5	0	0.0
Others	4,679	25.5	0	0.0
TOTAL	18,345		2	
Greenland				
Atassut (Liberal)	9,308	43.5	1	0.6
Siumut (Social Democratic)	9,148	42.8	1	0.6
Others	2,939	13.7	0	0.0
TOTAL	21,395		2	

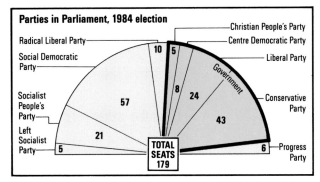

Parties in Parliament, 1984 election

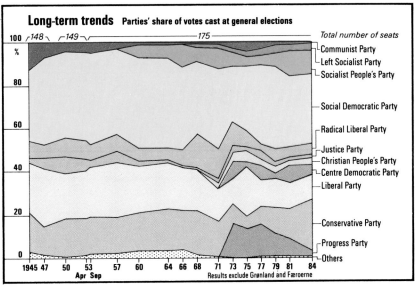

Long-term trends Parties' share of votes cast at general elections

Results exclude Grønland and Færoerne

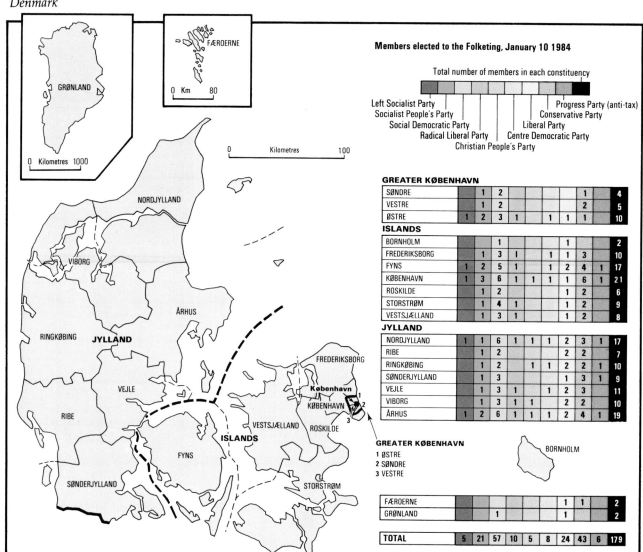

Members elected to the Folketing, January 10 1984

Total number of members in each constituency

Left Socialist Party · Socialist People's Party · Social Democratic Party · Radical Liberal Party · Christian People's Party · Centre Democratic Party · Liberal Party · Conservative Party · Progress Party (anti-tax)

	Left Socialist	Socialist People's	Social Democratic	Radical Liberal	Christian People's	Centre Democratic	Liberal	Conservative	Progress	Total
GREATER KØBENHAVN										
SØNDRE		1	2					1		4
VESTRE		1	2					2		5
ØSTRE	1	2	3	1			1	1	1	10
ISLANDS										
BORNHOLM		1						1		2
FREDERIKSBORG		1	3	1			1	1	3	10
FYNS	1	2	5	1			1	2	4	17
KØBENHAVN	1	3	6	1	1		1	1	6	21
ROSKILDE		1	2					1	2	6
STORSTRØM		1	4	1				1	2	9
VESTSJÆLLAND		1	3	1				1	2	8
JYLLAND										
NORDJYLLAND	1	1	6	1	1	1	2	3	1	17
RIBE		1	2				2	2		7
RINGKØBING		1	2		1	1	2	2	1	10
SØNDERJYLLAND		1	3				1	3	1	9
VEJLE		1	3	1		1	2	3		11
VIBORG		1	3	1	1		2	2		10
ÅRHUS	1	2	6	1	1	1	2	4	1	19
FÆROERNE							1	1		2
GRØNLAND		1					1			2
TOTAL	5	21	57	10	5	8	24	43	6	179

GREATER KØBENHAVN
1 ØSTRE
2 SØNDRE
3 VESTRE

Election results: percentage votes and seats gained since 1945[a]

Election year	1945		1947		1950		1953 (April)		1953 (Sept)		1957		1960		1964		1966	
Electorate	2,381,983		2,435,306		2,516,118		2,571,311		2,695,554		2,772,159		2,842,336		3,088,269		3,162,352	
Turnout %	86.0		85.6		81.6		80.5		80.4		83.3		85.6		85.2		88.4	
	V %	S	V %	S	V %	S	V %	S	V %	S	V %	S	V %	S	V %	S	V %	S
Communist Party	12.5	18	6.8	9	4.6	7	4.8	7	5.3	8	3.1	6	1.1	0	1.2	0	0.8	0
Left Socialist Party																		
Socialist People's Party													6.1	11	5.8	10	10.9	20
Social Democratic Party	32.8	48	40.0	57	39.6	59	40.4	61	41.3	74	39.4	70	42.1	76	41.9	76	38.3	69
Radical Liberal Party	8.2	11	6.9	10	8.2	12	8.6	13	7.8	14	7.8	14	5.8	11	5.3	10	7.3	13
Justice Party	1.9	3	4.5	6	8.2	12	5.6	9	3.5	6	5.3	9	2.2	0	1.3	0	0.7	0
Christian People's Party																		
Centre Democratic Party																		
Liberal Party	23.4	38	27.6	49	21.3	32	22.1	33	23.1	42	25.1	45	21.1	38	20.8	38	19.3	35
Conservative Party	18.2	26	12.4	17	17.8	27	17.3	26	16.8	30	16.6	30	17.9	32	20.1	36	18.7	34
Progress Party																		
Others	3.0	4	1.8	0	0.3	0	1.2	0	2.2	1	2.7	1	3.7	7		5		4
TOTAL SEATS		148		148		149		149		175		175		175		175		175

Election year	1968		1971		1973		1975		1977		1979		1981		1984	
Electorate	3,208,646		3,332,044		3,460,737		3,477,621		3,730,650		3,730,650		3,776,333		3,800,000[b]	
Turnout %	89.0		86.6		88.2		87.7		87.4		85.0		82.7		89.1	
	V %	S	V %	S	V %	S	V %	S	V %	S	V %	S	V %	S	V %	S
Communist Party	1.0	0	1.4	0	3.6	6	4.2	7	3.7	7	1.9	0	1.1	0	0.7	0
Left Socialist Party	2.0	4	1.6	0	1.5	0	2.1	4	2.7	5	3.7	6	2.7	5	2.7	5
Socialist People's Party	6.1	11	9.1	17	6.0	11	5.0	9	3.9	7	5.9	11	11.3	20	11.5	21
Social Democratic Party	34.1	62	37.3	70	25.6	46	29.9	53	37.0	65	38.3	68	32.9	59	31.6	56
Radical Liberal Party	15.0	27	14.3	27	11.2	20	7.1	13	3.6	6	5.4	10	5.1	9	5.5	10
Justice Party	0.7	0	1.7	0	2.9	5	1.8	0	3.3	6	2.6	5	1.5	0	1.5	0
Christian People's Party			2.0	0	4.0	7	5.3	9	3.4	6	2.6	5	2.3	4	2.7	5
Centre Democratic Party					7.8	13	2.2	3	6.4	10	3.2	6	8.3	15	4.6	8
Liberal Party	18.6	34	15.6	30	12.3	22	23.3	42	12.0	21	12.5	22	11.3	21	12.1	22
Conservative Party	20.4	37	16.7	31	9.2	16	5.5	10	8.5	15	12.5	22	14.5	26	23.4	42
Progress Party					15.9	28	13.6	24	14.6	26	11.0	20	8.9	16	3.6	6
Others		0		0		1		1		0	0.4	0	0.1	0	0.1	0
TOTAL SEATS		175		175		175		175		175		175		175		175

[a] Results exclude the Faeroe Islands and Greenland.
[b] Approximate.

Government

The present government, re-formed in January 1984, is a coalition of the Conservative, Liberal, Christian People's and Centre Democratic parties. The prime minister is Poul Schlüter (Conservative).

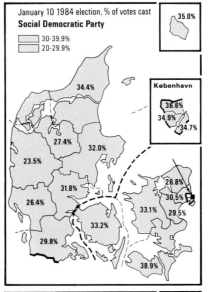

January 10 1984 election, % of votes cast
Social Democratic Party
- 30-39.9%
- 20-29.9%

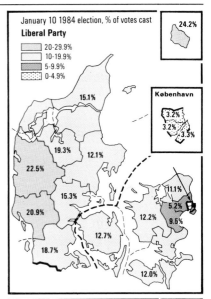

January 10 1984 election, % of votes cast
Liberal Party
- 20-29.9%
- 10-19.9%
- 5-9.9%
- 0-4.9%

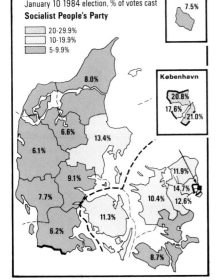

January 10 1984 election, % of votes cast
Socialist People's Party
- 20-29.9%
- 10-19.9%
- 5-9.9%

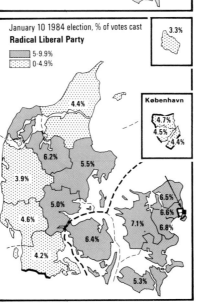

January 10 1984 election, % of votes cast
Radical Liberal Party
- 5-9.9%
- 0-4.9%

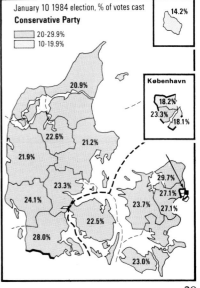

January 10 1984 election, % of votes cast
Conservative Party
- 20-29.9%
- 10-19.9%

Dominican Republic

The Dominican Republic has a directly elected president with executive powers. Democratic rule was re-established in 1966, following two military coups and foreign military intervention led by the United States of America.

Elections are held every four years for the presidency, the two houses of Congress and various local offices. Voters choose between rival party lists which incorporate candidates for each post. Ticket-splitting is not possible. The president and the 27 senators (one from each province) are elected by plurality (see page 2). The 120 members of the Chamber of Deputies are elected by proportional representation in 27 multi-member constituencies, using the Hare quota (see page 2) for distributing the seats. There are no by-elections: casual vacancies are filled by the next person on the party list. The minimum voting age is 18. Voting is, in theory, compulsory, though the law is not enforced in this respect.

Last elections: May 16 1982.

Next elections due: May 1986 (see Stop Press, page 159).

Main political parties

1. Liberation Party (PLD), left-wing nationalist
2. Revolutionary Party (PRD), Social Democrat
3. Social Christian Reformist Party (PR), Right of centre
4. Constitutional Action Party

President

The president is Salvador Jorge Blanco (PRD), elected in May 1982.

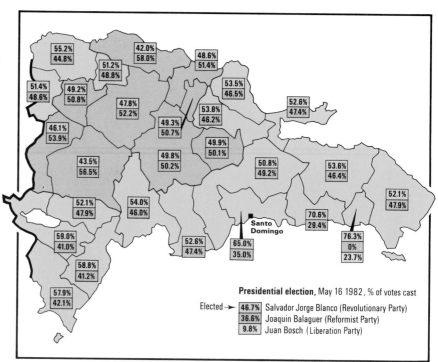

Presidential election, May 16 1982, % of votes cast

Elected → 46.7% Salvador Jorge Blanco (Revolutionary Party)
36.6% Joaquin Balaguer (Reformist Party)
9.8% Juan Bosch (Liberation Party)

Result of Presidential election of May 16 1982

	Votes	%
Salvador Jorge Blanco (PRD)	854,868	46.7
Joaquin Balaguer (PR)	669,176	36.6
Juan Bosch (PLD)	179,849	9.8
10 minor candidates – total	126,838	6.9
TOTAL	1,830,731	

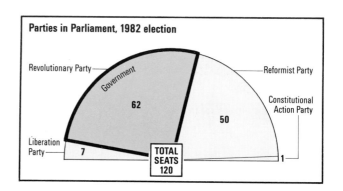

Parties in Parliament, 1982 election

Revolutionary Party — Government — 62
Reformist Party — 50
Liberation Party — 7
Constitutional Action Party — 1
TOTAL SEATS 120

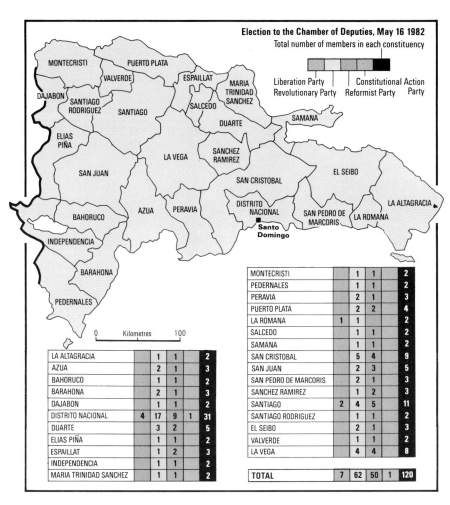

Election to the Chamber of Deputies, May 16 1982

Total number of members in each constituency

Liberation Party — Constitutional Action Party
Revolutionary Party — Reformist Party

MONTECRISTI		1	1		2
PEDERNALES		1	1		2
PERAVIA		2	1		3
PUERTO PLATA		2	2		4
LA ROMANA	1	1			2
SALCEDO		1	1		2
SAMANA		1	1		2
SAN CRISTOBAL		5	4		9
SAN JUAN		2	3		5
SAN PEDRO DE MACORIS		2	1		3
SANCHEZ RAMIREZ		1	2		3
SANTIAGO	2	4	5		11
SANTIAGO RODRIGUEZ		1	1		2
EL SEIBO		2	1		3
VALVERDE		1	1		2
LA VEGA		4	4		8

LA ALTAGRACIA		1	1		2
AZUA		2	1		3
BAHORUCO		1	1		2
BARAHONA		2	1		3
DAJABON		1	1		2
DISTRITO NACIONAL	4	17	9	1	31
DUARTE		3	2		5
ELIAS PIÑA		1	1		2
ESPAILLAT		1	2		3
INDEPENDENCIA		1	1		2
MARIA TRINIDAD SANCHEZ		1	1		2

TOTAL	7	62	50	1	120

Result of election to Chamber of Deputies of May 16 1982

The votes for the parties were as for the Presidential election, as the respective candidates were on the same party lists. The division of seats in the Chamber was as follows.

	Seats	%
Revolutionary Party (PRD)	62	51.7
Reformist Party (PR)	50	41.7
Liberation Party (PLD)	7	5.8
Constitutional Action Party	1	0.8
TOTAL	120	

Note

The report of the official Election Commission, from which the results of the 1982 elections are drawn, contains incomplete details of the votes of losing candidates. The percentages shown in the two analytical maps below, unlike the others in this book, are based on the combined vote of the two leading parties (who together polled 83.3 per cent) rather than on the total votes cast.

See also Stop Press, page 159.

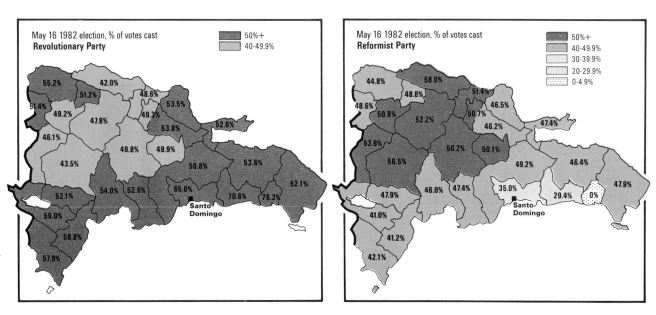

May 16 1982 election, % of votes cast
Revolutionary Party

50%+
40-49.9%

May 16 1982 election, % of votes cast
Reformist Party

50%+
40-49.9%
30-39.9%
20-29.9%
0-4.9%

Ecuador

A republic with a directly elected president, with executive powers. Democracy was restored in 1978, following a period of unconstitutional rule. The president is elected for a five-year term, and cannot be re-elected for a second term. He is chosen by a majoritarian vote (see page 2), a second ballot being held between the two leading candidates if no contender polls more than 50 per cent of the votes.

There is a single-chamber parliament, the Congress, or National Chamber of Representatives, also elected for a five-year term. It has 71 members, 12 of whom are elected nationally – at large – and the remaining 59 from 12 multi-member constituencies. In both cases proportional representation with the Hare quota (see page 2) is used. Voters choose beween party lists with no opportunity to vary the order of candidates. Members may not be elected for two consecutive terms. Casual vacancies are filled by co-opting the runner-up on the relevant party list. The minimum voting age is 18. Voting is compulsory for literate voters under 65.

Last Presidential election: First round, January 29 1984; second round, May 6 1984.

Last elections to Congress: January 29 1984.

Next elections due: January 1989 (partial election to Congress in June 1986). See Stop Press, page 159.

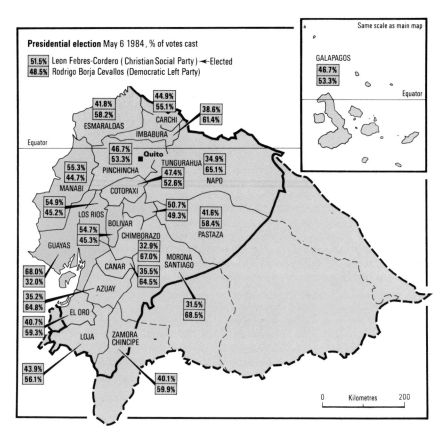

Presidential election May 6 1984 , % of votes cast

51.5% Leon Febres-Cordero (Christian Social Party) ◄Elected
48.5% Rodrigo Borja Cevallos (Democratic Left Party)

Percentage results of 1984 Presidential election

	%
1st round (January 29)	
Rodrigo Borja Cevallos (Democratic Left)	28.7
Leon Febres-Cordero (Christian Social)	27.2
7 other candidates – total	44.1
2nd round (May 6)	
Leon Febres-Cordero	51.5
Rodrigo Borja Cevallos	48.5

Main political parties

Altogether 17 parties contested the Congressional elections in 1984, many consisting of the personal followers of individual leaders. Thirteen obtained representation, and they are listed here in approximately left-right order.

1. Socialist Party
2. Popular Democratic Movement
3. Radical Alfarista Front
4. Democratic Left Party
5. Revolutionary Nationalist Party
6. Roldosista Party, supporters of late President Roldos
7. Left Broad Front
8. Christian Social Party
9. People's Democracy-Christian Democratic Union
10. Concentration of Popular Forces
11. Democratic Party
12. Liberal Party
13. Conservative Party

President

The president is Leon Febres-Cordero (Christian Social Party), who was elected in 1984.

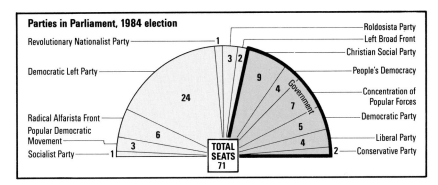

Parties in Parliament, 1984 election

Revolutionary Nationalist Party — 1
Democratic Left Party — 24
Radical Alfarista Front — 6
Popular Democratic Movement — 3
Socialist Party — 1

Roldosista Party
Left Broad Front
Christian Social Party — 3, 2
People's Democracy — 9
Concentration of Popular Forces — 4
Democratic Party — 7
Liberal Party — 5
Conservative Party — 4, 2

Government

TOTAL SEATS 71

Result of election to Congress of January 29 1984

	National Deputies		Prov. Deputies	
	% Votes	Seats	% Votes	Seats
Democratic Left Party	19.5	3	20.0	21
Christian Social Party	17.9	2	11.5	7
Concentration of Popular Forces	8.7	1	9.0	6
Radical Alfarista Front	8.0	1	8.8	5
Democratic Party	9.1	1	8.0	4
People's Democracy – CDU	6.6	1	7.3	3
Popular Democratic Movement	6.1	1	6.5	2
Roldosista Party	5.2	1	5.1	2
Left Broad Front	4.4	1	5.1	1
Liberal Party	3.7	0	6.0	4
Conservative Party	2.8	0	3.5	2
Revolutionary Nationalist Party	1.8	0	2.2	1
Socialist Party	1.6	0	1.8	1
Others	4.8	0	5.2	0
TOTAL		12		59

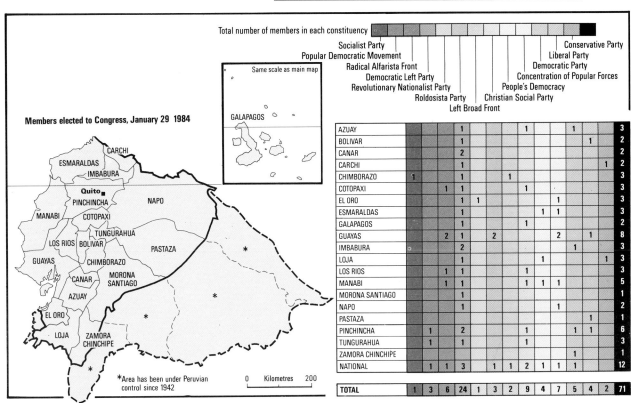

Members elected to Congress, January 29 1984

Total number of members in each constituency

Socialist Party
Popular Democratic Movement
Radical Alfarista Front
Democratic Left Party
Revolutionary Nationalist Party
Roldosista Party
Left Broad Front
Christian Social Party
People's Democracy
Concentration of Popular Forces
Democratic Party
Liberal Party
Conservative Party

GALAPAGOS — Same scale as main map

	SP	PDM	RAF	DLP	RNP	RP	LBF	CSP	PD	CPF	DP	LP	CP	Total
AZUAY				1				1			1			3
BOLIVAR				1								1		2
CANAR				2										2
CARCHI				1									1	2
CHIMBORAZO	1			1		1								3
COTOPAXI			1	1				1						3
EL ORO				1	1					1				3
ESMARALDAS				1					1	1				3
GALAPAGOS				1				1						2
GUAYAS		2		1		2				2		1		8
IMBABURA				2							1			3
LOJA				1				1					1	3
LOS RIOS			1	1					1					3
MANABI			1	1				1	1	1				5
MORONA SANTIAGO				1										1
NAPO				1							1			2
PASTAZA												1		1
PINCHINCHA		1		2				1				1	1	6
TUNGURAHUA		1		1				1						3
ZAMORA CHINCHIPE											1			1
NATIONAL	1	1	3		1	1	2	1	1	1				12
TOTAL	1	3	6	24	1	3	2	9	4	7	5	4	2	**71**

*Area has been under Peruvian control since 1942

0   Kilometres   200

Ecuador

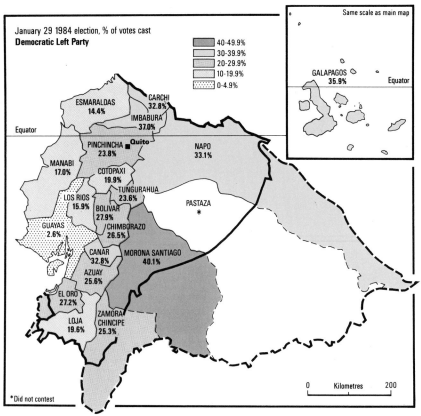

January 29 1984 election, % of votes cast
Democratic Left Party

40-49.9%
30-39.9%
20-29.9%
10-19.9%
0-4.9%

Same scale as main map

GALAPAGOS
35.9%
Equator

ESMARALDAS
14.4%
CARCHI
32.8%
IMBABURA
37.0%
Equator
PINCHINCHA
23.8%
■Quito
NAPO
33.1%
MANABI
17.0%
COTOPAXI
19.9%
TUNGURAHUA
23.6%
PASTAZA
*
LOS RIOS
15.9%
BOLIVAR
27.9%
CHIMBORAZO
26.5%
GUAYAS
2.6%
CANAR
32.8%
MORONA SANTIAGO
40.1%
AZUAY
25.6%
EL ORO
27.2%
ZAMORA
CHINCIPE
25.3%
LOJA
19.6%

0   Kilometres   200

*Did not contest

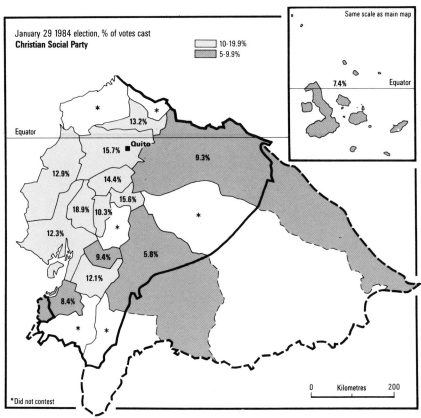

January 29 1984 election, % of votes cast
Christian Social Party

10-19.9%
5-9.9%

Same scale as main map

7.4%
Equator

*
*
13.2%
Equator
15.7% ■Quito
9.3%
12.9%
14.4%
18.9% **10.3%**
15.6%
*
12.3%
9.4% **5.8%**
*
12.1%
8.4%
*
*

0   Kilometres   200

*Did not contest

44

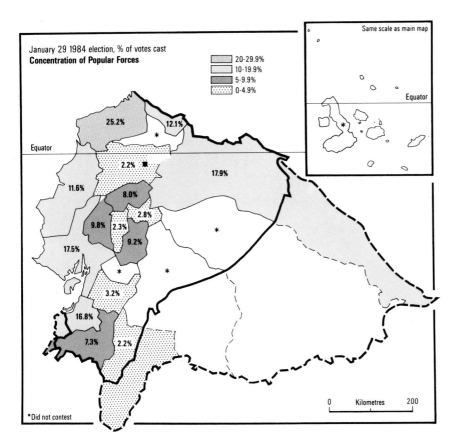

January 29 1984 election, % of votes cast
Concentration of Popular Forces

- 20-29.9%
- 10-19.9%
- 5-9.9%
- 0-4.9%

Same scale as main map

Equator

Equator

25.2%   12.1%

2.2%   17.9%

11.6%

8.0%

9.8% 2.3% 2.8%

17.5%   9.2%

3.2%

16.8%

7.3%   2.2%

*Did not contest

0   Kilometres   200

Fiji

A constitutional monarchy. The role of the British monarch is filled by a governor-general appointed on the advice of the Fiji government. The country became independent in 1970.

The government is responsible to a two-chamber parliament. The upper house, or Senate, of 22 members, is entirely nominated. The lower house, or House of Representatives, is elected on a plurality basis (see page 2) in single-member constituencies.

The population is almost equally divided between Fijians and Indians (who in fact are the larger group) and a much smaller number of people from other ethnic groups (mainly Europeans, part Europeans, Chinese and other South Sea Islanders). In order to maintain a balance between national interests and those of the different ethnic groups, there is an elaborate system of separate electoral rolls and different categories of (overlapping) constituencies. Each elector has four votes: one for the communal roll of his own ethnic group, the other three national roll votes for each of the three ethnic groups, including his own. There are, thus, six categories of constituency.

The House consists of 52 members: 22 Fijians, 22 Indians and 8 General (that is, other) representatives. For the Fijians and Indians 12 are elected by voters registered on the communal roll and 10 by voters on the national roll. For general elector representatives, three are elected by voters on the communal roll and five by voters on the national roll.

The term of office of the House is five years, with the possibility of early dissolution. Casual vacancies are filled by by-elections.

Last election: July 10–17 1982.

Next election due: July 1987.

Main political parties

1. Labour Party, a new party formed in 1985
2. National Federation Party
3. Western United Front
4. Alliance Party

Government

The present government, formed by the Alliance Party, was reconstituted after the 1982 election. The prime minister is Ratu Sir Kamisese Mara.

Result of election of July 10–17 1982

	% Votes	Seats	% Seats
Alliance Party	51.8	28	53.8
National Federation Party	41.2	22	42.3
Western United Front	3.9	2	3.8
Others	3.5	0	0.0
TOTAL		52	

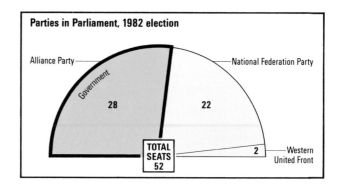

Parties in Parliament, 1982 election

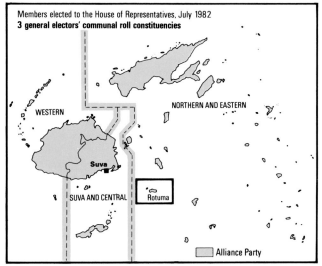

Members elected to the House of Representatives, July 1982
3 general electors' communal roll constituencies

WESTERN

NORTHERN AND EASTERN

Suva

SUVA AND CENTRAL

Rotuma

Alliance Party

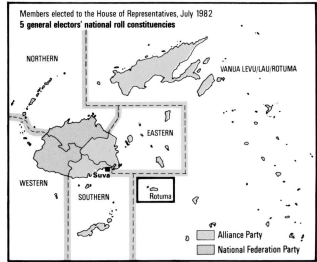

Members elected to the House of Representatives, July 1982
5 general electors' national roll constituencies

NORTHERN

VANUA LEVU/LAU/ROTUMA

EASTERN

Suva

WESTERN

SOUTHERN

Rotuma

Alliance Party
National Federation Party

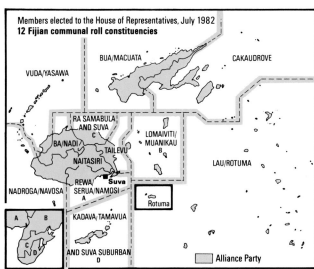

Members elected to the House of Representatives, July 1982
12 Fijian communal roll constituencies

BUA/MACUATA

CAKAUDROVE

VUDA/YASAWA

RA SAMABULA AND SUVA
C

BA/NADI

TAILEVU

LOMAIVITI/ MUANIKAU
B

NAITASIRI

LAU/ROTUMA

REWA/ SERUA/NAMOSI
A

Suva

NADROGA/NAVOSA

Rotuma

KADAVA/TAMAVUA

A B

C D

AND SUVA SUBURBAN
D

Alliance Party

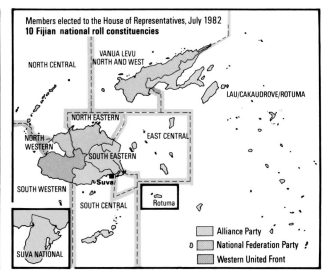

Members elected to the House of Representatives, July 1982
10 Fijian national roll constituencies

VANUA LEVU NORTH AND WEST

NORTH CENTRAL

LAU/CAKAUDROVE/ROTUMA

NORTH EASTERN

EAST CENTRAL

NORTH WESTERN

SOUTH EASTERN

SOUTH WESTERN

Suva

SOUTH CENTRAL

Rotuma

SUVA NATIONAL

Alliance Party
National Federation Party
Western United Front

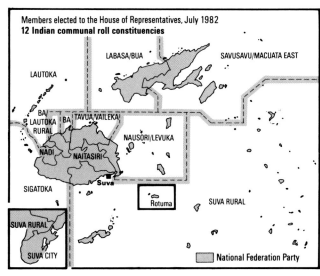

Members elected to the House of Representatives, July 1982
12 Indian communal roll constituencies

LABASA/BUA

SAVUSAVU/MACUATA EAST

LAUTOKA

BA/ LAUTOKA RURAL

BA

TAVUA/VAILEKA

NADI

NAUSORI/LEVUKA

NAITASIRI

Suva

SIGATOKA

Rotuma

SUVA RURAL

SUVA RURAL

SUVA CITY

National Federation Party

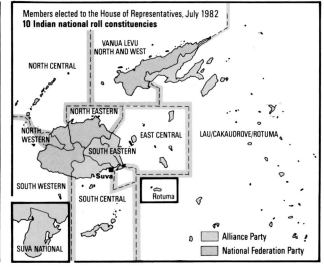

Members elected to the House of Representatives, July 1982
10 Indian national roll constituencies

VANUA LEVU NORTH AND WEST

NORTH CENTRAL

NORTH EASTERN

NORTH WESTERN

EAST CENTRAL

LAU/CAKAUDROVE/ROTUMA

SOUTH EASTERN

Suva

SOUTH WESTERN

SOUTH CENTRAL

Rotuma

SUVA NATIONAL

Alliance Party
National Federation Party

Finland

A republic, with a directly elected president without executive powers. The president is elected for a six-year term by an electoral college of 301, elected on the basis of proportional representation using the D'Hondt system (see page 2), by voters in the 15 provinces. The electors are chosen from party lists and are not legally bound to vote in the electoral college for their own party's nominee, though they normally do so, at least on the first ballot. Within the electoral college successive ballots are held, if necessary, until one nominee receives 151 votes.

The Finnish government is responsible to the *Eduskunta*, a one-chamber parliament of 200 members. It has a maximum term of four years, with the possibility of early dissolution. It is elected on a basis of proportional representation, using the D'Hondt system (see page 2) in multi-member constituencies, consisting of the 15 provinces. Voters cast their votes for individual candidates, within party lists, and thereby establish the rank order of candidates. Casual vacancies are filled by the runners-up within each party list. The minimum voting age is 18.

Last Presidential election: January 26 1982.

Next election due: January 1988.

Last parliamentary election: March 20–21 1983.

Next election due: January 1987.

Main political parties

1. People's Democratic League (SKDL), Communist Party
2. Social Democratic Party (SDP)
3. Centre Party (KP)
4. Liberal Party (LKP), merged with Centre Party in 1982
5. Swedish People's Party in Finland
6. Rural Party
7. National Coalition Party, Conservative
8. Christian League (SKL)
9. Constitutional Party
10. Greens

President
The president is Mauno Koivisto (Social Democratic Party), elected in January 1982.

Government

The present government, formed in May 1983, is a coalition of the Social Democratic, Centre, Swedish People's and Rural parties. The prime minister is Kalevi Sorsa (Social Democratic Party).

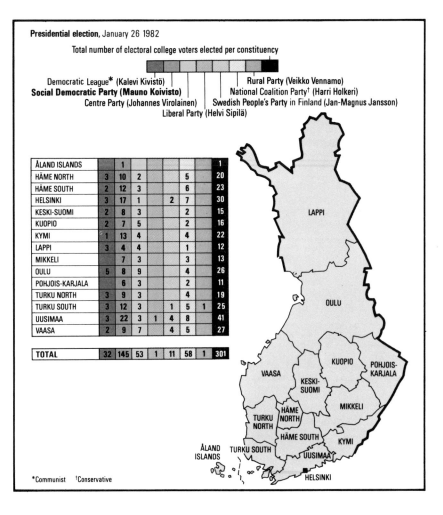

Presidential election, January 26 1982

Total number of electoral college voters elected per constituency

Democratic League* (Kalevi Kivistö) — **Social Democratic Party (Mauno Koivisto)** — Centre Party (Johannes Virolainen) — Liberal Party (Helvi Sipilä) — Rural Party (Veikko Vennamo) — National Coalition Party† (Harri Holkeri) — Swedish People's Party in Finland (Jan-Magnus Jansson)

	Democratic League*	Social Democratic Party	Centre Party	Liberal Party	Swedish People's Party	National Coalition Party†	Rural Party	TOTAL
ÅLAND ISLANDS		1						1
HÄME NORTH	3	10	2			5		20
HÄME SOUTH	2	12	3			6		23
HELSINKI	3	17	1		2	7		30
KESKI-SUOMI	2	8	3			2		15
KUOPIO	2	7	5			2		16
KYMI	1	13	4			4		22
LAPPI	3	4	4			1		12
MIKKELI		7	3			3		13
OULU	5	8	9			4		26
POHJOIS-KARJALA		6	3			2		11
TURKU NORTH	3	9	3			4		19
TURKU SOUTH	3	12	3		1	5	1	25
UUSIMAA	3	22	3	1	4	8		41
VAASA	2	9	7		4	5		27
TOTAL	32	145	53	1	11	58	1	301

*Communist †Conservative

48

Result of Presidential election of January 1982

	College seats	% Votes
Popular vote, January 17–18		
Social Democratic Party	145	43.3
National Coalition Party	58	18.7
Centre Party	53	16.9
People's Democratic League	32	11.0
Swedish People's Party	11	3.8
Rural Party	1	2.3
Liberal Party	1	1.8
Christian League	0	1.9
Others	0	0.3
Voting in Electoral College, January 26		
Mauno Koivisto (Social Democratic Party)		167
Harri Holkeri (National Coalition Party)		58
Johannes Virolainen (Centre Party)		53
Kalevi Kivistö (People's Democratic League)		11
Jan-Magnus Jansson (Swedish People's Party)		11
Helvi Sipilä (Liberal Party)		1

Result of parliamentary election of March 20–21 1983

Electorate: 3,951,932   Valid votes: 2,979,694 (75.4%)
Invalid votes: 13,276 (0.3%)

	Votes	%	Seats	%
Social Democratic Party	795,953	26.7	57	28.5
National Coalition Party	659,078	22.1	44	22.0
Centre Party[a]	525,207	17.6	38	19.0
People's Democratic League	416,270	13.8	27	13.5
Rural Party	288,711	9.7	17	8.5
Swedish People's Party	146,881	4.9	11	5.5
Christian League	90,410	3.0	3	1.5
Constitutional Party	11,104	0.4	1	0.5
Greens	42,045	1.4	2	1.0
Others	4,035	0.1	0	0.0
TOTAL	2,979,694		200	

[a] Including the Liberal Party.

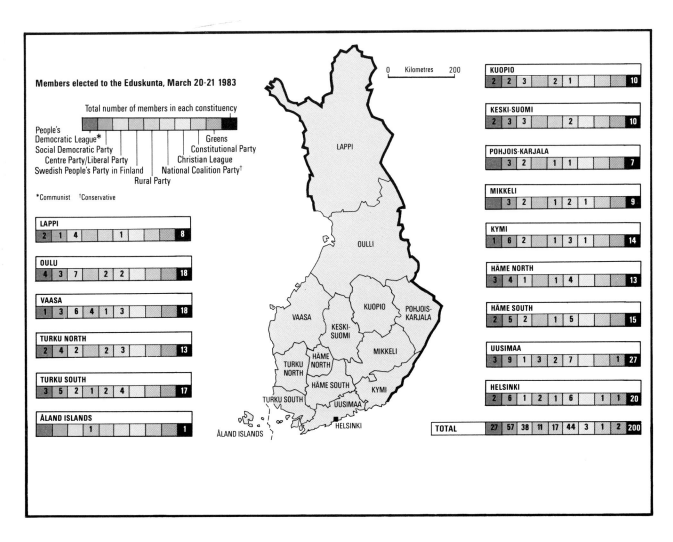

49

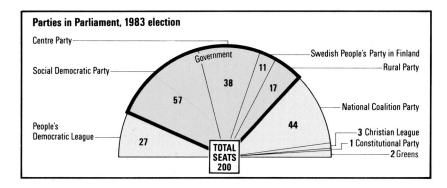

Parties in Parliament, 1983 election

Centre Party
Social Democratic Party
People's Democratic League

Government

Swedish People's Party in Finland
Rural Party
National Coalition Party

TOTAL SEATS 200

57 38 11 17 44 27

3 Christian League
1 Constitutional Party
2 Greens

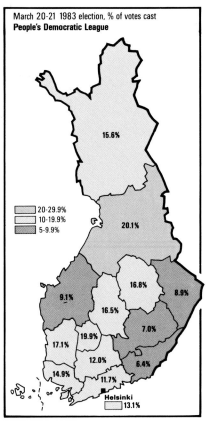

March 20-21 1983 election, % of votes cast
People's Democratic League

20-29.9%
10-19.9%
5-9.9%

15.6%
20.1%
16.8%
8.9%
9.1%
16.5%
7.0%
17.1%
19.9%
6.4%
12.0%
14.9%
11.7%
Helsinki 13.1%

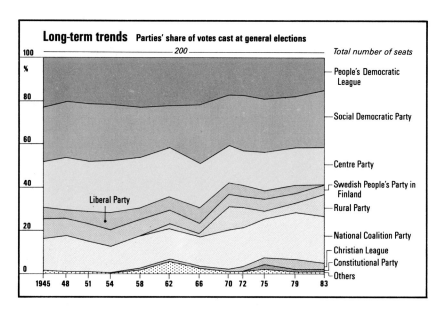

Long-term trends Parties' share of votes cast at general elections

Total number of seats
200

People's Democratic League
Social Democratic Party
Centre Party
Swedish People's Party in Finland
Rural Party
National Coalition Party
Christian League
Constitutional Party
Others

Liberal Party

1945 48 51 54 58 62 66 70 72 75 79 83

Election results: percentage votes and seats gained since 1945

Election year	1945		1948		1951		1954		1958		1962		1966		1970		1972		1975		1979		1983	
Electorate	2,284,249		2,420,287		2,448,239		2,526,969		2,606,258		2,714,838		2,800,461		3,094,359		3,178,169		3,741,460		3,858,553		3,951,932	
Turnout %	74.4		77.7		74.0		79.5		74.6		84.8		84.9		81.9		81.1		73.5		75.0		75.4	
	V %	S	V %	S	V %	S	V %	S	V %	S	V %	S	V %	S	V %	S	V %	S	V %	S	V %	S	V %	S
People's Democratic League	23.5	49	20.0	38	21.6	43	21.6	43	22.0	50	21.2	47	21.2	41	16.6	36	17.0	37	18.9	40	17.9	35	13.8	27
Social Democratic Party	25.1	50	26.3	54	26.5	53	26.2	54	23.2	48	19.5	38	27.2	55	23.4	51	25.8	55	24.9	54	23.9	52	26.7	57
Centre Party	21.4	49	24.2	56	23.3	51	24.1	53	23.1	48	23.0	53	21.2	49	17.1	37	16.4	35	17.6	39	17.3	36	17.6	38
Liberal Party	5.2	9	3.9	5	5.7	10	7.9	13	5.0	8	5.9	13	6.5	9	5.9	8	5.2	7	4.3	9	3.7	4		
Swedish People's Party	8.4	15	7.7	14	7.6	15	7.0	13	5.7	14	6.4	14	6.0	12	5.7	12	5.4	10	5.0	10	4.6	10	4.9	11
Rural Party											2.2	0	1.0	1	10.5	18	9.2	18	3.6	2	4.5	7	9.7	17
National Coalition Party	15.0	28	17.3	33	14.6	28	12.8	24	15.3	29	14.6	32	13.8	26	18.0	37	17.6	34	18.4	35	21.7	47	22.1	44
Christian League									0.2	0	0.8	0	0.4	0	1.1	1	2.5	4	3.3	9	4.8	9	3.0	3
Constitutional Party																			1.6	1	1.2	0	0.4	1
Others	1.5	0	0.8	0	0.9	0	0.4	0	2.5	3	5.6	3	2.6	7	1.6	0	1.0	0	2.5	1	0.5	0	1.4	2
TOTAL SEATS		200		200		200		200		200		200		200		200		200		200		200		200

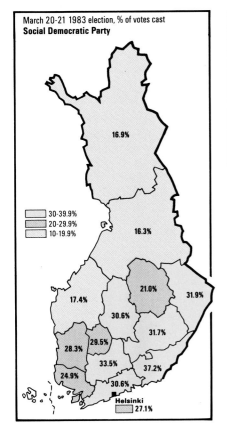

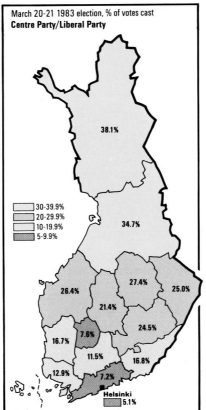

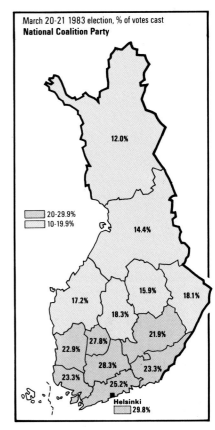

France

A republic, with a directly elected president who shares power with a government responsible to the Chamber of Deputies, the lower house of the two-chamber parliament. Under the Fifth Republic, established by General de Gaulle in 1958, the power of the president, who had hitherto always enjoyed majority support in the Chamber, had been pre-eminent. But in March 1986, in the legislative elections, a majority hostile to the president was elected. It is anticipated that henceforward the main power will be held by the prime minister and his government.

The president is elected for a seven-year term by a national ballot, held on a majoritarian basis (see page 2). If no candidate wins more than 50 per cent of the votes cast a second ballot is held between the two leading candidates.

The upper house, or Senate, with currently 318 members, is indirectly elected. The lower house, or Chamber of Deputies, with currently 577 members, is elected by proportional representation, using the D'Hondt system (see page 2). Voters choose between party lists in multi-member constituencies, with no possibility of varying the rank order of candidates. The constituencies are formed by the 95 *départements* of metropolitan France, as well as the nine overseas *départements* and *territoires*. Three of these use a majoritarian system, with two ballots. This was the system used for electing the entire Chamber in all the previous elections under the Fifth Republic before March 1986.

There is a 5 per cent threshold in each constituency before a party may qualify for seats. Casual vacancies, including when an elected member becomes a minister, are filled by promoting the next candidate on the relevant party list. The minimum voting age is 18. The Chamber is elected for a five-year term with the possibility of early dissolution.

Last Presidential election: April 26 and May 10 1981.

Next election due: April 1988.

Last parliamentary election: March 16 1986.

Next election due: March 1991.

Main political parties

1. Communist Party (PC)
2. Socialist Party (PS)
3. Movement of Left Radicals (MRG)
   Nos. 2 and 3 are allied.
4. Union for French Democracy (UDF), Centre Right
5. Rally for the Republic (RPF), Gaullist
   Nos. 4 and 5 are allied.
6. National Front (FN), extreme Right

President

The president, elected in May 1981, is François Mitterrand (Socialist Party).

Government

The present government, formed in March 1986, is a coalition of the Rally for the Republic (RPR) and the Union for French Democracy (UDF). The prime minister is Jacques Chirac (RPR).

See also Stop Press, page 159.

Result of Presidential election of April 26 and May 10 1981

	First round	%	Second round	%
Electorate	36,398,859		36,398,762	
Valid votes	29,038,117	79.8	30,350,568	83.4
Invalid votes	477,965	1.3	898,984	2.5
TOTAL VOTES	29,516,082	81.1	31,249,552	85.9
Candidates				
François Mitterrand (Socialist Party)	7,505,960	25.9	15,708,262	51.8
Valéry Giscard d'Estaing (Union for French Democracy)	8,222,432	28.3	14,642,306	48.2
Jacques Chirac (Gaullist RPR)	5,225,848	18.0		
Georges Marchais (Communist Party)	4,456,922	15.4		
Brice Lalonde (Ecologists)	1,126,254	3.9		
Arlette Laguiller (Trotskyist Lutte Ouvrière)	668,057	2.3		
Michel Crépeau (Left Radical)	642,847	2.2		
Michel Debré (Independent Gaullist)	481,821	1.7		
Marie-France Garaud (Independent Gaullist)	386,623	1.3		
Huguette Bouchardeau (Unified Socialist Party)	321,353	1.1		

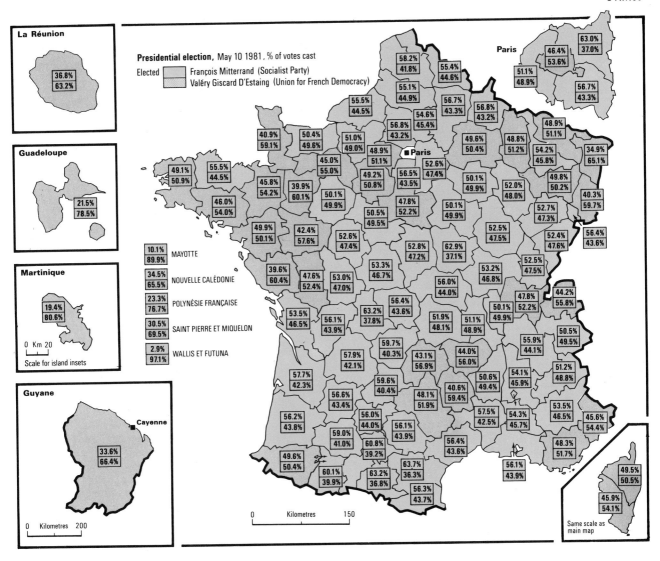

Presidential election, May 10 1981, % of votes cast

Elected
- François Mitterrand (Socialist Party)
- Valéry Giscard D'Estaing (Union for French Democracy)

La Réunion
36.8% / 63.2%

Guadeloupe
21.5% / 78.5%

Martinique
19.4% / 80.6%

0 Km 20
Scale for island insets

Guyane
Cayenne
33.6% / 66.4%

0 Kilometres 200

10.1% / 89.9%	MAYOTTE
34.5% / 65.5%	NOUVELLE CALÉDONIE
23.3% / 76.7%	POLYNÉSIE FRANÇAISE
30.5% / 69.5%	SAINT PIERRE ET MIQUELON
2.9% / 97.1%	WALLIS ET FUTUNA

Paris

0 Kilometres 150

Same scale as main map

Result of election to the Chamber of Deputies of March 16 1986

Electorate: 37,162,020 Valid votes: 27,825,239 (74.9%) Invalid votes: 1,269,690 (3.4%)

	Votes	%	Seats	%
Rally for the Republic	11,378,369	40.9	151	26.2
Union for French Democracy			127	22.0
Socialist Party and supporters	9,121,294	32.8	209	36.2
Movement of Left Radicals			7	1.2
Communist Party	2,724,381	9.8	35	6.1
National Front	2,705,497	9.7	34	5.9
Miscellaneous Right	1,055,253	3.8	14	2.4
Others	840,445	3.0	0	0.0
TOTAL	27,825,239		577	

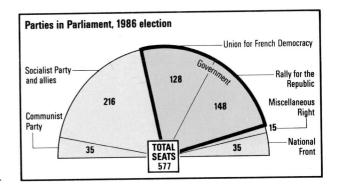

Parties in Parliament, 1986 election

- Union for French Democracy
- Socialist Party and allies — 216
- Communist Party — 35
- Government — 128
- 148
- Rally for the Republic
- Miscellaneous Right — 15
- National Front — 35
- TOTAL SEATS 577

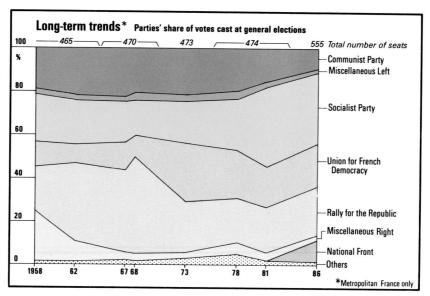

Long-term trends* Parties' share of votes cast at general elections

| | 465 | 470 | 473 | 474 | 555 *Total number of seats* |

- Communist Party
- Miscellaneous Left
- Socialist Party
- Union for French Democracy
- Rally for the Republic
- Miscellaneous Right
- National Front
- Others

100 %

80

60

40

20

0

1958   62   67 68   73   78 81   86

*Metropolitan France only

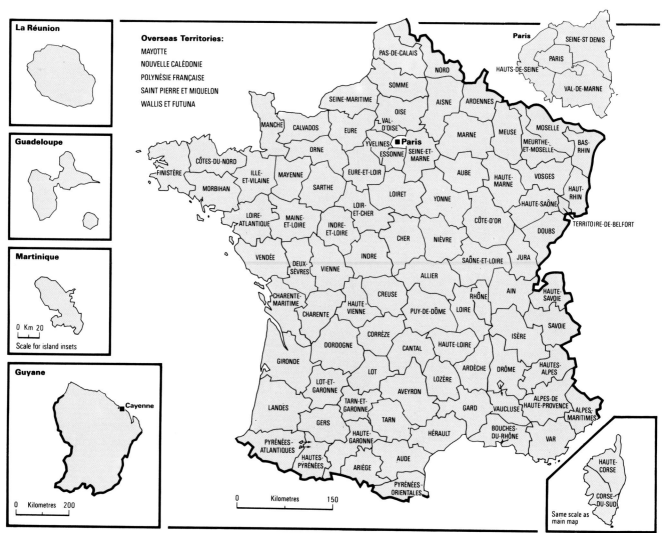

La Réunion

Guadeloupe

Martinique

0 Km 20

Scale for island insets

Guyane

Cayenne

0   Kilometres   200

Overseas Territories:

MAYOTTE
NOUVELLE CALÉDONIE
POLYNÉSIE FRANÇAISE
SAINT PIERRE ET MIQUELON
WALLIS ET FUTUNA

Paris

SEINE-ST DENIS
HAUTS-DE-SEINE
PARIS
VAL-DE-MARNE

PAS-DE-CALAIS
NORD
SOMME
SEINE-MARITIME
AISNE
ARDENNES
MANCHE
CALVADOS
EURE
OISE
VAL-D'OISE
MARNE
MEUSE
MOSELLE
ORNE
YVELINES
■ Paris
ESSONNE
SEINE-ET-MARNE
MEURTHE-ET-MOSELLE
BAS-RHIN
CÔTES-DU-NORD
AUBE
HAUTE-MARNE
VOSGES
FINISTÈRE
ILLE-ET-VILAINE
MAYENNE
EURE-ET-LOIR
HAUT-RHIN
MORBIHAN
SARTHE
LOIRET
YONNE
CÔTE-D'OR
HAUTE-SAÔNE
LOIRE-ATLANTIQUE
MAINE-ET-LOIRE
INDRE-ET-LOIRE
LOIR-ET-CHER
DOUBS
TERRITOIRE-DE-BELFORT
CHER
NIÈVRE
VENDÉE
DEUX-SÈVRES
VIENNE
INDRE
SAÔNE-ET-LOIRE
JURA
ALLIER
CHARENTE-MARITIME
CREUSE
RHÔNE
AIN
HAUTE-SAVOIE
CHARENTE
HAUTE-VIENNE
PUY-DE-DÔME
LOIRE
SAVOIE
CORRÈZE
ISÈRE
DORDOGNE
CANTAL
HAUTE-LOIRE
GIRONDE
LOT
ARDÈCHE
DRÔME
HAUTES-ALPES
LOT-ET-GARONNE
LOZÈRE
LANDES
TARN-ET-GARONNE
AVEYRON
GARD
VAUCLUSE
ALPES-DE-HAUTE-PROVENCE
ALPES-MARITIMES
GERS
TARN
HÉRAULT
BOUCHES-DU-RHÔNE
VAR
PYRÉNÉES-ATLANTIQUES
HAUTE-GARONNE
HAUTES-PYRÉNÉES
ARIÈGE
AUDE
PYRÉNÉES-ORIENTALES

HAUTE-CORSE
CORSE-DU-SUD

Same scale as main map

0   Kilometres   150

54

Election results: percentage votes and seats gained since 1958 (Metropolitan France only)

Election year	1958		1962		1967		1968		1973		1978		1981		1986	
Electorate	27,236,491		27,535,019		28,300,936		28,181,848		29,901.822		34,394,378		35,516,041		36,605,381	
Turnout %	74.6		66.6		79.1		78.6		79.4		81.7		69.9		75.1	
	V %	S	V %	S	V %	S	V %	S	V %	S	V %	S	V %	S	V %	S
Communist Party	19.2	10	21.8	41	22.5	72	20.0	33	21.4	73	20.6	86	16.1	43	9.7	32
Miscellaneous Left	1.3	0	2.4	2	2.2	3	3.9	0	3.3	2	3.3	0	1.3	0	1.5	0
Socialist Party and allies	22.8	67	20.3	108	18.9	118	16.5	57	19.2	100	25.0	112	37.8	281	32.8	211
Centre and Right Parties	11.2	57	8.9	36	12.6	38	10.3	26	26.5	105	21.8	125	19.3	63 }	42.0	125
Gaullist Party and allies	20.5	198	36.3	229	37.8	232	43.7	346	23.9	175	22.4	141	20.8	80 }		140
Miscellaneous Right	23.4	133	9.5	48	3.7	7	4.1	8	2.8	15	3.2	9	3.8	6	2.7	12
National Front															9.8	35
Others	1.4	0	0.9	1	2.3	0	1.4	0	2.8	3	2.9	1	2.0	1	1.5	0
TOTAL SEATS		465		465		470		470		473		474		474		555

Members elected to the Chamber of Deputies, March 16 1986

Total number of members in each constituency

Columns (left to right): ımunist Party; Socialist Party; ɔvement of Left Radicals; Union for French Democracy; Rally for the Republic; Miscellaneous Right; National Front; Total number of members in each constituency

Constituency	Communist Party	Socialist Party	Movement of Left Radicals	Union for French Democracy	Rally for the Republic	Miscellaneous Right	National Front	Total
		1	1	1	1			4
NE	1	2		1	1			5
ER	1	1		1	1			4
ES-DE HAUTE-PROVENCE		1			1			2
TES-ALPES		1		1				2
ES-MARITIMES		2		2	3		2	9
ÈCHE		1		1	1			3
ENNES		1		1	1			3
EGE		1			1			2
E		1		1	1			3
DE		2			1			3
YRON			1	1	1			3
CHES-DU-RHÔNE	2	5		4	1		4	16
VADOS		3		2	1			6
TAL		1			1			2
RENTE		2		1	1			4
RENTE-MARITIME		1	1	2	1			5
ER	1	1		1				3
RÈZE		1			2			3
SE-DU-SUD		1			1			2
JTE-CORSE			1		1			2
E-D'OR		2		1	2			5
ES-DU-NORD		2		2	1			5
EUSE		1			1			2
RDOGNE		1	1	1	1			4
JBS		2		1	2			5
ÔME		2		1	1			4
ONNE	1	4		2	2		1	10
EURE		3		1	1			5
EURE-ET-LOIR		2		1		1		4
FINISTÈRE		4		1	2	1		8
GARD	1	2		1			1	5
HAUTE-GARONNE		4		1	1	2		8
GERS		1		1				2
GIRONDE	1	4		2	3		1	11
HÉRAULT	1	3		1	1		1	7
ILLE-ET-VILAINE		3		3	1			7
INDRE		1			1	1		3
INDRE-ET-LOIRE		2		1	1	1		5
ISÈRE	1	3		2	2		1	9
JURA		1		1	1			3
LANDES		2			1			3
LOIR-ET-CHER		1		1	1			3
LOIRE	1	2		2	1		1	7
HAUTE-LOIRE				2				2
LOIRE-ATLANTIQUE		4		3	3			10
LOIRET		2		1	2			5
LOT		1			1			2
LOT-ET-GARONNE		1		1	1			3
LOZÈRE				2				2
MAINE-ET-LOIRE		2		3	2			7
MANCHE		2		1	2			5
MARNE	1	2		1	2			6
HAUTE-MARNE		1		1				2
MAYENNE		1		1	1			3
MEURTHE-ET-MOSELLE	1	3		2	1			7
MEUSE		1		1				2
MORBIHAN		2		3	1			6
MOSELLE		3		2	3	1	1	10
NIÈVRE		2		1				3
NORD	4	8		3	6		3	24
OISE		3		1	2		1	7
ORNE		1		1	1			3
PARIS		8		3	8		2	21
PAS-DE-CALAIS	2	6		1	2	2	1	14
PUY-DE-DÔME		3		2	1			6
PYRÉNÉES-ATLANTIQUES		3		1	2			6
HAUTES-PYRÉNÉES		1		2				3
PYRÉNÉES-ORIENTALES		1		1	1		1	4
BAS-RHIN		2		4	2		1	9
HAUT-RHIN		2		2	2		1	7
RHÔNE	1	5		3	3		2	14
HAUTE-SAÔNE		1			2			3
SAÔNE-ET-LOIRE		3		1	2			6
SARTHE		2		1	2			5
SAVOIE		1		1	1			3
HAUTE-SAVOIE		2		2	1			5
HAUTS-DE-SEINE	1	4		2	5		1	13
SEINE-MARITIME	1	5		3	2		1	12
SEINE-ET-MARNE	1	3		1	3		1	9
SEINE-ST DENIS	3	4		1	3		2	13
DEUX-SÈVRES		2		1	1			4
SOMME	1	2		1	1			5
TARN		2		1	1			4
TARN-ET-GARONNE		1			1			2
TERRITOIRE-DE-BELFORT		1		1				2
VAL-D'OISE	1	3		2	2		1	9
VAL-DE-MARNE	2	3	1	2	3		1	12
VAR		2		3	1		1	7
VAUCLUSE		1		1	1		1	4
VENDÉE		2		1	2			5
VIENNE		2		1	1			4
HAUTE-VIENNE	1	1		1	1	1		4
VOSGES		2			1			4
YONNE		1		1	1			3
YVELINES	1	4		1	4	1	1	12
METROPOLITAN FRANCE	32	205	6	125	140	12	35	555
OVERSEAS DEPARTMENTS								
GUADELOUPE	1	1				2		4
GUYANE		1			1			2
LA RÉUNION	2			1	1	1		5
MARTINIQUE		2		1	1			4
OVERSEAS TERRITORIES								
MAYOTTE				1				1
NOUVELLE CALEDONIE					2			2
POLYNÉSIE FRANÇAISE					2			2
SAINT PIERRE ET MIQUELON		1						1
WALLIS ET FUTUNA					1			1
TOTAL	35	210	6	128	148	15	35	577

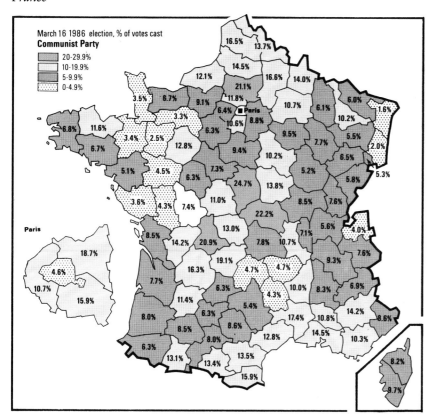

March 16 1986 election, % of votes cast
Communist Party

- 20-29.9%
- 10-19.9%
- 5-9.9%
- 0-4.9%

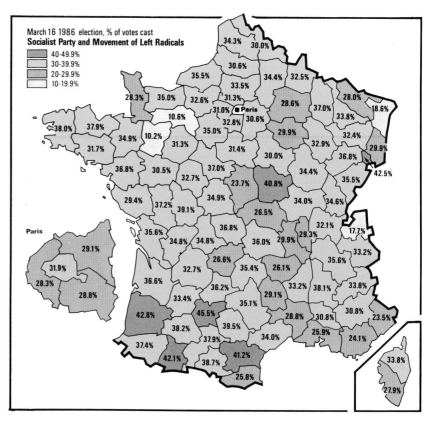

March 16 1986 election, % of votes cast
Socialist Party and Movement of Left Radicals

- 40-49.9%
- 30-39.9%
- 20-29.9%
- 10-19.9%

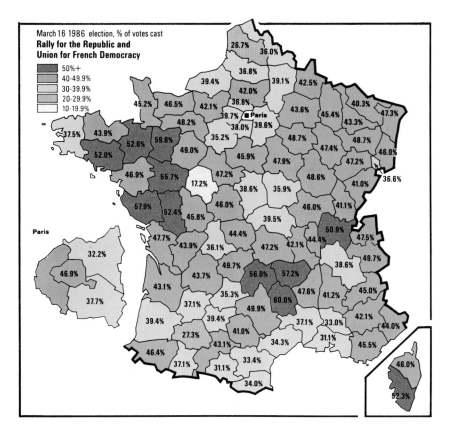

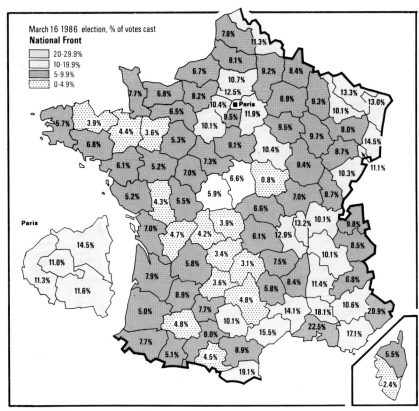

West Germany

The Federal Republic of Germany has an indirectly elected president with no executive powers. The government is responsible to a two-chamber parliament. The upper house, or *Bundesrat*, of 45 members, is indirectly elected.

The lower house, or *Bundestag*, is elected for a four-year term. Premature dissolution is possible only in narrowly defined circumstances. The normal membership is 498, plus 22 non-voting representatives indirectly elected by West Berlin. As a consequence of the mixed electoral system described below, the number of members may occasionally be increased.

The West German electoral system was designed to combine the benefits of single-member constituencies with those of a system of proportional representation. Each voter has two votes, one to choose his constituency representative, the other to choose between party lists. There are 248 constituencies in which members are elected on a plurality basis (see page 2). The remaining 248 members are chosen on a basis of proportional representation, using the D'Hondt system (see page 2), on a national basis. The voter casts his second vote between party lists, with no opportunity to vary the order of candidates.

The purpose of the national allocation of seats between party lists is to counteract the bias of the plurality system. If a party is over-represented among the constituency members it will be allocated relatively fewer seats from the party lists. Conversely, a party under-represented at the constituency level will be compensated nationally. There is one important qualification: a party needs to obtain at least 5 per cent of the party list votes, or to have won at least three seats at constituency level, before it is entitled to any of the party list seats.

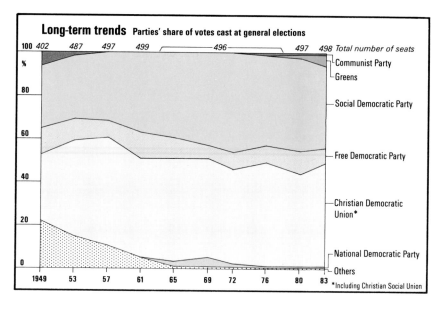

If a party is so over-represented at the constituency level that this cannot be rectified in the distribution of party list seats it is allowed to keep the extra seats. The minimum voting age is 18.

Last election: March 6 1983.

Next election due: March 1987.

Main political parties

1. Communist Party (DKP)
2. Greens
3. Social Democratic Party (SPD)
4. Free Democratic Party (FDP)
5. Christian Democratic Union/ Christian Social Union (CDU/CSU)
6. National Democratic Party (NDP), Neo-Nazi

Government

The present government, re-formed after the March 1983 election, is a coalition between the CDU, the CSU (which is the equivalent party in the state of Bavaria) and the FDP. The chancellor is Helmut Kohl (CDU).

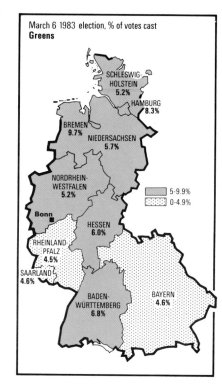

Election results: percentage votes and seats gained since 1949[a]

Election year	1949		1953		1957		1961		1965		1969		1972		1976		1980		1983	
Electorate	31,207,620		33,202,287		35,400,923		37,440,715		38,510,395		38,677,325		41,446,302		42,058,015		43,231,741		44,088,935	
Turnout %		76.5		83.0		84.5		84.3		84.7		85.2		90.4		89.9		87.8		88.3
	V %	S	V %	S	V %	S	V %	S	V %	S	V %	S	V %	S	V %	S	V %	S	V %	S
Communist Party	5.7	15	2.2	0									0.3	0	0.3	0	0.2	0	0.2	0
Greens																	1.5	0	5.6	27
Social Democratic Party	29.2	131	28.8	151	31.8	159	36.2	190	39.3	202	42.7	224	45.8	230	42.6	214	42.9	218	38.2	193
Free Democratic Party	11.9	52	9.5	48	7.7	41	12.8	67	9.5	49	5.8	30	8.4	41	7.9	39	10.6	53	7.0	34
Christian Democratic Union[b]	31.0	139	45.2	243	50.2	270	45.3	242	47.6	245	46.1	242	44.9	225	48.6	243	44.5	226	48.8	244
National Democratic Party									2.0	0	4.3	0	0.6	0	0.3	0	0.2	0	0.2	0
Others	22.2	115	14.5	45	10.4	17	5.7	0	1.6	0	0.9	0	0.7	0	0.2	0	0.1	0	0.1	0
TOTAL SEATS		452		487		487		499		496		496		496		496		497		498

[a] Excluding West Berlin.
[b] Including the Christian Social Union.

Result of election of March 6 1983

Electorate: 44,088,935   Valid votes: 38,940,687
(88.3%)   Invalid votes: 33,884 (0.8%)

	Votes[a]	%	Seats	%
Christian Democratic Union/CSU	18,998,545	48.8	244	49.0
Social Democratic Party	14,865,807	38.2	193	38.8
Free Democratic Party	2,706,942	7.0	34	6.8
Greens	2,167,431	5.6	27	5.4
National Democratic Party	91,095	0.2	0	0.0
Communist Party	64,986	0.2	0	0.0
Others	45,881	0.1	0	0.0
TOTAL	38,940,687		498	

[a] The party votes given are those cast for party lists, not an accumulation of constituency results.

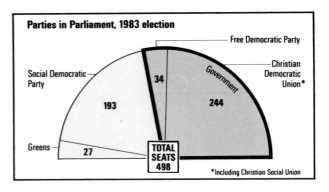

Parties in Parliament, 1983 election

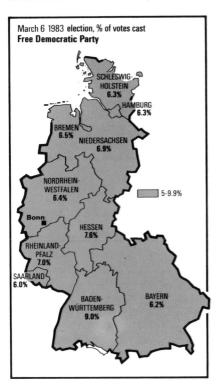

March 6 1983 election, % of votes cast
Free Democratic Party

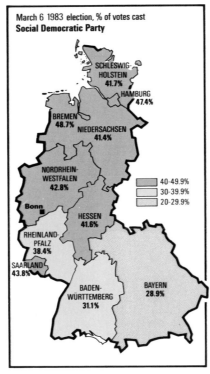

March 6 1983 election, % of votes cast
Social Democratic Party

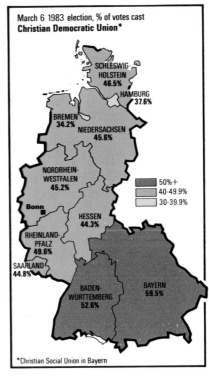

March 6 1983 election, % of votes cast
Christian Democratic Union*

*Christian Social Union in Bayern

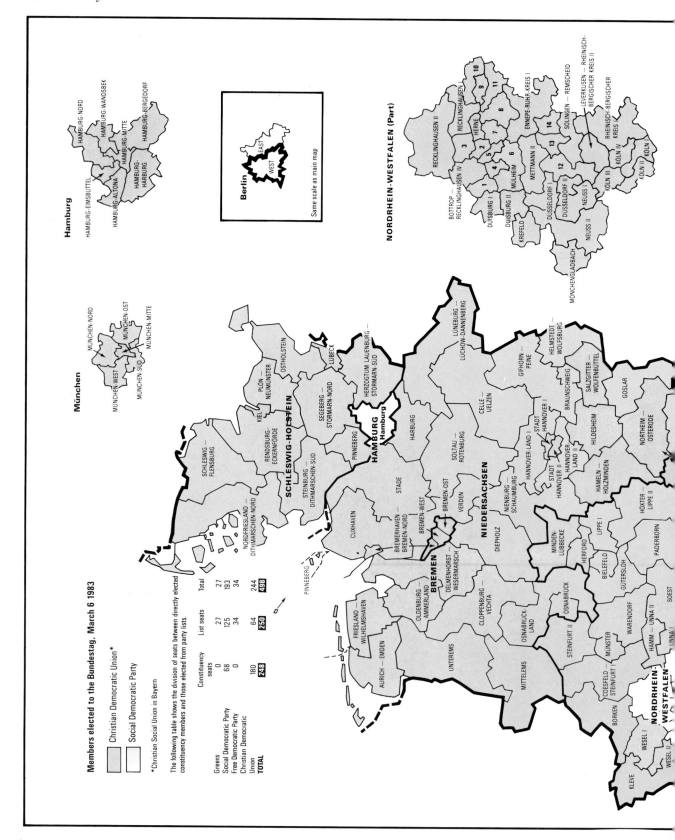

Hamburg

HAMBURG-NORD
HAMBURG-WANDSBEK
HAMBURG-MITTE
HAMBURG-BERGEDORF
HAMBURG-EIMSBÜTTEL
HAMBURG-ALTONA
HAMBURG-HARBURG

Berlin

EAST
WEST

Same scale as main map

NORDRHEIN-WESTFALEN (Part)

RECKLINGHAUSEN II
RECKLINGHAUSEN
HERNE
ENNEPE-RUHR-KREIS I
SOLINGEN — REMSCHEID
LEVERKUSEN — RHEINISCH-
BERGISCHER KREIS I
RHEINISCH-BERGISCHER KREIS II
BOTTROP — RECKLINGHAUSEN IV
DUISBURG I
DUISBURG II
KREFELD
MÜLHEIM
METTMANN II
DÜSSELDORF I
DÜSSELDORF II
NEUSS I
NEUSS II
KÖLN III
KÖLN IV
KÖLN II
KÖLN I
MÖNCHENGLADBACH

München

MÜNCHEN-NORD
MÜNCHEN-OST
MÜNCHEN-MITTE
MÜNCHEN-WEST
MÜNCHEN-SÜD

Members elected to the Bundestag, March 6 1983

Christian Democratic Union*

Social Democratic Party

*Christian Social Union in Bayern

The following table shows the division of seats between directly elected constituency members and those elected from party lists.

	Constituency seats	List seats	Total
Greens	0	27	27
Social Democratic Party	68	125	193
Free Democratic Party	0	34	34
Christian Democratic Union	180	64	244
TOTAL	**248**	**250**	**498**

SCHLESWIG-HOLSTEIN

OSTHOLSTEIN
LÜBECK
PLÖN — NEUMÜNSTER
SEGEBERG — STORMARN-NORD
HERZOGTUM LAUENBURG — STORMARN-SÜD
KIEL
RENDSBURG-ECKERNFÖRDE
SCHLESWIG — FLENSBURG
STEINBURG — DITHMARSCHEN-SÜD
PINNEBERG
NORDFRIESLAND — DITHMARSCHEN-NORD

HAMBURG

HARBURG

LÜNEBURG — LÜCHOW-DANNENBERG
GIFHORN — PEINE
HELMSTEDT — WOLFSBURG
SALZGITTER — WOLFENBÜTTEL
GOSLAR
CELLE — UELZEN
STADT HANNOVER I
BRAUNSCHWEIG
HILDESHEIM
NORTHEIM — OSTERODE
CUXHAVEN
STADE
SOLTAU — ROTENBURG
HANNOVER-LAND I
STADT HANNOVER II
HANNOVER LAND II
HAMELN — HOLZMINDEN
HÖXTER — LIPPE II
BREMERHAVEN — BREMEN-NORD
BREMEN-WEST
BREMEN-OST
VERDEN
NIENBURG — SCHAUMBURG
LIPPE I
PINNEBERG

NIEDERSACHSEN

BREMEN
DELMENHORST — WESERMARSCH
DIEPHOLZ
MINDEN-LÜBBECKE
HERFORD
BIELEFELD
GÜTERSLOH
PADERBORN
OLDENBURG — AMMERLAND
FRIESLAND — WILHELMSHAVEN
CLOPPENBURG — VECHTA
OSNABRÜCK-LAND
OSNABRÜCK
STEINFURT II
WARENDORF
SOEST
AURICH — EMDEN
UNTEREMS
MITTELEMS
COESFELD — STEINFURT I
MÜNSTER
HAMM — UNNA II
UNNA I
BORKEN
WESEL I
WESEL II
KLEVE

NORDRHEIN-WESTFALEN

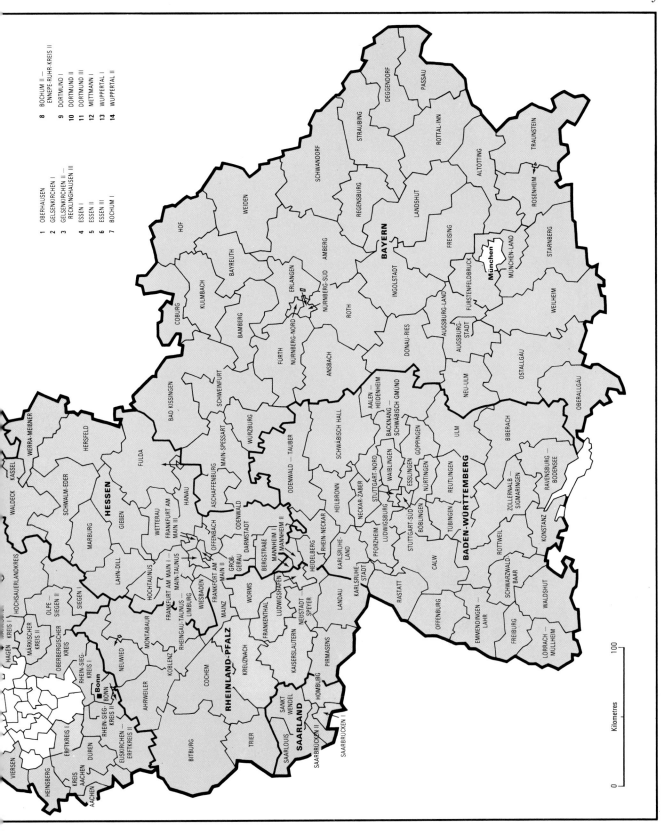

Greece

A republic, with an indirectly elected president without executive powers. Democratic rule was restored in 1974, following a period of military rule. The government is responsible to a single-chamber parliament, the *Vouli*, with 300 members.

Parliament is elected for a four-year term, but early dissolution is possible. 288 members are elected from 56 constituencies based on the 51 prefectures. (Attica is divided into five constituencies and Thessaloniki into two). All but five of these are multi-member, and the election is on the basis of proportional representation, using the Hagenbach-Bischoff quota (see page 3). In the single-member constituencies the plurality rule (see page 2) applies. If sufficient quotas are not achieved at constituency level the residual seats are allocated at regional level, using the Hare quota (see page 2). In addition, there are 12 national seats, also allocated on the basis of the Hare quota. The minimum voting age is 18.

Last election: June 2 1985.

Next election due: June 1989.

Main political parties

1. Communist Party of Greece (KKE)
2. Communist Party of Greece – Interior (KKE-Es), Euro-Communist
3. Panhellenic Socialist Movement (PASOK)
4. New Democracy Party (ND), Conservative

Government

The present government, re-elected in June 1985, is formed by PASOK. The prime minister is Andreas Papandreou.

Election results: percentage votes and seats gained since 1974

Election year	1974		1977		1981		1985	
Electorate	6,241,061		6,403,738		7,319,070		8,119,410	
Turnout %	78.6		80.1		77.5		78.4	
	V %	S	V %	S	V %	S	V %	S
Communist Party of Greece	9.5	5	9.4	11	10.9	13	9.9	12
Communist Party of Greece – Interior		3	2.7	2	1.3	0	1.8	1
PASOK	13.6	12	25.3	92	48.1	172	45.8	161
Union of the Centre	20.4	60	12.0	15	0.4	0		
New Democracy Party	54.4	220	41.8	173	35.9	115	40.9	126
Others	2.2	0	8.8	7	3.4	0	1.5	0
TOTAL SEATS		300		300		300		300

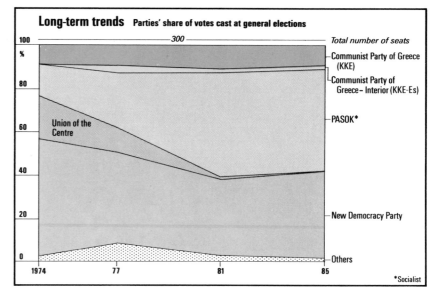

Long-term trends Parties' share of votes cast at general elections

Total number of seats
Communist Party of Greece (KKE)
Communist Party of Greece – Interior (KKE-Es)
PASOK*
New Democracy Party
Others
*Socialist

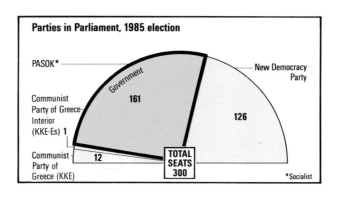

Parties in Parliament, 1985 election

PASOK*
New Democracy Party
Government 161
Communist Party of Greece– Interior (KKE-Es) 1
Communist Party of Greece (KKE) 12
126
TOTAL SEATS 300
*Socialist

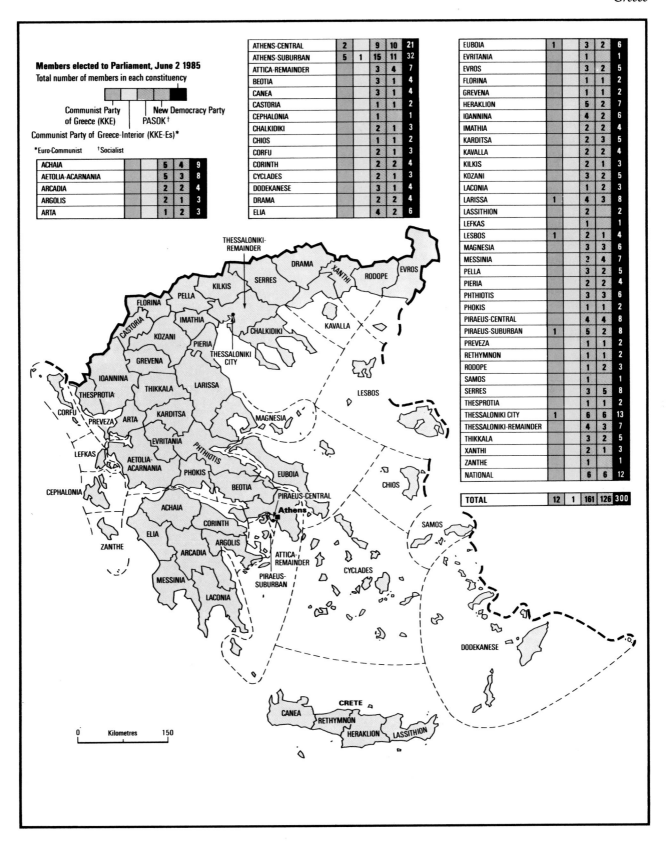

Members elected to Parliament, June 2 1985

Total number of members in each constituency

Communist Party of Greece (KKE)

Communist Party of Greece-Interior (KKE-Es)*

PASOK†

New Democracy Party

*Euro-Communist   †Socialist

	KKE	KKE-Es	PASOK	New Democracy	Total
ACHAIA			5	4	9
AETOLIA-ACARNANIA			5	3	8
ARCADIA			2	2	4
ARGOLIS			2	1	3
ARTA			1	2	3

	KKE	KKE-Es	PASOK	New Democracy	Total
ATHENS-CENTRAL	2		9	10	21
ATHENS-SUBURBAN	5	1	15	11	32
ATTICA-REMAINDER			3	4	7
BEOTIA			3	1	4
CANEA			3	1	4
CASTORIA			1	1	2
CEPHALONIA			1		1
CHALKIDIKI			2	1	3
CHIOS			1	1	2
CORFU			2	1	3
CORINTH			2	2	4
CYCLADES			2	1	3
DODEKANESE			3	1	4
DRAMA			2	2	4
ELIA			4	2	6

	KKE	KKE-Es	PASOK	New Democracy	Total
EUBOIA	1		3	2	6
EVRITANIA			1		1
EVROS			3	2	5
FLORINA			1	1	2
GREVENA			1	1	2
HERAKLION			5	2	7
IOANNINA			4	2	6
IMATHIA			2	2	4
KARDITSA			2	3	5
KAVALLA			2	2	4
KILKIS			2	1	3
KOZANI			3	2	5
LACONIA			1	2	3
LARISSA	1		4	3	8
LASSITHION			2		2
LEFKAS			1		1
LESBOS	1		2	1	4
MAGNESIA			3	3	6
MESSINIA			3	4	7
PELLA			3	2	5
PIERIA			2	2	4
PHTHIOTIS			3	3	6
PHOKIS			1	1	2
PIRAEUS-CENTRAL			4	4	8
PIRAEUS-SUBURBAN	1		5	2	8
PREVEZA			1	1	2
RETHYMNON			1	1	2
RODOPE			1	2	3
SAMOS			1		1
SERRES			3	5	8
THESPROTIA			1	1	2
THESSALONIKI CITY	1		6	6	13
THESSALONIKI-REMAINDER			4	3	7
THIKKALA			3	2	5
XANTHI			2	1	3
ZANTHE			1		1
NATIONAL			6	6	12

TOTAL	12	1	161	126	300

0   Kilometres   150

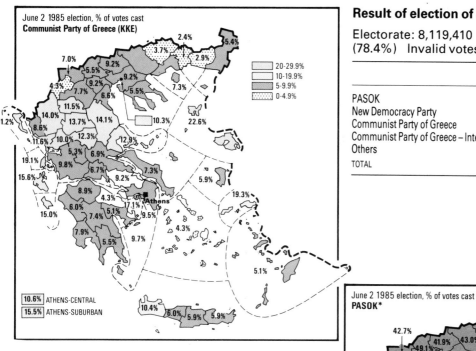

June 2 1985 election, % of votes cast
Communist Party of Greece (KKE)

Legend:
- 20-29.9%
- 10-19.9%
- 5-9.9%
- 0-4.9%

10.6% ATHENS-CENTRAL
15.5% ATHENS-SUBURBAN

Result of election of June 2 1985

Electorate: 8,119,410   Valid votes: 6,365,896
(78.4%)   Invalid votes: 57,313 (0.7%)

	Votes	%	Seats	%
PASOK	2,916,450	45.8	161	53.7
New Democracy Party	2,599,949	40.9	126	42.0
Communist Party of Greece	629,513	9.9	12	4.0
Communist Party of Greece – Interior	117,050	1.8	1	0.3
Others	102,934	1.5	0	0.0
TOTAL	6,365,896		300	

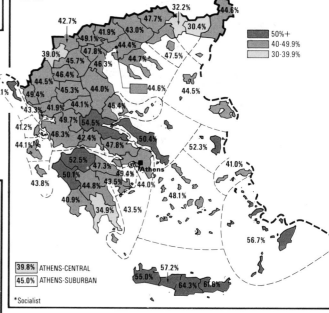

June 2 1985 election, % of votes cast
PASOK*

Legend:
- 50%+
- 40-49.9%
- 30-39.9%

39.8% ATHENS-CENTRAL
45.0% ATHENS-SUBURBAN

*Socialist

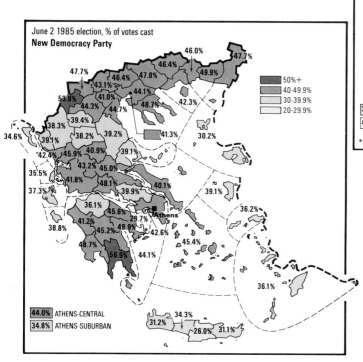

June 2 1985 election, % of votes cast
New Democracy Party

Legend:
- 50%+
- 40-49.9%
- 30-39.9%
- 20-29.9%

44.0% ATHENS-CENTRAL
34.8% ATHENS-SUBURBAN

Iceland

A republic, with a popularly elected president whose role is largely ceremonial. Parliament (the *Althingi*) consists of 60 members (52 before 1959). The prime minister is responsible to the Althingi and not to the president. Parliament's term is limited to four years, but there is a right of dissolution by the president, acting on the advice of the prime minister.

There are no by-elections; vacancies are filled by the next person on the party list of a member who dies or resigns. Vacancies are also filled for a temporary period on the same basis, for members who are unable, for example through illness, to attend parliament for at least two consecutive weeks.

After each election the Althingi chooses one-third of its members to form an Upper Chamber, the remaining two-thirds forming the Lower House, each chamber comprising party representatives on a proportional basis. The whole Althingi, sitting together, deals with the budget and other non-legislative business. Bills are debated separately in the two houses and must be passed by both before becoming law.

The president is elected for four years on a plurality basis. These elections are normally conducted on a non-party basis, and no sitting president has ever been opposed for re-election.

The minimum voting age is 20. For parliamentary elections the D'Hondt system of proportional representation (see page 2) is employed, with eight multi-member constituencies electing 49 members. The remaining 11 seats are filled on a national basis, with the aim of making the balance of party representation as proportional as possible. The 11 supplementary members are selected (also under the D'Hondt system) from among the runners-up in the constituencies. To qualify for supplementary seats a party must have won at least one seat at constituency level. Voters choose between party lists, but with the right to change the order of candidates. This right seldom affects the eventual outcome.

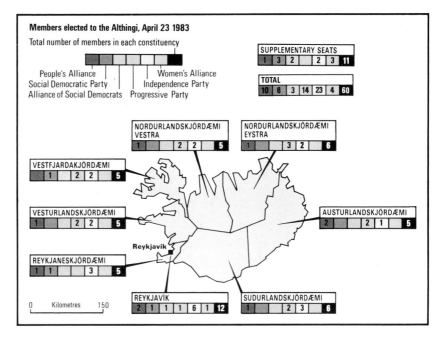

Last parliamentary election: April 23 1983.

Next election due: April 1987.

Last contested Presidential election: June 29 1980. (There was an unopposed election on June 30 1984.)

Next Presidential election due: June 1988.

Main political parties

1. Communist Party/People's Alliance
2. Union of Liberals and Leftists, breakaway from People's Alliance
3. Alliance of Social Democrats, breakaway from Social Democratic Party
4. Social Democratic Party
5. Progressive Party, a farmers' and co-operative party
6. Independence Party, Conservative
7. Women's Alliance, a new non-ideological list formed to fight the 1983 election

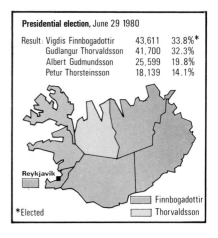

Government

The present government, formed in
May 1983, is a coalition between the
Independence Party and the
Progressive Party. The prime
minister is Steingrimur
Hermannsson (Progressive Party).
The president is Vigdis
Finnbogadottir.

Result of election of April 23 1983

Electorate: 150,977   Valid votes: 130,422 (86.4%)
Invalid votes: 3,342 (2.5%)

	Votes	%	Seats	%
People's Alliance	22,490	17.3	10	16.7
Alliance of Social Democrats	9,849	7.3	4	6.7
Social Democratic Party	15,214	11.7	6	10.0
Progressive Party	24,095	18.5	14	23.3
Independence Party	50,251	38.7	23	38.3
Women's Alliance	7,125	5.5	3	5.0
Others	1,398	1.0	0	0.0
TOTAL	130,422		60	

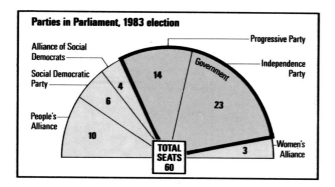

Parties in Parliament, 1983 election

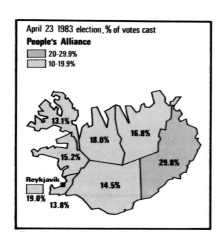

April 23 1983 election, % of votes cast
People's Alliance
- 20-29.9%
- 10-19.9%

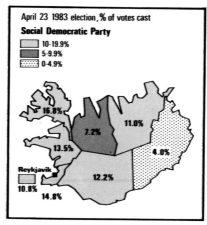

April 23 1983 election, % of votes cast
Social Democratic Party
- 10-19.9%
- 5-9.9%
- 0-4.9%

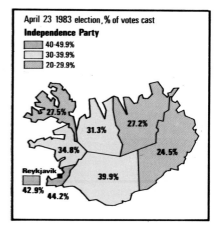

April 23 1983 election, % of votes cast
Independence Party
- 40-49.9%
- 30-39.9%
- 20-29.9%

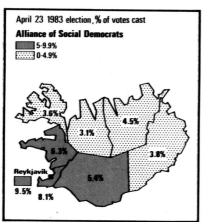

April 23 1983 election, % of votes cast
Alliance of Social Democrats
- 5-9.9%
- 0-4.9%

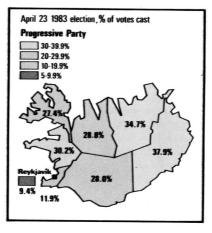

April 23 1983 election, % of votes cast
Progressive Party
- 30-39.9%
- 20-29.9%
- 10-19.9%
- 5-9.9%

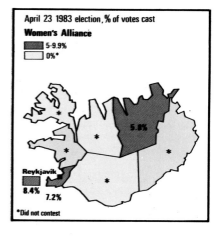

April 23 1983 election, % of votes cast
Women's Alliance
- 5-9.9%
- 0%*

*Did not contest

Election results: percentage votes and seats gained since 1946

Election year	1946		1949		1953		1956		June 1959		Oct. 1959		1963	
Electorate	77,640		82,481		87,601		91,618		95,050		95,637		99,798	
Turnout %	86.2		87.6		88.4		90.2		89.2		89.0		89.5	
	V %	S	V %	S	V %	S	V %	S	V %	S	V %	S	V %	S
Communists/People's Alliance	19.5	10	19.5	9	16.0	7	19.2	8	15.2	7	16.0	10	16.0	9
Union of Liberals and Leftists														
Alliance of Social Democrats														
Social Democratic Party	17.8	9	16.5	7	15.6	6	18.3	8	12.5	6	15.2	9	14.2	8
Progressive Party	23.1	13	24.5	17	21.9	16	15.6	17	27.2	19	25.7	17	28.2	19
Independence Party	39.5	20	39.5	19	37.1	21	42.4	19	42.5	20	39.7	24	41.4	24
Women's Alliance														
Others	0.1	0			9.3	2	4.5	0	2.5	0	3.4	0	0.2	0
TOTAL SEATS		52		52		52		52		52		60		60

Election year	1967		1971		1974		1978		1979		1983	
Electorate	107,101		118,289		126,388		137,782		142,073		150,977	
Turnout %	89.7		89.1		90.3		88.7		87.1		86.4	
	V %	S	V %	S	V %	S	V %	S	V %	S	V %	S
Communists/People's Alliance	13.9	9	17.1	10	18.3	11	22.9	14	19.7	11	17.3	10
Union of Liberals and Leftists	3.7	1	8.9	5	4.6	2	3.3	0				
Alliance of Social Democrats											7.3	4
Social Democratic Party	15.7	9	10.5	6	9.1	5	22.0	14	17.4	10	11.7	6
Progressive Party	28.1	18	25.3	17	24.9	17	16.9	12	24.9	17	18.5	14
Independence Party	37.5	23	36.2	22	42.7	25	32.7	20	35.4	21	38.7	23
Women's Alliance											5.5	3
Others	1.1	0	2.0	0	0.4	0	2.2	0	2.5	1	1.0	0
TOTAL SEATS		60		60		60		60		60		60

India

A republic, with an indirectly elected president without executive power. The government is responsible to a two-chamber parliament. The upper house, or *Rajya Sabha* (House of States), has 250 members, 238 of whom are indirectly elected from the 22 states and nine union territories which make up India's federal system. The remaining 12 are nominated by the president.

The *Lok Sabha*, the House of the People, is the more important chamber. It has 542 members elected on a plurality basis (see page 2), from single-member constituencies. 79 seats are reserved for members of Scheduled Castes and 40 for members of Scheduled Tribes (all Indians resident in these constituencies may vote for these members, but only candidates from the respective disadvantaged Castes or Tribes may stand).

The term of office of the Lok Sabha is five years but the president, acting on the advice of the prime minister, may order a premature dissolution. In 1976 the five-year term was extended for one year under the 'emergency' powers of Indira Gandhi's government. Casual vacancies are filled by by-elections. The minimum voting age is 21.

Because of the size of the country and of the electorate, and also because of climatic differences, polling is often staggered over two or three days. In the case of the December 1984 election, polling was postponed because of political unrest in the Punjab and Assam until September 1985 and December 1985 respectively. Voting was also postponed in seven other seats because of climatic conditions, election irregularities or, in the case of Bhopal, because of the chemical disaster. Polling in these seats took place in January, April and May 1985.

Results for all 542 seats are shown on the large constituency map. The

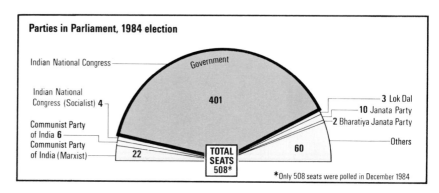

Parties in Parliament, 1984 election

Indian National Congress — Government
Indian National Congress (Socialist) **4**
Communist Party of India **6**
Communist Party of India (Marxist) **22**
401
TOTAL SEATS 508*
60
3 Lok Dal
10 Janata Party
2 Bharatiya Janata Party
Others
*Only 508 seats were polled in December 1984

smaller analytical maps are all based on the results for the 508 which polled in December 1984.

Last election held: December 24, 27 and 28 1984.

Next election due: December 1989.

Main political parties

1. Communist Party of India (Marxist) (CPM), originally a Maoist breakaway from the CPI
2. Communist Party of India (CPI), orthodox Commmunist
3. Indian National Congress (Socialist), Democratic Socialist
4. Indian National Congress, or Congress (I) Party
5. Lok Dal, People's Party
6. Janata Party
7. Bharatiya Janata Party, orthodox Hindu

Regional parties

Telugu Desam (Land of Telugu), Andhra Pradesh
Akali Dal, Punjab
Dravida Munnetra Kazhagam (DMK)
All-India Anna Dravida Munnetra Kazhagam (ADK)
The last two are in Tamil Nadu.
J & K National Conference, Jammu and Kashmir

Government

The government is formed by the Indian National Congress. The prime minister since October 31 1984 has been Rajiv Gandhi.

Election results: percentage votes and seats gained since 1952

Election year	1952		1957		1962		1967		1971		1977		1980		1984[b]	
Electorate	171,700,000		193,700,000		216,400,000		249,000,000		274,100,000		320,900,000		355,800,000		375,830,000	
Turnout %	61.7		63.7		55.4		61.3		55.3		60.5		56.9		63.4	
	V%	S	V%	S	V%	S	V%	S	V%	S	V%	S	V%	S	V%	S
Communist Party of India (Marxist)							4.2	19	5.1	23	4.3	22	6.2	36	6.0	22
Communist Party of India	3.3	6	8.9	27	9.9	29	5.2	23	4.7	23	2.8	7	2.6	11	2.6	6
Samvukta Socialist Party[a]							4.9	23	2.4	3						
Praja Socialist Party[a]/INC (Socialist)			10.4	19	6.8	12	3.1	13	1.0	2					1.5	4
Indian National Congress/Congress (I)	45.0	357	47.8	359	44.7	358	40.7	279	43.7	352	34.5	152	42.7	353	49.2	401
INC(C)/Lok Dal									10.4	16	1.7	3	5.3	13	6.0	3
Swatantra Party[a]					7.9	18	8.7	44	3.1	8						
Janata Party (Secular)													9.4	41	7.0	10
Janata Party											41.1	295	18.9	31		
Jan Sangh[a] Bharatiya Janata Party[a]	3.1	3	5.9	4	6.4	14	9.4	35	7.4	22					7.7	2
Others (incl. Independents)	48.6	123	27.0	85	24.3	63	23.8	84	22.2	69	15.6	63	14.9	42	20.1	60
TOTAL SEATS		489		494		494		520		518		542		527		508

[a] These parties combined to form the Janata Party in 1977.
[b] Figures relate to 508 seats for which polling took place in December 1984.

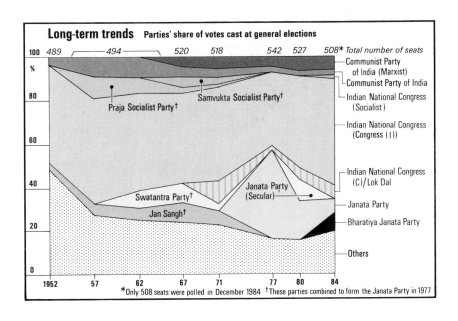

Long-term trends Parties' share of votes cast at general elections

*Only 508 seats were polled in December 1984 †These parties combined to form the Janata Party in 1977

Result of election of December 1984 (508 seats only)

Electorate: 375.83 million   Valid votes: 232,357,513 (63.4%)   Invalid votes: 6.01 million (1.6%)

	Votes	%	Seats	% Seats		Votes	%	Seats	% Seats
Indian National Congress	114,235,217	49.2	401	78.9	Dravida Munnetra Kazhagam				
Bharatiya Janata Party	17,836,438	7.7	2	0.4	(DMK)	5,428,514	2.3	1	0.2
Janata Party	16,197,490	7.0	10	2.0	All-India Anna DMK (ADK)	3,960,854	1.7	12	2.4
Communist Party of India					Indian National Congress				
(Marxist)	14,042,792	6.0	22	4.3	(Socialist)	3,390,540	1.5	4	0.8
Lok Dal	13,845,044	6.0	3	0.6	Others	8,316,137	3.6	14	2.8
Telugu Desam	9,536,632	4.1	28	5.5	Independents	19,487,260	8.4	5	1.0
Communist Party of India	6,080,595	2.6	6	1.2	TOTAL	232,357,513		508	

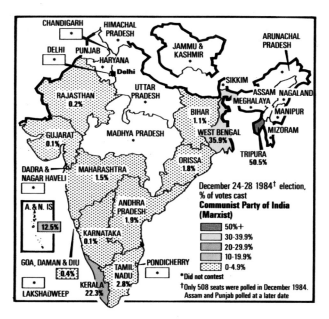

December 24-28 1984[†] election,
% of votes cast
**Communist Party of India
(Marxist)**

- 50%+
- 30-39.9%
- 20-29.9%
- 10-19.9%
- 0-4.9%

*Did not contest
[†]Only 508 seats were polled in December 1984.
Assam and Punjab polled at a later date

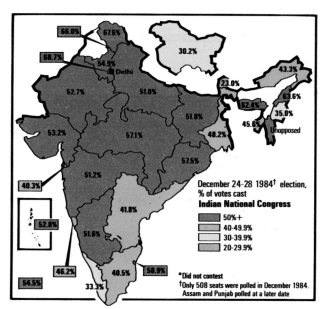

December 24-28 1984[†] election,
% of votes cast
Indian National Congress

- 50%+
- 40-49.9%
- 30-39.9%
- 20-29.9%

*Did not contest
[†]Only 508 seats were polled in December 1984.
Assam and Punjab polled at a later date

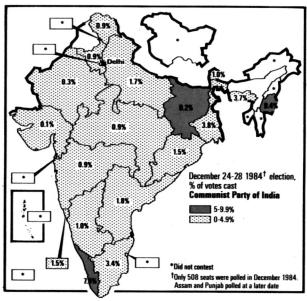

December 24-28 1984[†] election,
% of votes cast
Communist Party of India

- 5-9.9%
- 0-4.9%

*Did not contest
[†]Only 508 seats were polled in December 1984.
Assam and Punjab polled at a later date

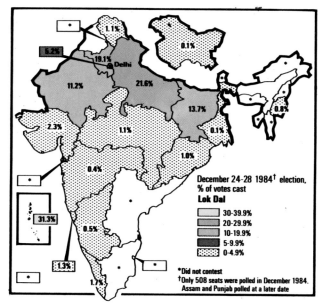

December 24-28 1984[†] election,
% of votes cast
Lok Dal

- 30-39.9%
- 20-29.9%
- 10-19.9%
- 5-9.9%
- 0-4.9%

*Did not contest
[†]Only 508 seats were polled in December 1984.
Assam and Punjab polled at a later date

Results, in seats, of constituencies polling January–December 1985

7 seats polling in January–May 1985	
Indian National Congress	4
Telugu Desam	2
Dravida Munnetra Kazhagam	1
13 Punjab seats polling on September 25 1985	
Indian National Congress	6
Akali Dal	7

14 Assam seats polling on December 16 1985	
Indian National Congress	4
Assam People's Council (AGP)	7
Indian National Congress (Socialist)	1
United Minorities Front (UMF)	1
Plains Tribal Council of Assam (PTCA)	1
TOTAL elected members	542

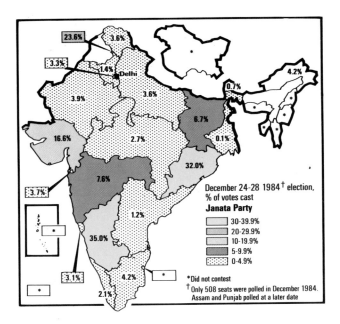

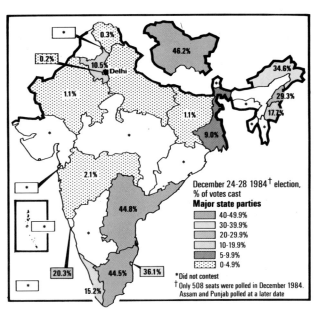

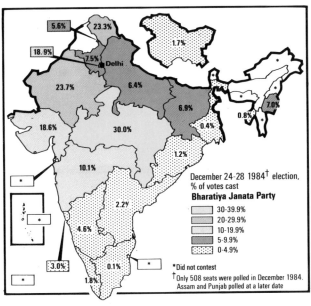

A variety of state-based parties contested the election, sometimes several in one state (in which case their support is aggregated in the above map). The most successful local parties were the J & K National Conference, which polled 46.2 per cent in Jammu and Kashmir, the Telugu Desam Party which polled 44.8 per cent in Andhra Pradesh, the Dravida Munnetra Kazhagam (DMK), 25.9 per cent in Tamil Nadu and 36.1 per cent in Pondicherry, and the All-India Anna Dravida Munnetra Kazhagam (ADK), with 18.4 per cent in Tamil Nadu. Independent candidates (not shown on this map) polled more than 50 per cent of the votes cast in Sikkim (72.4 per cent) and in Dadra and Nagar Haveli (56 per cent).

India

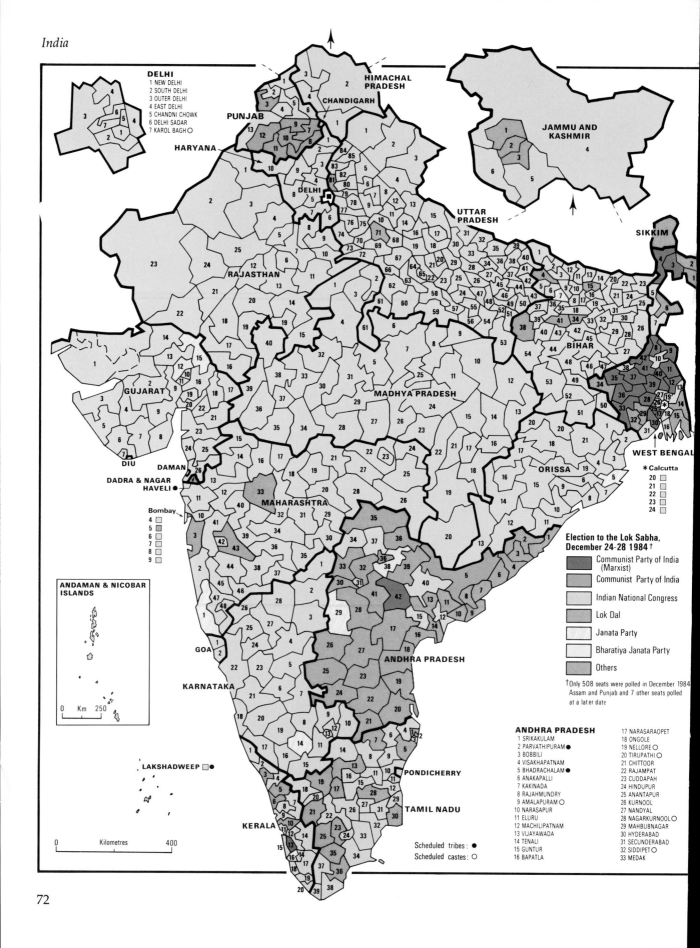

**Election to the Lok Sabha,
December 24-28 1984 †**

Communist Party of India
(Marxist)

Communist Party of India

Indian National Congress

Lok Dal

Janata Party

Bharatiya Janata Party

Others

†Only 508 seats were polled in December 1984
Assam and Punjab and 7 other seats polled
at a later date

* Calcutta

20	☐
21	☐
22	☐
23	☐
24	☐

Bombay

4	☐
5	☐
6	☐
7	☐
8	☐
9	☐

**ANDAMAN & NICOBAR
ISLANDS**

0   Km   250

LAKSHADWEEP ☐●

0   Kilometres   400

ANDHRA PRADESH

1 SRIKAKULAM	17 NARASARAOPET
2 PARVATHIPURAM ●	18 ONGOLE
3 BOBBILI	19 NELLORE ○
4 VISAKHAPATNAM	20 TIRUPATHI ○
5 BHADRACHALAM ●	21 CHITTOOR
6 ANAKAPALLI	22 RAJAMPAT
7 KAKINADA	23 CUDDAPAH
8 RAJAHMUNDRY	24 HINDUPUR
9 AMALAPURAM ○	25 ANANTAPUR
10 NARASAPUR	26 KURNOOL
11 ELURU	27 NANDYAL
12 MACHILIPATNAM	28 NAGARKURNOOL ○
13 VIJAYAWADA	29 MAHBUBNAGAR
14 TENALI	30 HYDERABAD
15 GUNTUR	31 SECUNDERABAD
16 BAPATLA	32 SIDDIPET ○
	33 MEDAK

Scheduled tribes: ●
Scheduled castes: ○

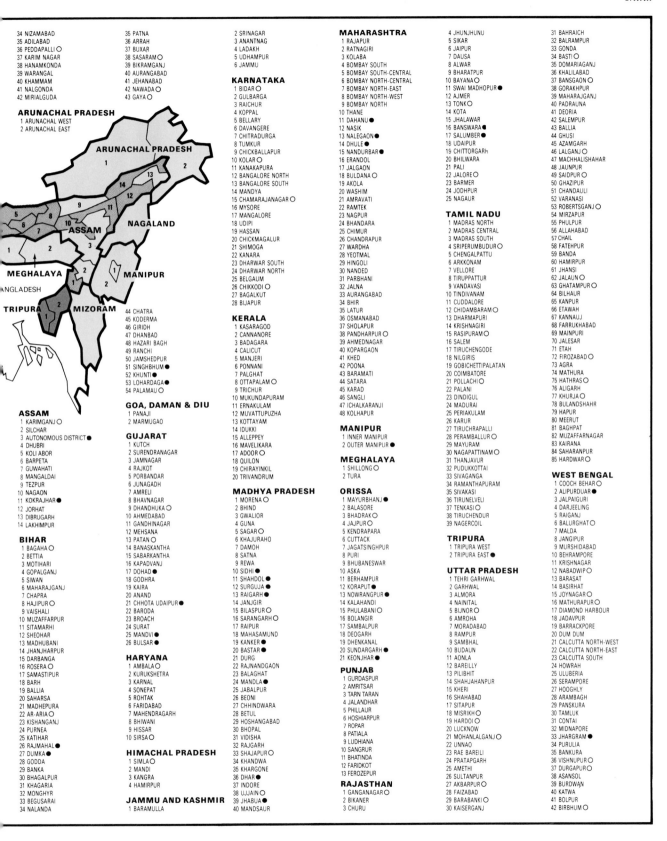

34 NIZAMABAD
35 ADILABAD
36 PEDDAPALLI ○
37 KARIM NAGAR
38 HANAMKONDA
39 WARANGAL
40 KHAMMAM
41 NALGONDA
42 MIRIALGUDA

ARUNACHAL PRADESH
1 ARUNACHAL WEST
2 ARUNACHAL EAST

ASSAM
1 KARIMGANJ ○
2 SILCHAR
3 AUTONOMOUS DISTRICT ●
4 DHUBRI
5 KOLI ABOR
6 BARPETA
7 GUWAHATI
8 MANGALDAI
9 TEZPUR
10 NAGAON
11 KOKRAJHAR ●
12 JORHAT
13 DIBRUGARH
14 LAKHIMPUR

BIHAR
1 BAGAHA ○
2 BETTIA
3 MOTIHARI
4 GOPALGANJ
5 SIWAN
6 MAHARAJGANJ
7 CHAPRA
8 HAJIPUR ○
9 VAISHALI
10 MUZAFFARPUR
11 SITAMARHI
12 SHEOHAR
13 MADHUBANI
14 JHANJHARPUR
15 DARBANGA
16 ROSERA ○
17 SAMASTIPUR
18 BARH
19 BALLIA
20 SAHARSA
21 MADHEPURA
22 AR-ARIA ○
23 KISHANGANJ
24 PURNEA
25 KATIHAR
26 RAJMAHAL ●
27 DUMKA ●
28 GODDA
29 BANKA
30 BHAGALPUR
31 KHAGARIA
32 MONGHYR
33 BEGUSARAI
34 NALANDA

35 PATNA
36 ARRAH
37 BUXAR
38 SASARAM ○
39 BIKRAMGANJ
40 AURANGABAD
41 JEHANABAD
42 NAWADA ○
43 GAYA ○

JAMMU AND KASHMIR
1 BARAMULLA
2 SRINAGAR
3 ANANTNAG
4 LADAKH
5 UDHAMPUR
6 JAMMU

KARNATAKA
1 BIDAR ○
2 GULBARGA
3 RAICHUR
4 KOPPAL
5 BELLARY
6 DAVANGERE
7 CHITRADURGA
8 TUMKUR
9 CHICKBALLAPUR
10 KOLAR ○
11 KANAKAPURA
12 BANGALORE NORTH
13 BANGALORE SOUTH
14 MANDYA
15 CHAMARAJANAGAR ○
16 MYSORE
17 MANGALORE
18 UDIPI
19 HASSAN
20 CHICKMAGALUR
21 SHIMOGA
22 KANARA
23 DHARWAR SOUTH
24 DHARWAR NORTH
25 BELGAUM
26 CHIKKODI ○
27 BAGALKUT
28 BIJAPUR

KERALA
1 KASARAGOD
2 CANNANORE
3 BADAGARA
4 CALICUT
5 MANJERI
6 PONNANI
7 PALGHAT
8 OTTAPALAM ○
9 TRICHUR
10 MUKUNDAPURAM
11 ERNAKULAM
12 MUVATTUPUZHA
13 KOTTAYAM
14 IDUKKI
15 ALLEPPEY
16 MAVELIKARA
17 ADOOR ○
18 QUILON
19 CHIRAYINKIL
20 TRIVANDRUM

GOA, DAMAN & DIU
1 PANAJI
2 MARMUGAO

GUJARAT
1 KUTCH
2 SURENDRANAGAR
3 JAMNAGAR
4 RAJKOT
5 PORBANDAR
6 JUNAGADH
7 AMRELI
8 BHAVNAGAR
9 DHANDHUKA ○
10 AHMEDABAD
11 GANDHINAGAR
12 MEHSANA
13 PATAN
14 BANASKANTHA
15 SABARKANTHA
16 KAPADVANJ
17 DOHAD ●
18 GODHRA
19 KAIRA
20 ANAND
21 CHHOTA UDAIPUR ●
22 BARODA
23 BROACH
24 SURAT
25 MANDVI ○
26 BULSAR ●

HARYANA
1 AMBALA ○
2 KURUKSHETRA
3 KARNAL
4 SONEPAT
5 ROHTAK
6 FARIDABAD
7 MAHENDRAGARH
8 BHIWANI
9 HISSAR
10 SIRSA ○

HIMACHAL PRADESH
1 SIMLA ○
2 MANDI
3 KANGRA
4 HAMIRPUR

MADHYA PRADESH
1 MORENA ○
2 BHIND
3 GWALIOR
4 GUNA
5 SAGAR ○
6 KHAJURAHO
7 DAMOH
8 SATNA
9 REWA
10 SIDHI
11 SHAHDOL ●
12 SURGUJA ●
13 RAIGARH ●
14 JANJGIR
15 BILASPUR ○
16 SARANGARH ○
17 RAIPUR
18 MAHASAMUND
19 KANKER ●
20 BASTAR ●
21 DURG
22 RAJNANDGAON
23 BALAGHAT
24 MANDLA ●
25 JABALPUR
26 BEONI
27 CHHINDWARA
28 BETUL
29 HOSHANGABAD
30 BHOPAL
31 VIDISHA
32 RAJGARH
33 SHAJAPUR ○
34 KHANDWA
35 KHARGONE
36 DHAR ●
37 INDORE
38 UJJAIN ○
39 JHABUA ●
40 MANDSAUR

MAHARASHTRA
1 RAJAPUR
2 RATNAGIRI
3 KOLABA
4 BOMBAY SOUTH
5 BOMBAY SOUTH-CENTRAL
6 BOMBAY NORTH-CENTRAL
7 BOMBAY NORTH-EAST
8 BOMBAY NORTH-WEST
9 BOMBAY NORTH
10 THANE
11 DAHANU ●
12 NASIK
13 NALEGAON ●
14 DHULE ●
15 NANDURBAR ●
16 ERANDOL
17 JALGAON
18 BULDANA ○
19 AKOLA
20 WASHIM
21 AMRAVATI
22 RAMTEK
23 NAGPUR
24 BHANDARA
25 CHIMUR
26 CHANDRAPUR
27 WARDHA
28 YEOTMAL
29 HINGOLI
30 NANDED
31 PARBHANI
32 JALNA
33 AURANGABAD
34 BHIR
35 LATUR
36 OSMANABAD
37 SHOLAPUR
38 PANDHARPUR ○
39 AHMEDNAGAR
40 KOPARGAON
41 KHED
42 POONA
43 BARAMATI
44 SATARA
45 KARAD
46 SANGLI
47 ICHALKARANJI
48 KOLHAPUR

MANIPUR
1 INNER MANIPUR
2 OUTER MANIPUR ●

MEGHALAYA
1 SHILLONG ○
2 TURA

ORISSA
1 MAYURBHANJ ●
2 BALASORE
3 BHADRAK ○
4 JAJPUR ○
5 KENDRAPARA
6 CUTTACK
7 JAGATSINGHPUR
8 PURI
9 BHUBANESWAR
10 ASKA
11 BERHAMPUR
12 KORAPUT ●
13 NOWRANGPUR ●
14 KALAHANDI
15 PHULABANI ○
16 BOLANGIR
17 SAMBALPUR
18 DEOGARH
19 DHENKANAL
20 SUNDARGARH ●
21 KEONJHAR ●

PUNJAB
1 GURDASPUR
2 AMRITSAR
3 TARN TARAN
4 JALANDHAR
5 PHILLAUR
6 HOSHIARPUR
7 ROPAR
8 PATIALA
9 LUDHIANA
10 SANGRUR
11 BHATINDA
12 FARIDKOT
13 FEROZEPUR

RAJASTHAN
1 GANGANAGAR ○
2 BIKANER
3 CHURU
4 JHUNJHUNU
5 SIKAR
6 JAIPUR
7 DAUSA
8 ALWAR
9 BHARATPUR
10 BAYANA ○
11 SWAI MADHOPUR ○
12 AJMER
13 TONK
14 KOTA
15 JHALAWAR
16 BANSWARA ●
17 SALUMBER ●
18 UDAIPUR
19 CHITTORGARH
20 BHILWARA
21 PALI
22 JALORE ○
23 BARMER
24 JODHPUR
25 NAGAUR

TAMIL NADU
1 MADRAS NORTH
2 MADRAS CENTRAL
3 MADRAS SOUTH
4 SRIPERUMBUDUR ○
5 CHENGALPATTU
6 ARKKONAM
7 VELLORE
8 TIRUPPATTUR
9 VANDAVASI
10 TINDIVANAM
11 CUDDALORE
12 CHIDAMBARAM ○
13 DHARMAPURI
14 KRISHNAGIRI
15 RASIPURAM ○
16 SALEM
17 TIRUCHENGODE
18 NILGIRIS
19 GOBICHETTIPALATAN
20 COIMBATORE
21 POLLACHI ○
22 PALANI
23 DINDIGUL
24 MADURAI
25 PERIAKULAM
26 KARUR
27 TIRUCHRAPALLI
28 PERAMBALLUR ○
29 MAYURAM
30 NAGAPATTINAM ○
31 THANJAVUR
32 PUDUKKOTTAI
33 SIVAGANGA
34 RAMANTHAPURAM
35 SIVAKASI
36 TIRUNELVELI
37 TENKASI ○
38 TIRUCHENDUR
39 NAGERCOIL

TRIPURA
1 TRIPURA WEST
2 TRIPURA EAST ●

UTTAR PRADESH
1 TEHRI GARHWAL
2 GARHWAL
3 ALMORA
4 NAINITAL
5 BIJNOR ○
6 AMROHA
7 MORADABAD
8 RAMPUR
9 SAMBHAL
10 BUDAUN
11 AONLA
12 BAREILLY
13 PILIBHIT
14 SHAHJAHANPUR
15 KHERI
16 SHAHABAD
17 SITAPUR
18 MISRIKH ○
19 HARDOI
20 LUCKNOW
21 MOHANLALGANJ ○
22 UNNAO
23 RAE BAREILI
24 PRATAPGARH
25 AMETHI
26 SULTANPUR
27 AKBARPUR ○
28 FAIZABAD
29 BARABANKI ○
30 KAISERGANJ
31 BAHRAICH
32 BALRAMPUR
33 GONDA
34 BASTI ○
35 DOMARIAGANJ
36 KHALILABAD
37 BANSGAON ○
38 GORAKHPUR
39 MAHARAJGANJ
40 PADRAUNA
41 DEORIA
42 SALEMPUR
43 BALLIA
44 GHUSI
45 AZAMGARH
46 LALGANJ ○
47 MACHHALISHAHAR
48 JAUNPUR
49 SAIDPUR ○
50 GHAZIPUR
51 CHANDAULI ○
52 VARANASI
53 ROBERTSGANJ ○
54 MIRZAPUR
55 PHULPUR
56 ALLAHABAD
57 CHAIL
58 FATEHPUR
59 BANDA
60 HAMIRPUR
61 JHANSI
62 JALAUN
63 GHATAMPUR ○
64 BILHAUR
65 KANPUR
66 ETAWAH
67 KANNAUJ
68 FARRUKHABAD
69 MAINPURI
70 JALESAR
71 ETAH
72 FIROZABAD ○
73 AGRA
74 MATHURA
75 HATHRAS ○
76 ALIGARH
77 KHURJA ○
78 BULANDSHAHR
79 HAPUR
80 MEERUT
81 BAGHPAT
82 MUZAFFARNAGAR
83 KAIRANA
84 SAHARANPUR
85 HARDWAR ○

WEST BENGAL
1 COOCH BEHAR ○
2 ALIPURDUAR ●
3 JALPAIGURI
4 DARJEELING
5 RAIGANJ
6 BALURGHAT ○
7 MALDA
8 JANGIPUR
9 MURSHIDABAD
10 BEHRAMPORE
11 KRISHNAGAR
12 NABADWIP ○
13 BARASAT
14 BASIRHAT
15 JOYNAGAR ○
16 MATHURAPUR ○
17 DIAMOND HARBOUR
18 JADAVPUR
19 BARRACKPORE
20 DUM DUM
21 CALCUTTA NORTH-WEST
22 CALCUTTA NORTH-EAST
23 CALCUTTA SOUTH
24 HOWRAH
25 ULUBERIA
26 SERAMPORE
27 HOOGHLY
28 ARAMBAGH
29 PANSKURA
30 TAMLUK
31 CONTAI
32 MIDNAPORE
33 JHARGRAM ●
34 PURULIA
35 BANKURA
36 VISHNUPUR ○
37 DURGAPUR ○
38 ASANSOL
39 BURDWAN
40 KATWA
41 BOLPUR
42 BIRBHUM ○

44 CHATRA
45 KODERMA
46 GIRIDH
47 DHANBAD
48 HAZARI BAGH
49 RANCHI
50 JAMSHEDPUR
51 SINGHBHUM ●
52 KHUNTI ●
53 LOHARDAGA ●
54 PALAMAU ○

Map labels: ARUNACHAL PRADESH, ASSAM, NAGALAND, MANIPUR, MEGHALAYA, ANGLADESH, TRIPURA, MIZORAM

Republic of Ireland

A republic, with a directly elected president without executive powers. The president serves for seven years and is restricted to two terms. He is elected, on a majoritarian basis, using the alternative vote (see page 2).

There is a two-chamber parliament, the upper house of which, the *Seanad*, with 60 members, is partly nominated and partly indirectly elected. The government is responsible to the lower house, or *Dáil*, which has 166 members. Its term of office is five years, with the possibility of early dissolution. It is elected by proportional representation, using the single transferable vote system (see page 2). The 41 constituencies return three, four or five members. Voters number the candidates in the order of their preference. Casual vacancies are filled by by-elections in which the whole constituency participates, using the alternative vote. The minimum voting age is 18.

Last Presidential election: October 21 1983 (unopposed).

Result of Presidential election of October 21 1983
Patrick J. Hillery, unopposed.

Last parliamentary election: November 24 1982.

Next Presidential election due: October 1990.

Next parliamentary election due: November 1987.

Main political parties

1. Workers' Party
2. Labour Party
3. Fine Gael
4. Progressive Democratic Party, formed in 1985
5. Fianna Fáil

Result of election of November 24 1982

Electorate: 2,336,035   Valid votes: 1,688,719 (72.3%)   Invalid votes: 12,382 (0.5%). The results refer to first preference votes.

	Votes	%	Seats	%
Fianna Fáil	763,312	45.2	75	45.2
Fine Gael	662,284	39.2	70	42.2
Labour Party	158,115	9.4	16	9.6
Sinn Fein (Workers' Party)	54,888	3.2	2	1.2
Others	50,120	3.0	3	1.8
TOTAL	1,701,101		166	

Note: The invalid votes are, unlike in other countries, included in the party totals shown above.

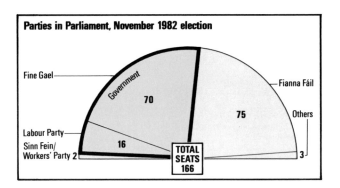

Parties in Parliament, November 1982 election

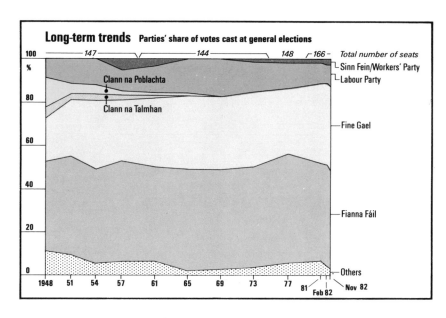

Long-term trends Parties' share of votes cast at general elections

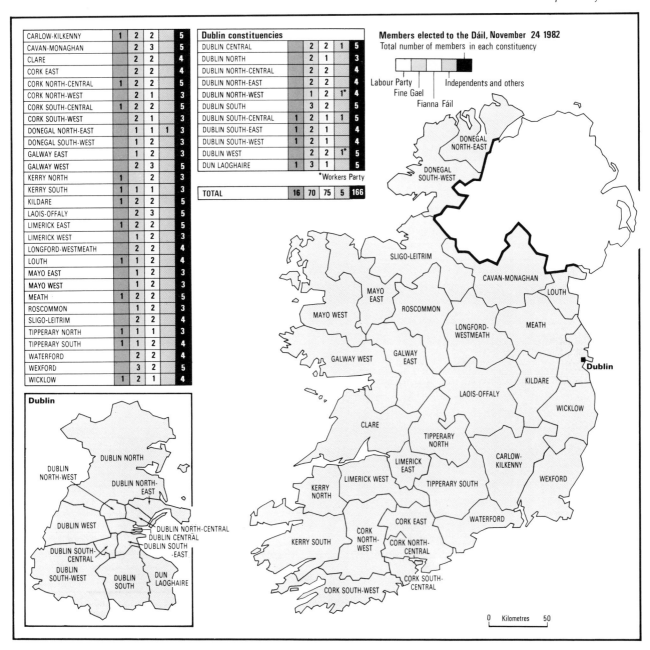

	Labour Party	Fine Gael	Fianna Fáil	Independents and others	Total
CARLOW-KILKENNY	1	2	2		5
CAVAN-MONAGHAN		2	3		5
CLARE		2	2		4
CORK EAST		2	2		4
CORK NORTH-CENTRAL	1	2	2		5
CORK NORTH-WEST		2	1		3
CORK SOUTH-CENTRAL	1	2	2		5
CORK SOUTH-WEST		2	1		3
DONEGAL NORTH-EAST		1	1	1	3
DONEGAL SOUTH-WEST		1	2		3
GALWAY EAST		1	2		3
GALWAY WEST		2	3		5
KERRY NORTH	1		2		3
KERRY SOUTH	1	1	1		3
KILDARE	1	2	2		5
LAOIS-OFFALY		2	3		5
LIMERICK EAST	1	2	2		5
LIMERICK WEST		1	2		3
LONGFORD-WESTMEATH		2	2		4
LOUTH	1	1	2		4
MAYO EAST		1	2		3
MAYO WEST		1	2		3
MEATH	1	2	2		5
ROSCOMMON		1	2		3
SLIGO-LEITRIM		2	2		4
TIPPERARY NORTH	1	1	1		3
TIPPERARY SOUTH	1	1	2		4
WATERFORD		2	2		4
WEXFORD		3	2		5
WICKLOW	1	2	1		4

Dublin constituencies	Labour Party	Fine Gael	Fianna Fáil	Independents and others	Total
DUBLIN CENTRAL		2	2	1	5
DUBLIN NORTH		2	1		3
DUBLIN NORTH-CENTRAL		2	2		4
DUBLIN NORTH-EAST		2	2		4
DUBLIN NORTH-WEST		1	2	1*	4
DUBLIN SOUTH		3	2		5
DUBLIN SOUTH-CENTRAL	1	2	1	1	5
DUBLIN SOUTH-EAST	1	2	1		4
DUBLIN SOUTH-WEST	1	2	1		4
DUBLIN WEST		2	2	1*	5
DUN LAOGHAIRE	1	3	1		5

*Workers Party

| TOTAL | 16 | 70 | 75 | 5 | 166 |

Members elected to the Dáil, November 24 1982

Total number of members in each constituency

Labour Party | Fine Gael | Fianna Fáil | Independents and others

Government

The present government, formed in December 1982, is a coalition of Fine Gael and Labour. The prime minister (*Taoiseach*) is Garret FitzGerald.

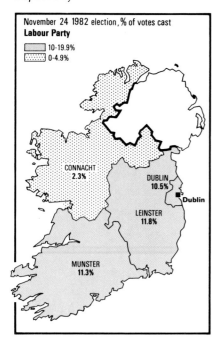

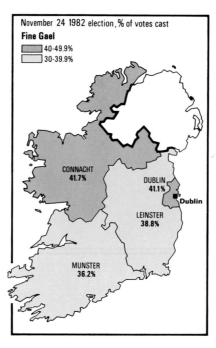

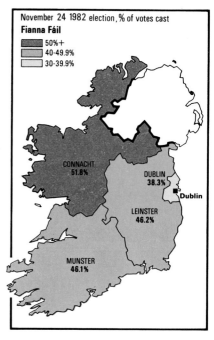

Election results: percentage votes and seats gained since 1948 (first preference votes only)

Election year	1948		1951		1954		1957		1961		1965		1969		1973		1977		1981		1982 (Feb.)		1982 (Nov.)	
Electorate	1,800,210		1,785,144		1,763,209		1,738,278		1,670,080		1,683,019		1,735,388		1,783,604		2,118,606		2,275,450		2,275,450		2,336,035	
Turnout %	73.5		74.6		75.7		70.6		69.9		74.5		76.0		75.7		75.5		75.5		73.2		72.3	
	V %	S	V %	S	V %	S	V %	S	V %	S	V %	S	V %	S	V %	S	V %	S	V %	S	V %	S	V %	S
Sinn Fein/Workers' Party									5.3	4	3.1	0			1.1	0	1.7	0	1.7	1	2.2	3	3.2	2
Labour Party	8.7	14	11.4	16	12.1	19	9.1	12	12.0	16	15.4	22	17.0	18	13.7	19	11.6	17	9.9	15	9.1	15	9.4	16
Clann na Poblachta	13.3	10	4.1	2	3.9	3	1.7	1	1.1	1	0.8	1												
Clann na Talmhan	5.5	7	2.9	6	3.0	5	2.4	3	1.5	2														
Fine Gael	19.8	31	25.8	40	32.0	50	26.6	40	32.0	47	34.1	47	34.1	47	35.1	54	30.5	43	36.5	65	37.3	63	39.2	70
Fianna Fáil	41.9	68	46.3	69	43.4	65	48.3	78	43.8	70	47.7	72	45.7	75	46.2	69	50.6	84	45.3	78	47.3	81	45.2	75
Others	10.9	17	9.6	14	5.7	5	6.6	9	6.4	8	2.1	2	3.2	1	3.9	2	5.6	4	6.7	7	4.1	4	3.0	3
TOTAL SEATS		147		147		147		147		144		144		144		144		148		166		166		166

Israel

A republic, with an indirectly elected president without executive powers. The government is responsible to the *Knesset*, a single-chamber parliament, with 120 members.

The *Knesset* serves a four-year term, with the possibility of early dissolution. It is elected by proportional representation, using the D'Hondt system (see page 2). The whole country forms a single constituency, and there is a minimum threshold of 1 per cent. The voter chooses between party lists with no possibility of varying the rank order of candidates. Casual vacancies are filled by co-opting the runner-up in the relevant party list. The minimum age for voting is 18.

Arabs who are Israeli citizens have voting rights, but in the occupied territories of the West Bank and Gaza only Israelis are able to vote.

Last election: July 23 1984.

Next election due: July 1988.

Main political parties

1. Hadash, Communist
2. Progressive List for Peace, Arab-Jewish list
3. Civil Rights Movement
4. Mapam, left-wing Labour, split off from Labour Party again in 1984
5. Labour Party
6. Shinui, or Change
7. National Religious Party
8. Tami, or Israel Tradition Movement
9. Likud, or Consolidation
10. Agudat, or Union of Israel
11. Shas, or Sephardic Torah Guardians
12. Ometz, or Courage
13. Morasha, Rally of Religious Zionism
14. Tehiya, or Revival
15. Kach Movement, anti-Arab extremist party

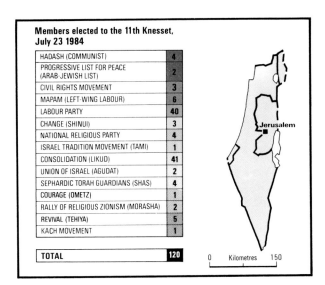

Members elected to the 11th Knesset, July 23 1984

HADASH (COMMUNIST)	4
PROGRESSIVE LIST FOR PEACE (ARAB-JEWISH LIST)	2
CIVIL RIGHTS MOVEMENT	3
MAPAM (LEFT-WING LABOUR)	6
LABOUR PARTY	40
CHANGE (SHINUI)	3
NATIONAL RELIGIOUS PARTY	4
ISRAEL TRADITION MOVEMENT (TAMI)	1
CONSOLIDATION (LIKUD)	41
UNION OF ISRAEL (AGUDAT)	2
SEPHARDIC TORAH GUARDIANS (SHAS)	4
COURAGE (OMETZ)	1
RALLY OF RELIGIOUS ZIONISM (MORASHA)	2
REVIVAL (TEHIYA)	5
KACH MOVEMENT	1
TOTAL	**120**

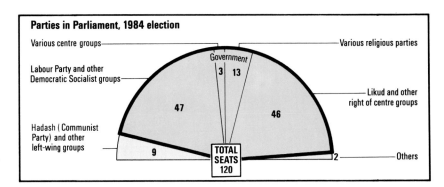

Parties in Parliament, 1984 election

Various centre groups — Government — Various religious parties
Labour Party and other Democratic Socialist groups
3 13
47 46
Likud and other right of centre groups
Hadash (Communist Party) and other left-wing groups
9 **TOTAL SEATS 120** 2 — Others

Government

The present government is a coalition between the Labour, Likud, National Religious, Shinui, Shas, Ometz and Morasha parties, with Shimon Peres (Labour) as prime minister. By prior agreement, Yitzhak Shamir (Likud) was to take over the premiership in September 1986.

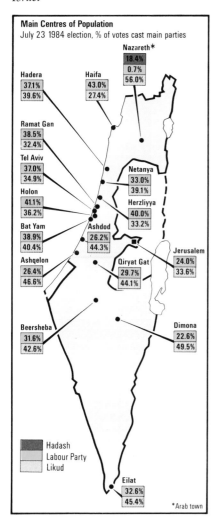

Main Centres of Population
July 23 1984 election, % of votes cast main parties

Nazareth*
18.4%
0.7%
56.0%

Hadera
37.1%
39.6%

Haifa
43.0%
27.4%

Ramat Gan
38.5%
32.4%

Tel Aviv
37.0%
34.9%

Netanya
33.0%
39.1%

Holon
41.1%
36.2%

Herzliyya
40.0%
33.2%

Bat Yam
38.9%
40.4%

Ashdod
26.2%
44.3%

Jerusalem
24.0%
33.6%

Ashqelon
26.4%
46.6%

Qiryat Gat
29.7%
44.1%

Beersheba
31.6%
42.6%

Dimona
22.6%
49.5%

Hadash
Labour Party
Likud

Eilat
32.6%
45.4%

*Arab town

Result of election of July 23 1984

Electorate: 2,654,613   Valid votes: 2,073,321 (78.1%)
Invalid votes: 18,081 (0.7%)

	Votes	%	Seats	%
Labour Alignment[a]	724,074	34.9	44	36.6
Likud	661,302	31.9	41	34.1
Tehiya	83,037	4.0	5	4.2
National Religious Party	73,530	3.5	4	3.3
Hadash	69,815	3.4	4	3.3
Shas	63,605	3.1	4	3.3
Shinui	54,747	2.6	3	2.5
Civil Rights Movement	49,698	2.4	3	2.5
Yahad[b]	46,302	2.2	3	2.5
Progessive List for Peace	38,012	1.8	2	1.7
Agudat	36,079	1.7	2	1.7
Morasha	33,287	1.6	2	1.7
Tami	31,103	1.5	1	0.8
Kach Movement	25,907	1.2	1	0.8
Ometz	23,845	1.2	1	0.8
Others	58,978	2.8	0	0.0
TOTAL	2,073,321		120	

[a] Included Mapam which won six seats, but subsequently split off from Labour.
[b] Yahad subsequently merged with Labour.

Note
Although the votes are cumulated nationally to allocate the seats, they are counted, and published, at lower levels, which enables a breakdown to be made by various categories – not all of them geographical. In the accompanying maps and diagrams, the support for the two largest parties Labour and Likud (and, where appropriate, for Hadash, which has a strong following among Arab voters), is shown for the following: large urban centres, old towns and cities, new towns and cities, old rural settlements (mainly *kibbutzim*), new rural settlements and non-Jewish settlements.

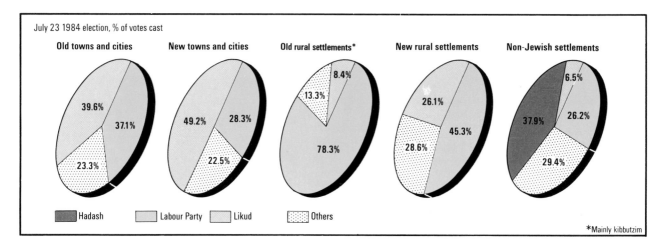

July 23 1984 election, % of votes cast

Old towns and cities
39.6%
37.1%
23.3%

New towns and cities
49.2%
28.3%
22.5%

Old rural settlements*
8.4%
13.3%
78.3%

New rural settlements
26.1%
45.3%
28.6%

Non-Jewish settlements
6.5%
26.2%
37.9%
29.4%

Hadash   Labour Party   Likud   Others

*Mainly kibbutzim

Election results: percentage votes and seats gained since 1949 (simplified categorisation of parties)

Election year	1949		1951		1955		1959		1961		1965		1969		1973		1977		1981		1984	
Electorate	506,567		924,885		1,057,795		1,218,483		1,274,280		1,449,709		1,758,685		2,037,478		2,236,293		2,490,014		2,654,613	
Turnout %	85.8		74.3		80.7		79.6		79.0		83.2		77.8		76.9		78.2		77.8		78.1	
	V %	S	V %	S	V %	S	V %	S	V %	S	V %	S	V %	S	V %	S	V %	S	V %	S	V %	S
Communists and other left-wing groups	3.5	4	4.0	5	4.5	6	2.8	3	4.2	5	8.5	10	8.5	10	11.3	12	7.0	7	5.4	5	7.6	9
Labour and other Democratic Socialist groups	53.5	67	54.5	65	52.6	64	56.2	68	52.7	63	55.0	67	49.7	60	42.7	54	26.0	33	36.6	47	37.1	47
Various centre groups																	15.2	18	2.5	2	2.6	3
Various religious parties	12.2	16	11.8	15	13.8	17	14.6	18	15.4	18	14.0	17	14.7	18	12.1	15	13.9	17	11.9	13	11.4	13
Likud and other right of centre groups	20.8	26	26.0	32	27.2	33	24.3	31	27.4	34	21.3	26	26.0	32	30.2	39	35.3	45	41.0	53	36.0	46
Others	10.0	7	3.5	3	1.9	0	2.2	0	0.3	0	1.3	0	1.1	0	3.5	0	2.7	0	2.7	0	5.2	2
TOTAL SEATS		120		120		120		120		120		120		120		120		120		120		120

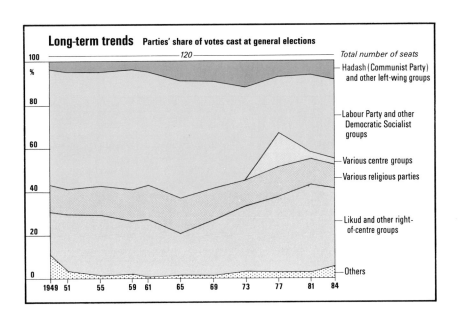

Long-term trends Parties' share of votes cast at general elections

Total number of seats

Hadash (Communist Party) and other left-wing groups

Labour Party and other Democratic Socialist groups

Various centre groups

Various religious parties

Likud and other right-of-centre groups

Others

Italy

A republic, with an indirectly elected president without executive powers. The government is responsible to the two-chamber parliament. The upper house, or Senate, has 315 members elected by proportional representation using the D'Hondt system (see page 2), plus five nominated members and former presidents of the republic *ex officio*.

The Chamber of Deputies has 630 members elected by proportional representation, using the Imperiali quota (see page 3). There are 31 multi-member constituencies and one (Val d'Aosta) returning a single member who is chosen on a plurality basis (see page 2). There is a two-stage distribution of seats. In each constituency the seats are allocated to parties according to the number of electoral quotas which they achieve. Residual seats and votes are transferred to a national pool, where the seats are allocated on a highest remainder basis (see page 2). To be eligible for seats from the national pool a party must have polled at least 300,000 votes nationally and have achieved at least one electoral quota.

The minimum voting age is 18. Voters choose between party lists, but are able to vary the order of candidates to a considerable extent. Casual vacancies are filled by the co-option of the next highest candidate in the relevant party list. The Chamber serves for five years, with a limited possibility of early dissolution.

Last election: June 26 1983.

Next election due: June 1988.

Result of election of June 26 1983

Electorate: 43,925,763   Valid votes: 36,890,319 (84.0%)   Invalid votes: 2,216,086 (5.0%)

	Votes	%	Seats	%
Christian Democratic Party	12,145,800	32.9	225	35.7
Communist Party[a]	11,028,158	29.9	198	31.3
Socialist Party	4,222,487	11.4	73	11.6
Italian Social Movement	2,511,722	6.8	42	6.7
Republican Party	1,872,536	5.1	29	4.6
Social Democratic Party	1,507,431	4.1	23	3.7
Liberal Party	1,065,833	2.9	16	2.5
Radical Party	809,672	2.2	11	1.7
Proletarian Democracy Party	541,493	1.5	7	1.1
Others	1,185,187	3.2	6	1.0
TOTAL	36,890,319		630	

[a] Including the Socialist Party of Proletarian Unity.

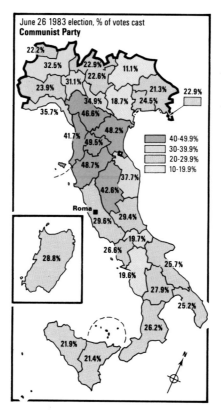

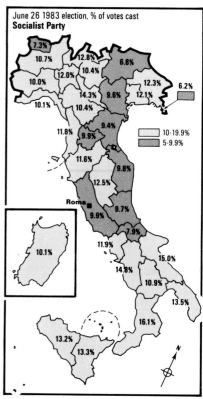

80

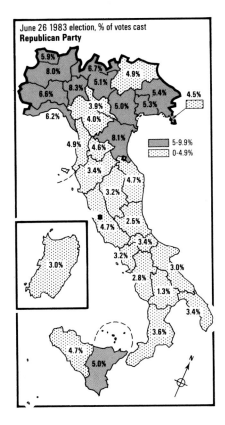

June 26 1983 election, % of votes cast
Republican Party

5-9.9%
0-4.9%

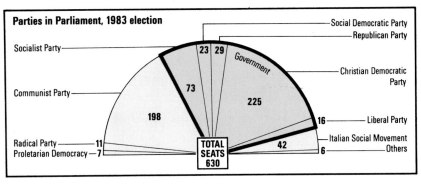

Parties in Parliament, 1983 election

Social Democratic Party
Republican Party
Socialist Party
Christian Democratic Party
Communist Party
Liberal Party
Italian Social Movement
Radical Party
Proletarian Democracy
Others
Government

23 29
73
198   225
16
42
6

11
7

TOTAL SEATS 630

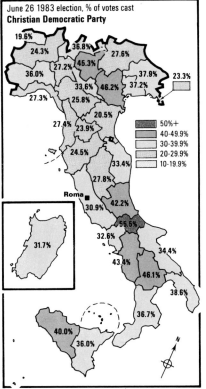

June 26 1983 election, % of votes cast
Christian Democratic Party

50%+
40-49.9%
30-39.9%
20-29.9%
10-19.9%

Roma

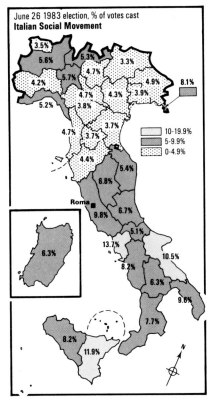

June 26 1983 election, % of votes cast
Italian Social Movement

10-19.9%
5-9.9%
0-4.9%

Roma

Main political parties

1. Proletarian Democracy Party (DP)
2. Radical Party (PR)
3. Communist Party (PCI)
4. Socialist Party (PSI)
5. Social Democratic Party (PSDI)
6. Republican Party (PRI)
7. Christian Democratic Party (DC)
8. Liberal Party (PLI)
9. Monarchist Party, merged with MSI in 1972
10. Italian Social Movement (MSI), Neo-Fascist

Government

The present government, formed in July 1983, is a coalition of the Christian Democratic, Socialist, Social Democratic, Republican and Liberal parties. The prime minister is Bettino Craxi (Socialist).

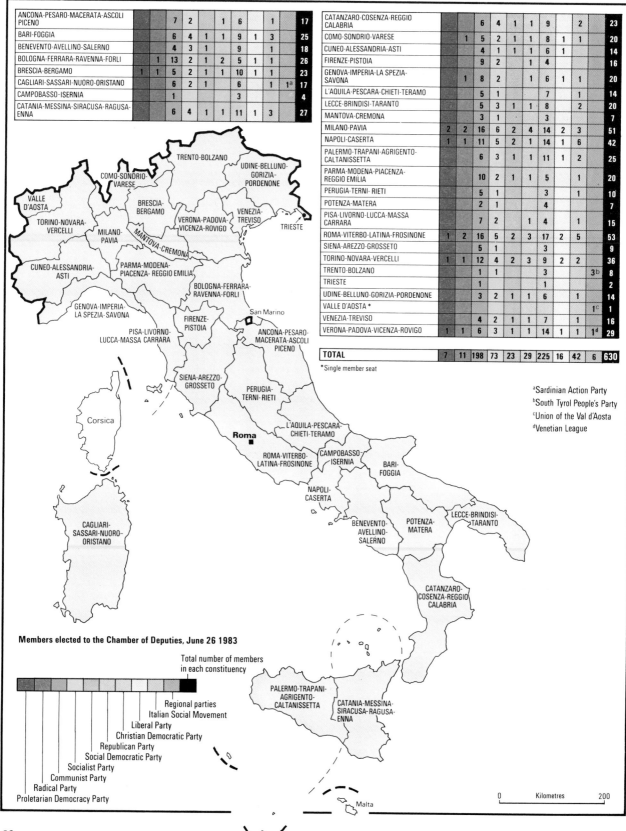

Constituency	Proletarian Democracy Party	Radical Party	Communist Party	Socialist Party	Social Democratic Party	Republican Party	Christian Democratic Party	Liberal Party	Italian Social Movement	Regional parties	Total
ANCONA-PESARO-MACERATA-ASCOLI PICENO			7	2		1	6		1		17
BARI-FOGGIA			6	4	1	1	9	1	3		25
BENEVENTO-AVELLINO-SALERNO			4	3	1		9		1		18
BOLOGNA-FERRARA-RAVENNA-FORLI		1	13	2	1	2	5	1	1		26
BRESCIA-BERGAMO	1	1	5	2	1	1	10	1	1		23
CAGLIARI-SASSARI-NUORO-ORISTANO			6	2	1		6		1	1a	17
CAMPOBASSO-ISERNIA			1				3				4
CATANIA-MESSINA-SIRACUSA-RAGUSA-ENNA			6	4	1	1	11	1	3		27
CATANZARO-COSENZA-REGGIO CALABRIA			6	4	1	1	9		2		23
COMO-SONDRIO-VARESE		1	5	2	1	1	8	1	1		20
CUNEO-ALESSANDRIA-ASTI			4	1	1	1	6	1			14
FIRENZE-PISTOIA			9	2		1	4				16
GENOVA-IMPERIA-LA SPEZIA-SAVONA		1	8	2		1	6	1	1		20
L'AQUILA-PESCARA-CHIETI-TERAMO			5	1			7		1		14
LECCE-BRINDISI-TARANTO			5	3	1	1	8		2		20
MANTOVA-CREMONA			3	1			3				7
MILANO-PAVIA	2	2	16	6	2	4	14	2	3		51
NAPOLI-CASERTA	1	1	11	5	2	1	14	1	6		42
PALERMO-TRAPANI-AGRIGENTO-CALTANISSETTA			6	3	1	1	11	1	2		25
PARMA-MODENA-PIACENZA-REGGIO EMILIA			10	2	1	1	5		1		20
PERUGIA-TERNI-RIETI			5	1			3		1		10
POTENZA-MATERA			2	1			4				7
PISA-LIVORNO-LUCCA-MASSA CARRARA			7	2		1	4		1		15
ROMA-VITERBO-LATINA-FROSINONE	1	2	16	5	2	3	17	2	5		53
SIENA-AREZZO-GROSSETO			5	1			3				9
TORINO-NOVARA-VERCELLI	1	1	12	4	2	3	9	2	2		36
TRENTO-BOLZANO			1	1			3			3b	8
TRIESTE			1				1				2
UDINE-BELLUNO-GORIZIA-PORDENONE			3	2	1	1	6		1		14
VALLE D'AOSTA *										1c	1
VENEZIA-TREVISO			4	2	1	1	7		1		16
VERONA-PADOVA-VICENZA-ROVIGO	1	1	6	3	1	1	14	1	1	1d	29
TOTAL	7	11	198	73	23	29	225	16	42	6	**630**

*Single member seat

a Sardinian Action Party
b South Tyrol People's Party
c Union of the Val d'Aosta
d Venetian League

Members elected to the Chamber of Deputies, June 26 1983

Total number of members in each constituency

Regional parties
Italian Social Movement
Liberal Party
Christian Democratic Party
Republican Party
Social Democratic Party
Socialist Party
Communist Party
Radical Party
Proletarian Democracy Party

0   Kilometres   200

Election results: percentage votes and seats gained since 1945

Election year	1946		1948		1953		1958		1963		1968		1972		1976		1979		1983	
Electorate	28,005,449		29,117,554		30,267,080		32,436,022		34,201,660		35,566,681		37,049,654		40,423,131		42,181,664		43,925,763	
Turnout %		82.2		90.2		89.5		91.1		89.9		89.4		90.1		90.8		86.8		84.0
	V %	S	V %	S	V %	S	V %	S	V %	S	V %	S	V %	S	V %	S	V %	S	V %	S
Proletarian Democracy Party													0.7		1.5	6	1.4	6	1.5	7
Radical Party															1.1	4	3.5	18	2.2	11
Communist Party	18.9	104	31.0	131	22.6	143	22.7	140	25.3	166	26.9	177	27.2	179	34.4	227	30.4	201	29.9	198
Socialist Party	20.7	115		52	12.7	75	14.2	84	13.8	87	14.5	91	9.6	61	9.6	57	9.8	62	11.4	73
Democratic Social Party			7.1	33	4.5	19	4.6	22	6.1	32			5.1	29	3.4	15	3.8	21	4.1	23
Republican Party	4.8	25	2.5	9	1.6	5	1.4	6	1.4	6	2.0	9	2.9	14	3.1	14	3.0	15	5.1	29
Christian Democratic Party	35.2	207	48.5	305	40.1	263	42.4	273	38.2	260	39.0	266	38.7	267	38.7	263	38.3	261	32.9	225
Liberal Party	6.8	41	3.8	19	3.0	13	3.5	17	7.0	40	5.8	31	3.9	21	1.3	5	1.9	9	2.9	16
Monarchist Party	2.8	16	2.8	14	6.8	40	2.2	11	1.7	8	1.3	6	8.7	56	6.1	35	5.3	31	6.8	42
Italian Social Movement			2.0	6	5.8	29	4.8	24	5.1	27	4.4	24								
Others	10.8	48	2.3	5	2.9	3	4.2	19	1.4	4	6.1	26	3.2	3	0.8	4	2.6	6	3.2	6
TOTAL SEATS		556		574		590		596		630		630		630		630		630		630

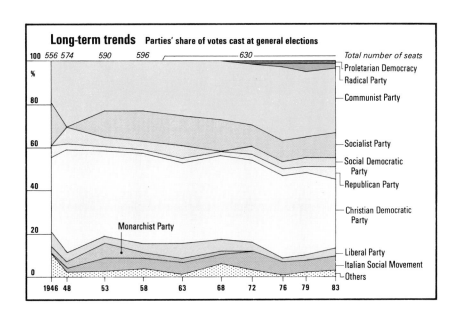

Long-term trends Parties' share of votes cast at general elections

Total number of seats

Proletarian Democracy
Radical Party
Communist Party
Socialist Party
Social Democratic Party
Republican Party
Christian Democratic Party
Monarchist Party
Liberal Party
Italian Social Movement
Others

556 574 590 596 630

1946 48 53 58 63 68 72 76 79 83

Jamaica

A constitutional monarchy, the British monarch's role being filled by a governor-general appointed on the advice of the Jamaican government.

The government is responsible to a two-chamber parliament. The upper house, or Senate, of 21 members, is entirely nominated. The lower house, or House of Representatives, of 60 members is elected on a plurality basis (see page 2) in single-member constituencies. Its term of office is five years, with the possibility of early dissolution. The minimum voting age is 18. Casual vacancies are filled by by-elections.

The most recent election, in December 1983, was boycotted by the main opposition party, the People's National Party, on the grounds that the government had gone back on an earlier undertaking in provoking an early dissolution. In consequence, the Government candidate was returned unopposed in 54 out of the 60 constituencies.

Result of election of December 15 1983

Electorate: 990,586   Electors in six contested seats: 90,019   Valid votes: 26,055 (28.9%)   Invalid votes: 488 (0.5%)

	Votes	%	Seats
Jamaica Labour Party	23,363	89.7	6
Independents and others	2,692	10.3	0
TOTAL contested	26,055		6

Note: Due to the boycott by the main opposition party, the People's National Movement, only six out of 60 seats were contested. The candidate for the Jamaica Labour Party was elected in each case, and a JLP member was returned unopposed for each of the other 54 seats.

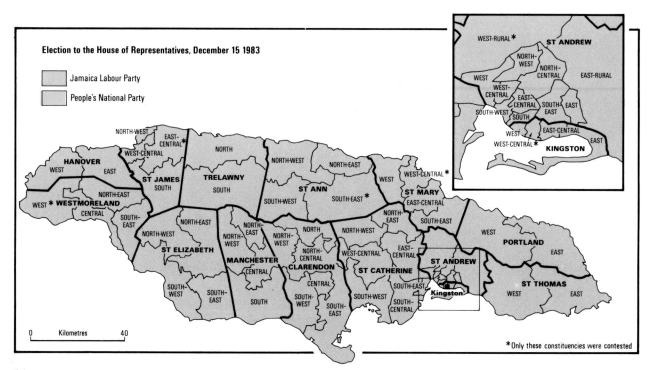

Election to the House of Representatives, December 15 1983

Jamaica Labour Party

People's National Party

*Only these constituencies were contested

Last election: December 15 1983.

Next election due: December 1988.

Main political parties

1. People's National Party (PNP), Social Democratic
2. Jamaica Labour Party (JLP), Right of Centre

Government

The present government, reconstituted after the December 1983 election, is formed by the Jamaica Labour Party. The prime minister is Edward Seaga.

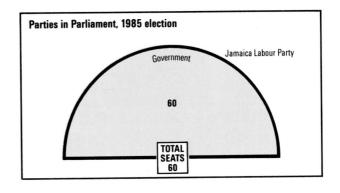

Parties in Parliament, 1985 election

Japan

A constitutional monarchy since 1947, when a democratic constitution was adopted.

The government is responsible to a two-chamber parliament, or Diet, both of which are directly elected. The upper house, or House of Councillors, has 252 members. 152 of these are elected on a plurality basis (see page 2), while the remaining 100 are elected by proportional representation.

The lower house, or House of Representatives, has 511 members, elected on a plurality basis from 130 multi-member constituencies. Japan, uniquely, uses the single non-transferable vote system (see page 2), which means that the voter can support only one candidate even though there is more than one vacancy to fill. Casual vacancies are filled by by-elections. The minimum voting age is 20. The term of office of the House of Representatives is four years, with the possibility of early dissolution.

Last election: December 18 1983.

Next election due: December 1987 (see Stop Press, page 159).

Main political parties

1. Japan Communist Party
2. Japan Socialist Party (JSP)
3. Democratic Socialist Party (DSP)
4. Social Democratic Federation (Shaminren) (SDF)
5. Clean Government Party (Komeito)
6. New Liberal Club (NLC)
7. Liberal Democratic Party

Government

The present government is formed by the Liberal Democratic Party. The prime minister is Yasuhiro Nakasone.

Result of election of December 18 1983

Electorate: 84,252,608   Valid votes: 56,779,690 (67.4%)   Invalid votes: 461,130 (0.8%)

	Votes	%	Seats	%
Liberal Democratic Party	25,982,781	45.8	251	49.1
Japan Socialist Party	11,065,080	19.5	110	21.5
Clean Government Party	5,745,750	10.1	59	11.5
Japan Commmunist Party	5,302,485	9.3	25	4.9
Democratic Socialist Party	4,129,907	7.3	39	7.6
New Liberal Club	1,341,584	2.4	8	1.6
Social Democratic Federation	381,045	0.7	3	0.6
Other parties	62,323	0.1	0	0.0
Independents	2,768,735	4.9	16	3.1
TOTAL	56,779,690		511	

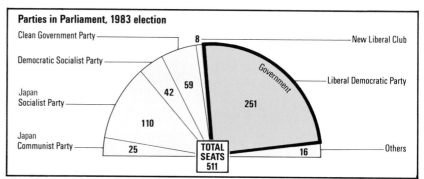

Parties in Parliament, 1983 election

Note: The figure for the Democratic Socialist Party includes 3 seats for the Social Democratic Federation.

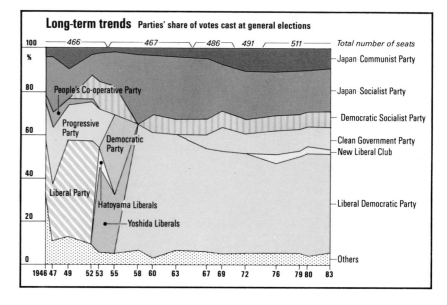

Long-term trends Parties' share of votes cast at general elections

86

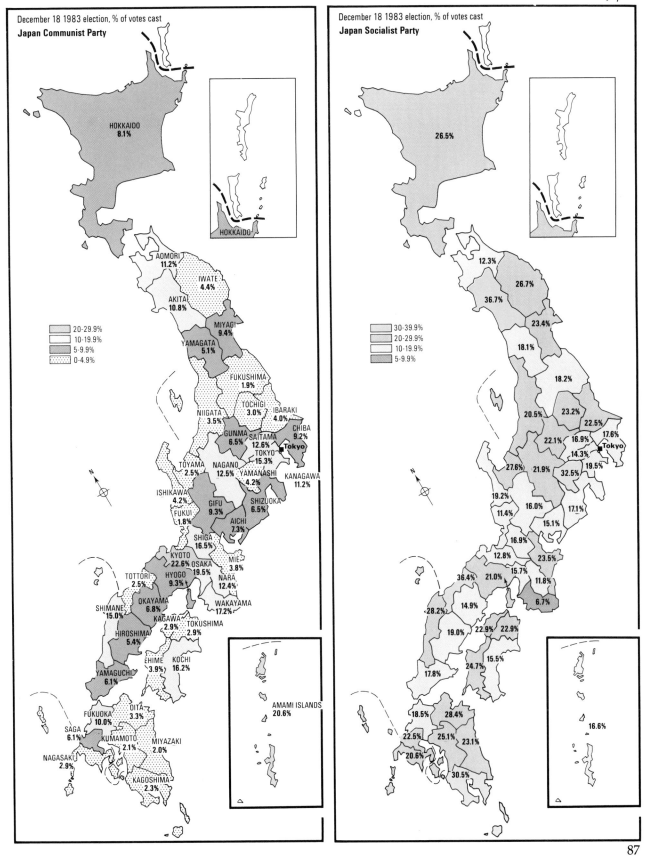

December 18 1983 election, % of votes cast
Japan Communist Party

HOKKAIDO
8.1%

20-29.9%
10-19.9%
5-9.9%
0-4.9%

AOMORI
11.2%

IWATE
4.4%

AKITA
10.8%

MIYAGI
9.4%

YAMAGATA
5.1%

FUKUSHIMA
1.9%

TOCHIGI
3.0%

IBARAKI
4.0%

NIIGATA
3.5%

GUNMA
6.5%

SAITAMA
12.6%

CHIBA
9.2%

TOKYO
15.3%

Tokyo

TOYAMA
2.5%

NAGANO
12.5%

YAMANASHI
4.2%

KANAGAWA
11.2%

ISHIKAWA
4.2%

GIFU
9.3%

SHIZUOKA
6.5%

FUKUI
1.8%

AICHI
7.3%

SHIGA
16.5%

KYOTO
22.6%

OSAKA
19.5%

MIE
3.8%

TOTTORI
2.5%

HYOGO
9.3%

NARA
12.4%

SHIMANE
15.0%

OKAYAMA
6.8%

KAGAWA
2.9%

WAKAYAMA
17.2%

TOKUSHIMA
2.9%

HIROSHIMA
5.4%

EHIME
3.9%

KOCHI
16.2%

YAMAGUCHI
6.1%

FUKUOKA
10.0%

OITA
3.3%

AMAMI ISLANDS
20.6%

SAGA
6.1%

KUMAMOTO
2.1%

MIYAZAKI
2.0%

NAGASAKI
2.9%

KAGOSHIMA
2.3%

HOKKAIDO

December 18 1983 election, % of votes cast
Japan Socialist Party

26.5%

30-39.9%
20-29.9%
10-19.9%
5-9.9%

12.3%

26.7%

36.7%

23.4%

18.1%

18.2%

20.5%

23.2%

22.5%

17.6%

22.1%

16.9%

Tokyo

14.3%

27.6%

21.9%

32.5%

19.5%

19.2%

16.0%

17.1%

11.4%

15.1%

16.9%

12.8%

23.5%

36.4%

21.0%

15.7%

11.8%

28.2%

14.9%

22.9%

22.9%

6.7%

19.0%

15.5%

17.8%

24.7%

18.5%

28.4%

16.6%

22.5%

25.1%

23.1%

20.6%

30.5%

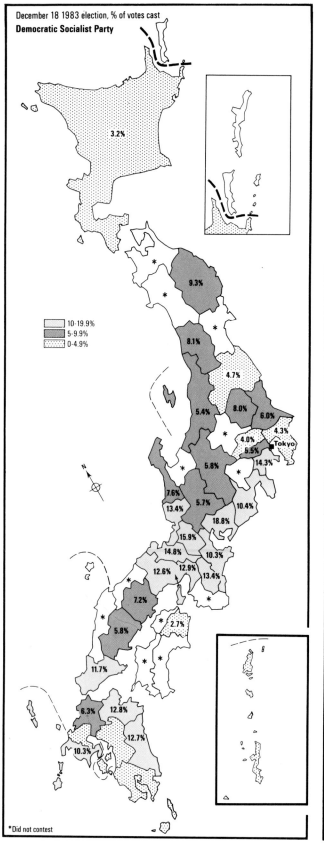

December 18 1983 election, % of votes cast
Democratic Socialist Party

3.2%

9.3%

8.1%

4.7%

5.4%   8.0%   6.0%

4.3%

4.0%   Tokyo

5.5%

14.3%

5.8%

7.6%

13.4%   5.7%

10.4%

18.8%

15.9%

14.8%   10.3%

12.6%   12.9%   13.4%

7.2%

5.8%   2.7%

11.7%

6.3%   12.8%

12.7%

10.3%

10-19.9%
5-9.9%
0-4.9%

*Did not contest

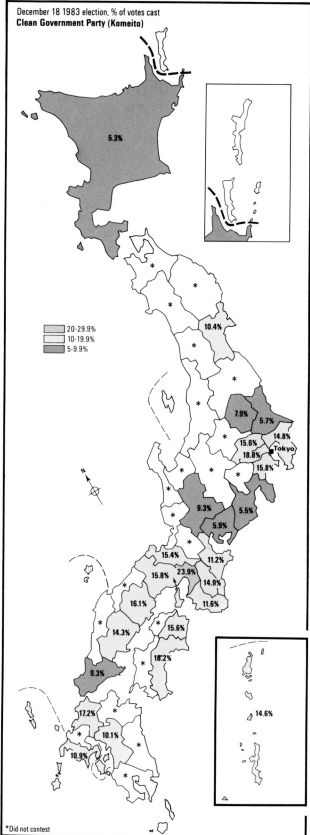

December 18 1983 election, % of votes cast
Clean Government Party (Komeito)

5.3%

10.4%

7.9%   5.7%

15.6%   14.8%

18.8%   Tokyo

15.8%

9.3%   5.5%

5.9%

15.4%   11.2%

15.8%   23.9%

14.9%

16.1%   11.6%

14.3%   15.6%

18.2%

9.3%

17.2%

10.1%

10.9%

14.6%

20-29.9%
10-19.9%
5-9.9%

*Did not contest

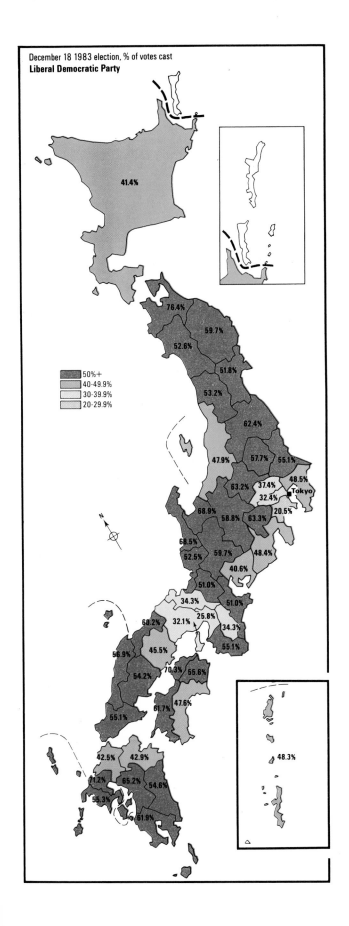

December 18 1983 election, % of votes cast
Liberal Democratic Party

41.4%

76.4%
59.7%
52.6%
51.8%
53.2%
62.4%

50%+
40-49.9%
30-39.9%
20-29.9%

47.9%
57.7% 55.1%
48.5%
63.2% 37.4% Tokyo
32.4%
68.9% 20.5%
58.8% 63.3%
68.5%
52.5% 59.7% 48.4%
40.6%
51.0%
34.3%
51.0%
25.8%
60.2% 32.1%
34.3%
56.9% 45.5% 55.1%
54.2% 70.3% 55.6%
47.6%
61.7%
55.1%

42.5% 42.9%
71.2% 65.2% 54.6%
55.3%
61.9%

48.3%

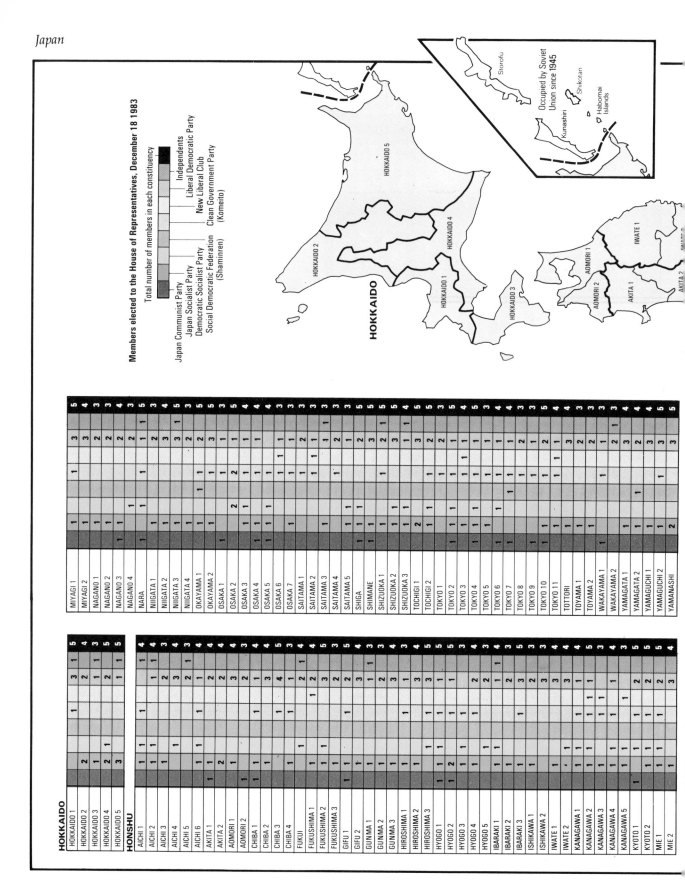

Members elected to the House of Representatives, December 18 1983

Total number of members in each constituency

Japan Communist Party
Japan Socialist Party
Democratic Socialist Party
Social Democratic Federation (Shaminren)
Independents
Liberal Democratic Party
New Liberal Club
Clean Government Party (Komeito)

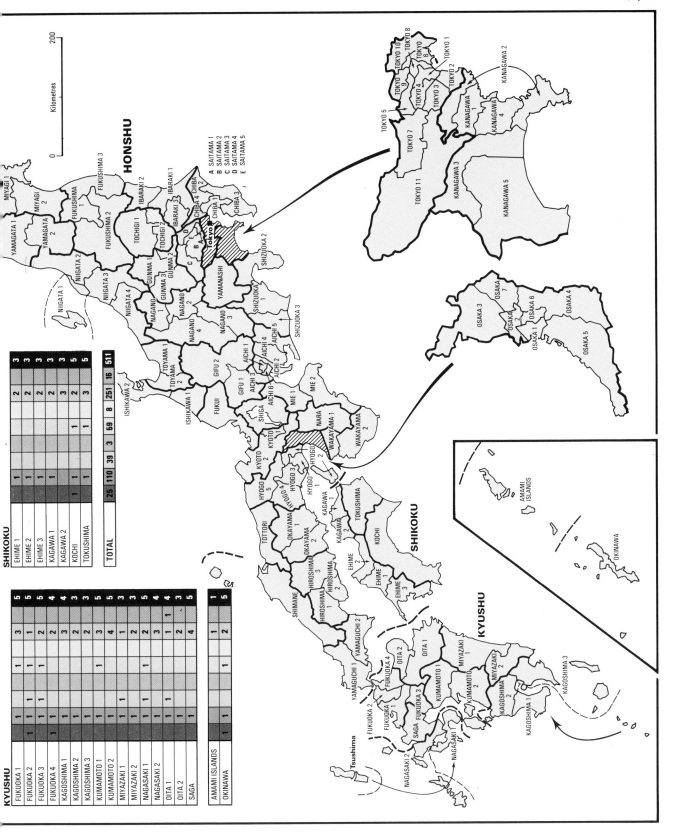

Election results: percentage votes and seats gained since 1946

Election year	1946		1947		1949		1952		1953		1955		1958		1960		1963		1967	
Electorate	36,878,420		40,907,493		42,105,300		46,772,584		47,090,167		49,235,375		52,013,529		54,312,993		58,281,676		62,992,796	
Turnout %		70.8		66.9		72.7		75.6		73.5		75.2		76.4		72.7		70.4		73.0
	V %	S	V %	S	V %	S	V %	S	V %	S	V %	S	V %	S	V %	S	V %	S	V %	S
Japan Communist Party	3.9	5	3.7	4	9.8	35	2.5	0	1.9	1	2.0	2	2.5	1	2.9	3	4.0	5	4.8	5
Japan Socialist Party	17.8	94	26.2	143	13.5	48	9.9	54	13.1	72	15.4	89 }	32.9	166	27.6	145	28.6	144	27.9	140
Democratic Socialist Party							11.4	57	13.5	66	13.9	67 }			8.8	17	7.3	23	7.4	30
People's Co-operative Party	3.2	14	7.0	31	3.4	14	1.1	2												
Clean Government Party																			5.4	25
New Liberal Club																				
Progressive Party	18.7	94	25.4	121	15.7	69	18.2	85	17.9	76										
Democratic Party											36.6	185 }								
Liberal Party	24.4	141	26.7	131	43.9	264	47.9	240					57.8	287	57.6	296	53.9	283	48.8	277
Hatoyama Liberals									8.8	35										
Yoshida Liberals									38.9	199	26.6	112								
Liberal Democratic Party																				
Others	32.0	118	10.9	36	13.5	36	9.1	28	5.9	17	5.7	12	6.7	13	3.2	6	6.3	12	5.8	9
TOTAL SEATS		466		466		466		466		466		467		467		467		467		486

Election year	1969		1972		1976		1979		1980		1983	
Electorate	61,260,424		73,769,637		77,926,588		80,169,924		80,925,034		84,252,608	
Turnout %		67.8		71.1		72.6		67.4		72.9		67.4
	V %	S	V %	S	V %	S	V %	S	V %	S	V %	S
Japan Communist Party	6.8	14	10.5	38	10.4	17	10.4	39	9.8	29	9.3	25
Japan Socialist Party	21.4	90	21.9	118	20.7	123	19.7	107	19.3	107	19.5	110
Democratic Socialist Party	7.7	31	7.0	19	6.3	29	6.8	35	6.6	32	7.3	39
People's Co-operative Party												
Clean Government Party	10.9	47	8.5	29	10.9	55	9.8	57	9.0	33	10.1	59
New Liberal Club					4.2	17	3.0	4	3.0	12	2.4	8
Progressive Party												
Democratic Party												
Liberal Party												
Hatoyama Liberals	47.6	288	46.9	271	41.8	249	44.6	248	47.9	284	45.8	251
Yoshida Liberals												
Liberal Democratic Party												
Others	5.5	16	5.3	16	5.8	21	5.7	21	4.4	14	5.7	19
TOTAL SEATS		486		491		511		511		511		511

Luxembourg

A constitutional monarchy, with an hereditary Grand Duke. The government is responsible to a single-chamber parliament, the Chamber of Deputies, with 64 members.

The Chamber is elected for a five-year term, with the possibility of early dissolution. The country is divided into four multi-member constituencies, and the voter has as many votes to cast as there are members to be elected. Votes may be freely divided, if the voter desires, between candidates from several different party lists (*Panachage*, see page 3). Up to two votes (but no more) may be given to the same candidate. The seat allocation is based on proportional representation, using the Hagenbach-Bischoff quota (see page 3). Casual vacancies are filled by co-opting the runner-up within the relevant party list. The minimum voting age is 18, and voting is compulsory.

Last election: June 17 1984.

Next election due: June 1989.

Main political parties

1. Communist Party (PCL)
2. The Green Alternative
3. Socialist Party (POSL)
4. Christian Social Party (PCS)
5. Democratic Party (PD), Liberal

Government

The present government is a coalition of the Christian Social and Socialist Parties. It was formed in June 1984, and the prime minister is Jacques Santer (PCS).

Result of election of June 17 1984

Electorate: 215,792   Valid voters: 173,928 (80.6%)

	Votes[a]	%	Seats	%
Christian Social Party	1,149,310	34.8	25	39.1
Socialist Party	1,106,755	33.6	21	32.8
Democratic Party	615,637	18.7	14	21.9
The Green Alternative	169,856	5.1	2	3.1
Communist Party	166,063	4.9	2	3.1
Others	87,818	2.9	0	0.0
TOTAL	3,295,439		64	

[a] As each elector may cast up to 25 votes, the total number recorded is many times the size of the electorate.

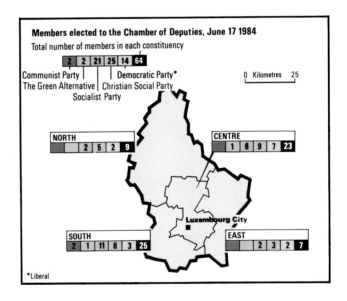

Members elected to the Chamber of Deputies, June 17 1984

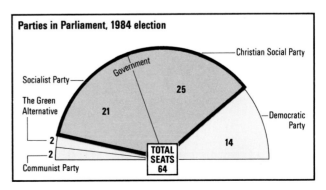

Parties in Parliament, 1984 election

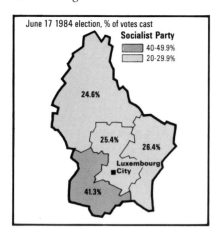

June 17 1984 election, % of votes cast
Socialist Party
- ▦ 40-49.9%
- ☐ 20-29.9%

24.6%
25.4%
26.4%
Luxembourg City
41.3%

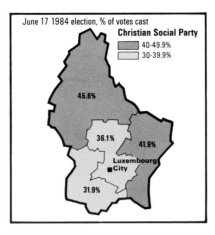

June 17 1984 election, % of votes cast
Christian Social Party
- ▦ 40-49.9%
- ☐ 30-39.9%

45.8%
36.1%
41.9%
Luxembourg City
31.9%

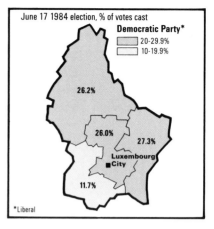

June 17 1984 election, % of votes cast
Democratic Party*
- ▦ 20-29.9%
- ☐ 10-19.9%

26.2%
26.0%
27.3%
Luxembourg City
11.7%

*Liberal

Election results: percentage votes and seats gained since 1954

Election year	1954		1959		1964		1968		1974		1979		1984	
Electorate	183,590		188,286		191,788		192,601		205,817		212,615		215,792	
Turnout %	88.3		87.9		85.1		83.2		85.2		82.7		80.6	
%	V %	S	V %	S	V %	S	V %	S	V %	S	V %	S	V	S
Communist Party	8.9	3	9.1	3	12.5	5	15.5	6	10.5	5	5.8	2	4.9	2
Socialist Party	35.1	17	34.9	17	37.7	21	32.3	18}	29.1	17	24.3	14	33.6	21
Social Democratic Party									9.2	5	6.0	2		
The Green Alternative											1.0	0	5.1	2
Popular Independent Movement					6.0	2	0.4	0}	22.2	14	21.3	15	18.7	14
Democratic Party	10.8	6	18.5	11	10.6	6	16.6	11}						
Christian Social Party	42.4	26	36.9	21	33.3	22	35.3	21	27.9	18	34.5	24	34.8	25
Others	2.8	0	0.7	0					1.1	0	6.9	2	2.9	0
TOTAL SEATS		52		52		56		56		59		59		64

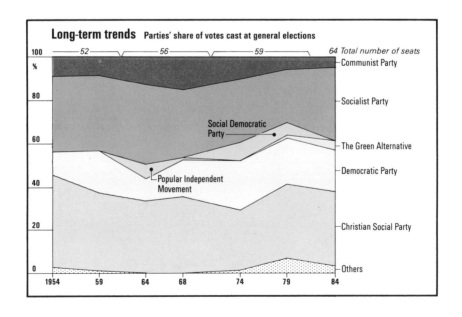

Long-term trends Parties' share of votes cast at general elections

52 — 56 — 59 — 64 Total number of seats
Communist Party
Socialist Party
Social Democratic Party
The Green Alternative
Popular Independent Movement
Democratic Party
Christian Social Party
Others

1954 59 64 68 74 79 84

Netherlands

A constitutional monarchy. The government is responsible to a two-chamber parliament, the *States General*. The First Chamber, with 75 members, is indirectly elected. The Second Chamber, with 150 members, is elected by proportional representation, using the D'Hondt system (see page 2) for allocating the seats. The whole country forms a single constituency, though the votes are counted locally and then aggregated at the national level. Voters choose between rival party lists with a possibility of amending the order of candidates. There is a very low threshold, of 0.66 per cent, before a party can qualify to be allocated a seat. The minimum voting age is 18. The term of office of the Second Chamber is four years, with the possibility of early dissolution. Casual vacancies are filled by co-opting the runner-up in the relevant party list.

Last election: September 8 1982.

Next election due: May 1986 (see Stop Press, page 160).

Main political parties

1. Communist Party
2. Pacifist Socialist Party
3. Radical Party
4. Labour Party
5. Democrats '66
6. Christian Democratic Appeal
7. Liberal Party
8. Evangelical Progressive People's Party
9. Reformational Political Federation
10. Reformed Political Association
11. State Reform Party
   Nos. 8–11 are Calvinist parties.
12. Centre Party, extreme Right

Result of election of September 8 1982

Electorate: 10,216,634   Valid votes: 8,236,536 (80.6%)
Invalid votes: 63,791 (0.6%)

	Votes	%	Seats	%
Labour Party	2,503,517	30.4	47	31.3
Christian Democratic Appeal	2,420,441	29.4	45	30.0
Liberal Party	1,900,763	23.1	36	24.0
Democrats '66	351,278	4.3	6	4.0
Pacifist Socialist Party	187,567	2.3	3	2.0
State Reform Party	156,636	1.9	3	2.0
Communist Party	147,753	1.8	3	2.0
Radical Party	136,446	1.7	2	1.3
Reformational Political Federation	124,235	1.5	2	1.3
Reformed Political Association	67,163	0.8	1	0.7
Centre Party	68,423	0.8	1	0.7
Evangelical Progressive People's Party	56,466	0.7	1	0.7
Others	115,848	1.4	0	0.0
TOTAL	8,236,536		150	

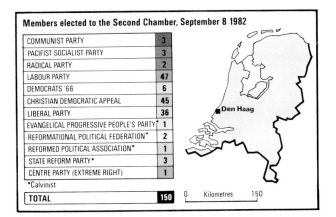

Members elected to the Second Chamber, September 8 1982

COMMUNIST PARTY	3
PACIFIST SOCIALIST PARTY	3
RADICAL PARTY	2
LABOUR PARTY	47
DEMOCRATS '66	6
CHRISTIAN DEMOCRATIC APPEAL	45
LIBERAL PARTY	36
EVANGELICAL PROGRESSIVE PEOPLE'S PARTY*	1
REFORMATIONAL POLITICAL FEDERATION*	2
REFORMED POLITICAL ASSOCIATION*	1
STATE REFORM PARTY*	3
CENTRE PARTY (EXTREME RIGHT)	1
*Calvinist	
TOTAL	150

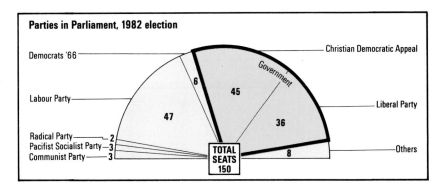

Parties in Parliament, 1982 election

Election results: percentage votes and seats gained since 1946

Election year	1946		1948		1952		1956		1959		1963		1967		1971		1972		1977		1981		1982	
Electorate	5,275,888		5,433,633		5,792,679		6,125,210		6,427,864		6,748,611		7,452,776		8,048,726		8,916,947		9,506,318		10,040,121		10,216,634	
Turnout %		90.2		90.8		92.1		93.5		93.3		92.7		92.3		78.5		82.9		87.5		86.6		80.6
	V %	S	V %	S	V %	S	V %	S	V %	S	V %	S	V %	S	V %	S	V %	S	V %	S	V %	S	V %	S
Communist Party	10.6	10	7.7	8	6.2	6	4.7	7	2.4	3	2.8	4	3.6	5	3.9	6	4.5	7	1.7	2	2.1	3	1.8	3
Pacifist Socialist Party									1.8	2	3.0	4	2.9	4	1.4	2	1.5	2	0.9	1	2.1	3	2.3	3
Radical Party															1.8	2	4.8	7	1.7	3	2.0	3	1.7	2
Labour Party	28.3	28	25.6	27	29.0	30	32.7	50	30.4	48	28.0	43	23.6	37	24.6	39	27.3	43	33.8	53	28.3	44	30.4	47
Democrats '66													4.5	7	6.8	11	4.2	6	5.4	8	11.1	17	4.3	6
Christian Democratic Appeal																			31.9	49	30.8	48	29.4	45
Catholic People's Party	30.8	32	31.0	32	28.7	30	31.7	49	31.6	49	31.9	50	26.5	42	21.8	35	17.7	27						
Christian Historical Union	7.8	8	9.2	9	8.9	9	8.4	13	8.1	12	8.6	13	8.1	12	6.3	10	4.8	7						
Anti-Revolutionary Party	12.9	13	13.2	13	11.3	12	9.9	15	9.4	14	8.7	13	9.9	15	8.6	13	8.8	14						
Liberal Party	6.4	6	7.9	8	8.8	9	8.8	13	12.2	19	10.3	16	10.7	17	10.3	16	14.4	22	17.9	28	17.3	26	23.1	36
Evangelical Progressive People's Party																							0.7	1
Reformational Political Federation																			0.6	0	1.5	2	1.5	2
Reformed Political Association					0.7	0	0.6	6	0.7	0	0.9	1	1.6	1	1.6	2	1.8	2	1.0	1	0.8	1	0.8	1
State Reform Party	2.1	2	2.4	2	2.4	2	2.3	3	2.2	3	2.3	3	2.0	3	2.3	3	2.2	3	2.1	3	2.0	3	1.9	3
Centre Party																							0.8	1
Others	1.0	1	2.9	1	4.1	2	0.8	0	1.3	0	3.7	3	7.4	7	10.4	11	7.9	10	2.9	2	2.0	0	1.4	0
TOTAL SEATS		100		100		100		150		150		150		150		150		150		150		150		150

Government

The present government, formed in November 1982, is a coalition of Christian Democrats and Liberals, with Ruud Lubbers (Christian Democrat) as prime minister.

Note

Though the seats are all allocated on a national basis, figures are published showing the breakdown of votes in each of the provinces. The maps showing the geographical distribution of party support are based on these figures.

See also Stop Press, page 160.

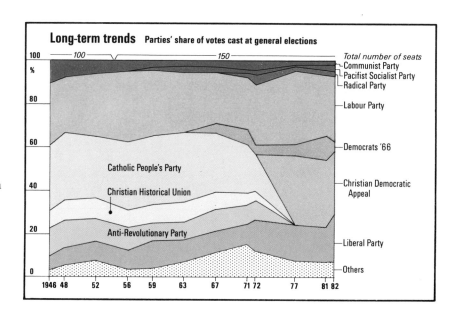

Long-term trends Parties' share of votes cast at general elections

Total number of seats
Communist Party
Pacifist Socialist Party
Radical Party
Labour Party
Democrats '66
Christian Democratic Appeal
Catholic People's Party
Christian Historical Union
Anti-Revolutionary Party
Liberal Party
Others

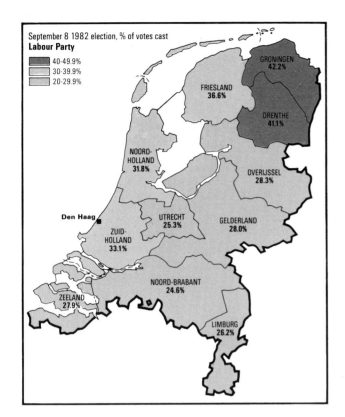

September 8 1982 election, % of votes cast
Labour Party

- 40-49.9%
- 30-39.9%
- 20-29.9%

GRONINGEN 42.2%
FRIESLAND 36.6%
DRENTHE 41.1%
NOORD-HOLLAND 31.8%
OVERIJSSEL 28.3%
Den Haag
UTRECHT 25.3%
GELDERLAND 28.0%
ZUID-HOLLAND 33.1%
NOORD-BRABANT 24.6%
ZEELAND 27.9%
LIMBURG 26.2%

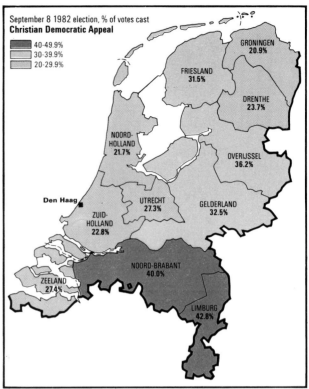

September 8 1982 election, % of votes cast
Christian Democratic Appeal

- 40-49.9%
- 30-39.9%
- 20-29.9%

GRONINGEN 20.9%
FRIESLAND 31.5%
DRENTHE 23.7%
NOORD-HOLLAND 21.7%
OVERIJSSEL 36.2%
Den Haag
UTRECHT 27.3%
GELDERLAND 32.5%
ZUID-HOLLAND 22.8%
NOORD-BRABANT 40.0%
ZEELAND 27.4%
LIMBURG 42.8%

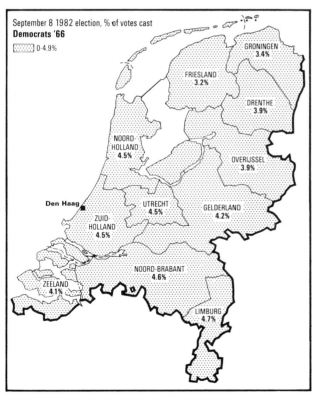

September 8 1982 election, % of votes cast
Democrats '66

- 0-4.9%

GRONINGEN 3.4%
FRIESLAND 3.2%
DRENTHE 3.9%
NOORD-HOLLAND 4.5%
OVERIJSSEL 3.9%
Den Haag
UTRECHT 4.5%
GELDERLAND 4.2%
ZUID-HOLLAND 4.5%
NOORD-BRABANT 4.6%
ZEELAND 4.1%
LIMBURG 4.7%

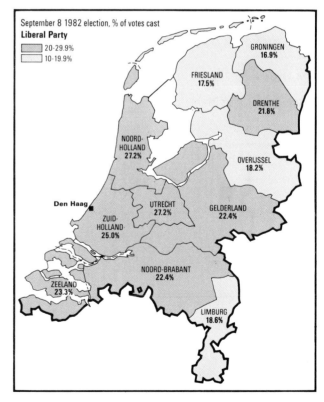

September 8 1982 election, % of votes cast
Liberal Party

- 20-29.9%
- 10-19.9%

GRONINGEN 16.9%
FRIESLAND 17.5%
DRENTHE 21.8%
NOORD-HOLLAND 27.2%
OVERIJSSEL 18.2%
Den Haag
UTRECHT 27.2%
GELDERLAND 22.4%
ZUID-HOLLAND 25.0%
NOORD-BRABANT 22.4%
ZEELAND 23.3%
LIMBURG 18.6%

New Zealand

A constitutional monarchy, with the role of the British monarch being filled by a governor-general, appointed on the advice of the New Zealand government.

The government is responsible to a single-chamber parliament, the House of Representatives. It is elected on a plurality basis (see page 2). Its term of office is three years, with the possibility of early dissolution. The 95 members are elected in single-member constituencies: 91 of these are general constituencies, the remaining four being reserved for voters of Maori descent. Maori voters have the option of registering to vote in a general or a Maori constituency. The minimum voting age is 18. Casual vacancies are filled by by-elections.

Last election: July 14 1984.

Next election due: July 1987.

Main political parties

1. Labour Party
2. Social Credit Party (called New Zealand Democratic Party since 1985)
3. National Party, Conservative
4. New Zealand Party, right-wing Conservative

Government

The present government, elected in July 1984, is formed by the Labour Party. The prime minister is David Lange.

Result of election of July 14 1984

Electorate: 2,111,651   Valid votes: 1,929,201 (91.4%)

	Votes	%	Seats	%
Labour Party	829,154	43.0	56	58.9
National Party	692,494	35.9	37	38.9
New Zealand Party	236,385	12.3	0	0.0
Social Credit Party	147,162	7.6	2	2.1
Other	24,006	1.2	0	0.0
TOTAL	1,929,201		95	

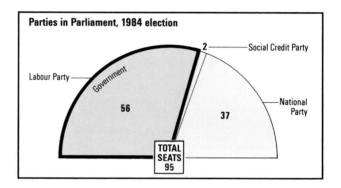

Parties in Parliament, 1984 election

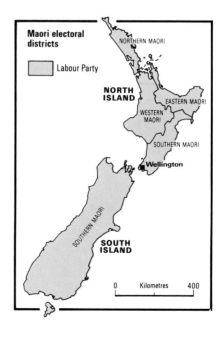

Maori electoral districts

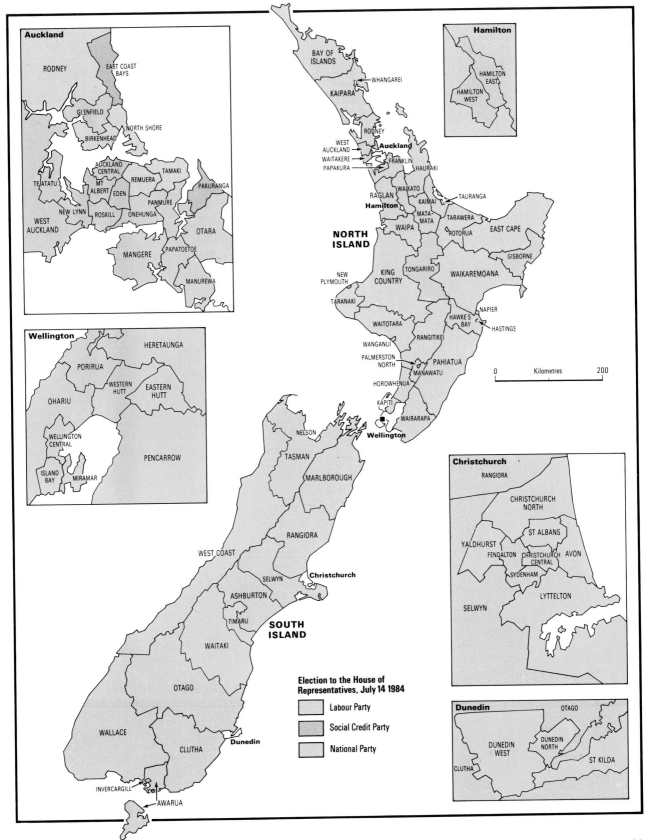

Auckland

RODNEY
EAST COAST BAYS
GLENFIELD
NORTH SHORE
BIRKENHEAD
AUCKLAND CENTRAL
TAMAKI
MT ALBERT
REMUERA
TE ATATU
EDEN
PAKURANGA
NEW LYNN
ROSKILL
PANMURE
ONEHUNGA
WEST AUCKLAND
OTARA
MANGERE
PAPATOETOE
MANUREWA

Hamilton

HAMILTON EAST
HAMILTON WEST

BAY OF ISLANDS
WHANGAREI
KAIPARA
RODNEY
WEST AUCKLAND
Auckland
WAITAKERE
FRANKLIN
PAPAKURA
HAURAKI
WAIKATO
RAGLAN
KAIMAI
TAURANGA
Hamilton
MATA-MATA
TARAWERA
WAIPA
ROTORUA
EAST CAPE
NORTH ISLAND
GISBORNE
NEW PLYMOUTH
KING COUNTRY
TONGARIRO
WAIKAREMOANA
TARANAKI
NAPIER
WAITOTARA
HAWKE'S BAY
HASTINGS
RANGITIKEI
WANGANUI
PALMERSTON NORTH
PAHIATUA
MANAWATU
HOROWHENUA
KAPITI
WAIRARAPA
Wellington

Wellington

HERETAUNGA
PORIRUA
WESTERN HUTT
EASTERN HUTT
OHARIU
WELLINGTON CENTRAL
PENCARROW
ISLAND BAY
MIRAMAR

NELSON
TASMAN
MARLBOROUGH
RANGIORA
WEST COAST
Christchurch
SELWYN
Christchurch
ASHBURTON
RANGIORA
TIMARU
CHRISTCHURCH NORTH
SOUTH ISLAND
YALDHURST
ST ALBANS
WAITAKI
FENDALTON
CHRISTCHURCH CENTRAL
AVON
SYDENHAM
OTAGO
SELWYN
LYTTELTON

WALLACE
CLUTHA
Dunedin

Election to the House of Representatives, July 14 1984

Labour Party
Social Credit Party
National Party

INVERCARGILL
AWARUA

Dunedin

OTAGO
DUNEDIN WEST
DUNEDIN NORTH
ST KILDA
CLUTHA

0   Kilometres   200

99

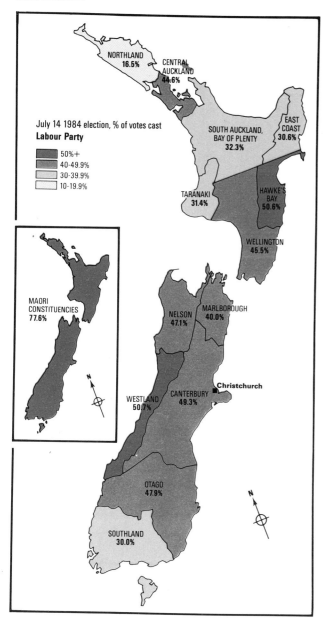

July 14 1984 election, % of votes cast
Labour Party

	50%+
	40-49.9%
	30-39.9%
	10-19.9%

NORTHLAND
16.5%

CENTRAL
AUCKLAND
44.6%

SOUTH AUCKLAND,
BAY OF PLENTY
32.3%

EAST
COAST
30.6%

TARANAKI
31.4%

HAWKE'S
BAY
50.6%

WELLINGTON
45.5%

MAORI
CONSTITUENCIES
77.6%

NELSON
47.1%

MARLBOROUGH
40.0%

Christchurch

WESTLAND
50.7%

CANTERBURY
49.3%

OTAGO
47.9%

SOUTHLAND
30.0%

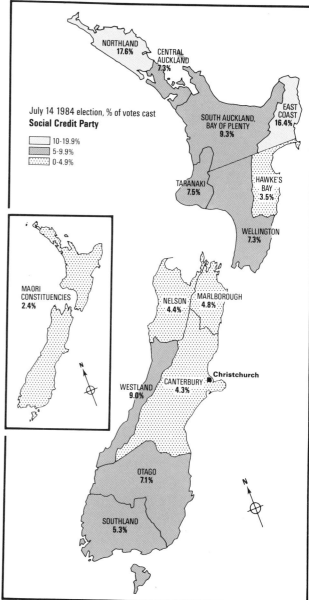

July 14 1984 election, % of votes cast
Social Credit Party

	10-19.9%
	5-9.9%
	0-4.9%

NORTHLAND
17.6%

CENTRAL
AUCKLAND
7.3%

SOUTH AUCKLAND,
BAY OF PLENTY
9.3%

EAST
COAST
16.4%

TARANAKI
7.5%

HAWKE'S
BAY
3.5%

WELLINGTON
7.3%

MAORI
CONSTITUENCIES
2.4%

NELSON
4.4%

MARLBOROUGH
4.8%

WESTLAND
9.0%

CANTERBURY
4.3%

Christchurch

OTAGO
7.1%

SOUTHLAND
5.3%

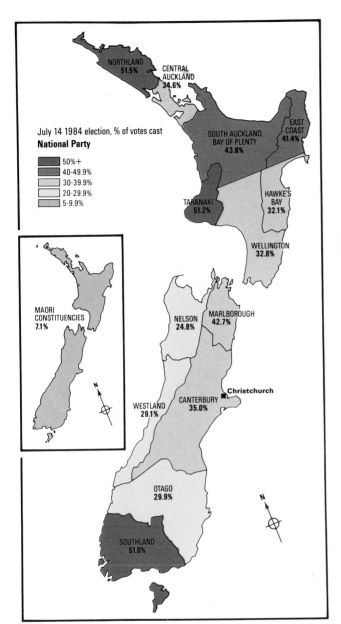

July 14 1984 election, % of votes cast
National Party

- 50%+
- 40-49.9%
- 30-39.9%
- 20-29.9%
- 5-9.9%

NORTHLAND
51.5%

CENTRAL
AUCKLAND
34.6%

EAST
COAST
41.4%

SOUTH AUCKLAND,
BAY OF PLENTY
43.8%

TARANAKI
51.2%

HAWKE'S
BAY
32.1%

WELLINGTON
32.8%

MAORI
CONSTITUENCIES
7.1%

NELSON
24.8%

MARLBOROUGH
42.7%

WESTLAND
29.1%

CANTERBURY
35.0%

Christchurch

OTAGO
29.9%

SOUTHLAND
51.0%

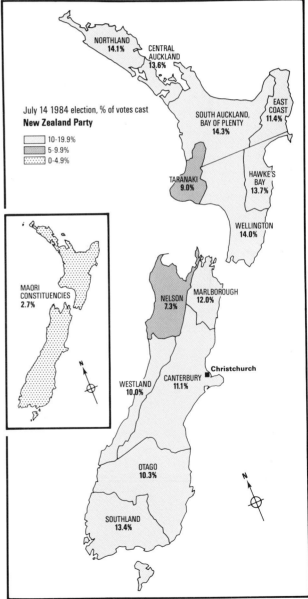

July 14 1984 election, % of votes cast
New Zealand Party

- 10-19.9%
- 5-9.9%
- 0-4.9%

NORTHLAND
14.1%

CENTRAL
AUCKLAND
13.6%

EAST
COAST
11.4%

SOUTH AUCKLAND,
BAY OF PLENTY
14.3%

TARANAKI
9.0%

HAWKE'S
BAY
13.7%

WELLINGTON
14.0%

MAORI
CONSTITUENCIES
2.7%

NELSON
7.3%

MARLBOROUGH
12.0%

WESTLAND
10.0%

CANTERBURY
11.1%

Christchurch

OTAGO
10.3%

SOUTHLAND
13.4%

Election results: percentage votes and seats gained since 1946

Election year	1946		1949		1951		1954		1957		1960		1963	
Electorate	1,081,898		1,148,748		1,205,772		1,209,670		1,244,748		1,303,955		1,332.371	
Turnout %		96.8		93.4		88.7		90.7		93.0		89.8		89.9
	V %	S	V %	S	V %	S	V %	S	V %	S	V %	S	V %	S
Labour Party	51.3	42	47.2	34	45.8	30	44.1	35	48.3	41	43.4	34	43.7	35
Social Credit Party							11.1	0	7.2	0	8.6	0	7.9	0
National Party	48.4	38	51.9	46	54.0	50	44.3	45	44.2	39	47.6	46	47.1	45
New Zealand Party														
Others	0.3	0	0.9	0	0.1	0	0.5	0	0.3	0	0.4	0	1.3	0
TOTAL SEATS		80		80		80		80		80		80		80

Election year	1966		1969		1972		1975		1978		1981		1984	
Electorate	1,399,720		1,519,889		1,583,256		1,953,050		2,057,840		2,034,747		2,111,651	
Turnout %		86.1		88.2		88.5		82.1		83.1		88.5		93.7
	V %	S	V %	S	V %	S	V %	S	V %	S	V %	S	V %	S
Labour Party	41.4	35	44.2	39	48.4	55	39.6	32	40.4	40	39.0	43	43.0	56
Social Credit Party	14.5	1	9.1	0	6.7	0	7.4	0	16.1	1	20.7	2	7.6	2
National Party	43.6	44	45.2	45	41.5	32	47.6	55	39.8	51	38.8	47	35.9	37
New Zealand Party													12.3	0
Others	0.4	0	1.5	0	3.5	0	5.4	0	3.7	0	1.6	0	1.2	0
TOTAL SEATS		80		84		87		87		92		92		95

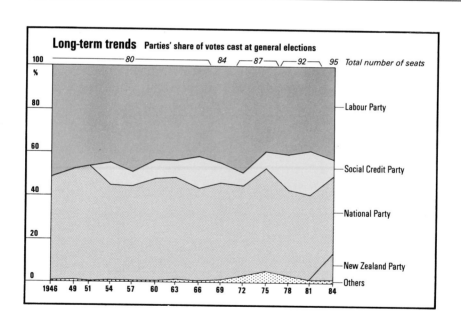

Norway

A constitutional monarchy. Parliament (the *Storting*) consists of 157 members and is elected every four years in September. There is no right of dissolution, and no provision for by-elections, casual vacancies being filled by substitutes nominated at the same time as the original candidates.

For certain purposes the Storting becomes a two-chamber parliament. At its first meeting after each election, it elects from among its own members 39 to form the *Lagting*, while the remainder constitute the *Odelsting*. Proposed laws are discussed separately in each chamber, but otherwise the Storting sits as a single body.

Since 1978 the minimum voting age has been 18. Before 1946 it was 23, when it was reduced to 21. Between 1969 and 1978 it was 20.

The electoral system is one of proportional representation in nineteen multi-member constituencies (these coincide with the counties which form the principal units of local government).

Until 1953 the D'Hondt system (see page 2) was used to allocate seats, but since then it has been replaced by a modified Sainte-Laguë system (see page 3). Voters choose between rival party lists, but do not have the option of varying the order of candidates in the lists.

Last election: September 8–9 1985.

Next election due: September 1989.

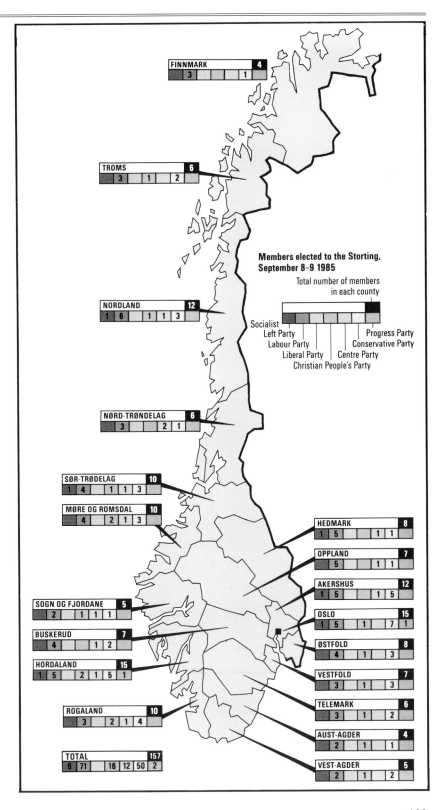

Members elected to the Storting, September 8–9 1985

Total number of members in each county

Socialist Left Party
Labour Party
Liberal Party
Christian People's Party
Centre Party
Conservative Party
Progress Party

FINNMARK 4 — 3 1
TROMS 6 — 3 1 2
NORDLAND 12 — 1 6 1 1 3
NØRD-TRØNDELAG 6 — 3 2 1
SØR-TRØDELAG 10 — 1 4 1 1 3
MØRE OG ROMSDAL 10 — 4 2 1 3
SOGN OG FJORDANE 5 — 2 1 1 1
BUSKERUD 7 — 4 1 2
HORDALAND 15 — 1 5 2 1 5 1
ROGALAND 10 — 3 2 1 4
HEDMARK 8 — 1 5 1 1
OPPLAND 7 — 5 1 1
AKERSHUS 12 — 1 5 1 5
OSLO 15 — 1 5 1 7 1
ØSTFOLD 8 — 4 1 3
VESTFOLD 7 — 3 1 3
TELEMARK 6 — 3 1 2
AUST-AGDER 4 — 2 1 1
VEST-AGDER 5 — 2 1 2
TOTAL 157 — 6 71 16 12 50 2

103

Main political parties

1. Communist Party
2. Socialist People's Party, a left-wing breakaway from Labour
3. Socialist Left Party, a left-wing breakaway from Labour, which incorporated the Socialist People's Party and, temporarily, the Communist Party
4. Labour Party
5. Liberal Party
6. Liberal People's Party (formerly New People's Party), a pro-EEC breakaway from the Liberal Party
7. Christian People's Party
8. Centre Party (formerly Farmers' Party)
9. Conservative Party
10. Progress Party (formerly Anders Lange's Party), a right-wing anti-tax party

Government

The present government, formed in May 1986, is a minority Labour government. The prime minister is Gro Harlem Brundtland.

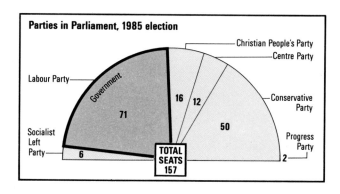

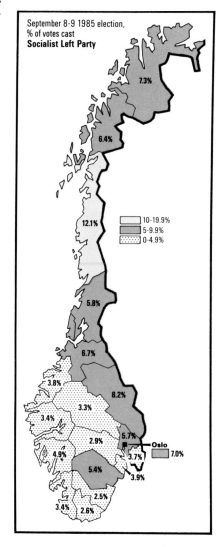

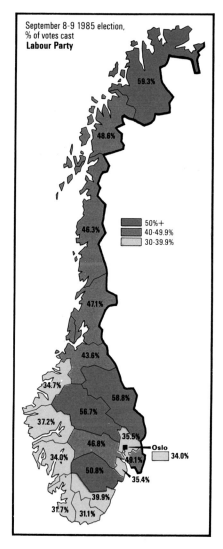

Result of election of September 8–9 1985

Electorate: 3,097,382   Valid votes: 2,511,729 (81.1%)
Invalid votes: 3,577 (0.1%)

	Votes	%	Seats	%
Labour Party	1,033,650	41.2	71	45.3
Conservative Party	755,159	30.1	50	31.8
Christian People's Party	208,315	8.3	16	10.2
Centre Party	169,223	6.7	12	7.6
Socialist Left Party	135,191	5.4	6	3.8
Progress Party	92,635	3.7	2	1.3
Liberal Party	77,919	3.1	0	0.0
Liberal People's Party	12,413	0.5	0	0.0
Communist Party	4,048	0.2	0	0.0
Others	23,176	0.9	0	0.0
TOTAL	2,511,729		157	

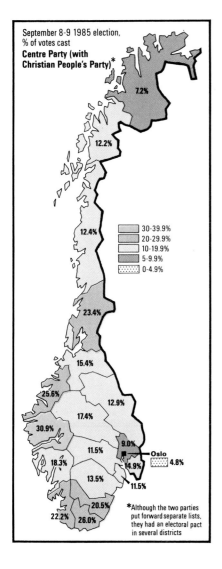

September 8-9 1985 election, % of votes cast
Centre Party (with Christian People's Party)*

30-39.9%
20-29.9%
10-19.9%
5-9.9%
0-4.9%

*Although the two parties put forward separate lists, they had an electoral pact in several districts

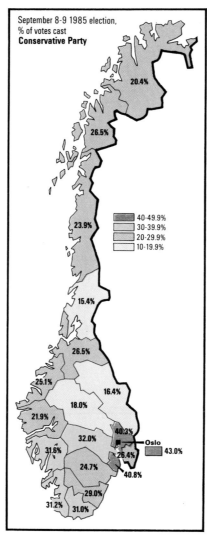

September 8-9 1985 election, % of votes cast
Conservative Party

40-49.9%
30-39.9%
20-29.9%
10-19.9%

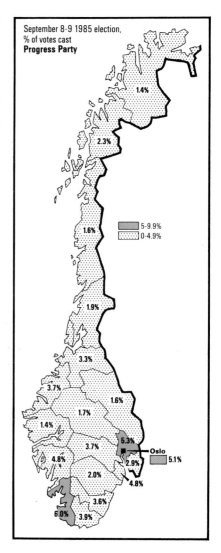

September 8-9 1985 election, % of votes cast
Progress Party

5-9.9%
0-4.9%

Election results: percentage votes and seats gained since 1945

Election year	1945 V%	1945 S	1949 V%	1949 S	1953 V%	1953 S	1957 V%	1957 S	1961 V%	1961 S	1965 V%	1965 S	1969 V%	1969 S	1973 V%	1973 S	1977 V%	1977 S	1981 V%	1981 S	1985 V%	1985 S
Electorate	1,961,977		2,159,005		2,256,799		2,298,376		2,340,495		2,406,866		2,579,566		2,686,676		2,780,190		3,003,093		3,097,382	
Turnout %		75.7		81.4		78.9		77.9		78.6		85.1		83.7		80.1		82.8		81.9		81.1
Communist Party	11.9	11	5.8	0	5.1	3	3.4	1	2.9	0	1.4	0	1.0	0			0.4	0	0.3	0	0.2	0
Socialist People's Party									2.4	2	6.0	2	3.4	0	11.2	16						
Socialist Left Party																	4.2	2	4.9	4	5.4	6
Labour Party	41.0	76	45.7	85	46.7	77	48.3	78	46.8	74	43.1	68	46.5	74	35.3	62	42.3	76	37.2	65	41.2	71
Liberal Party	13.8	20	12.4	21	10.0	15	9.6	15	7.2	14	10.2	18	9.4	13	2.3	2	2.4	2	3.2	2	3.1	0
Liberal People's Party	–		–		–		–		–		–		–		3.4	1	1.0	0	0.5	0	0.5	0
Christian People's Party	7.9	8	8.4	9	10.5	14	10.2	12	9.3	15	7.8	13	7.8	14	11.9	20	9.7	22	8.9	15	8.3	16
Centre Party	8.0	10	4.9	12	8.8	14	8.6	15	6.8	16	9.4	18	9.0	20	6.8	21	8.0	12	4.2	11	6.7	12
Conservative Party	17.0	25	15.9	23	18.4	27	16.8	29	19.3	29	20.3	31	18.8	29	17.2	29	24.5	41	31.7	54	30.1	50
Progress Party															5.0	4	1.9	0	4.5	4	3.7	2
Joint non-Socialist lists			6.1		8.5		2.9		5.2		1.8		3.8		6.0		4.8		3.6			
Others	0.3	0	0.7	0	0.0	0	0.2	0	0.2	0	0.0	0	0.2	0	0.9	0	0.9	0	0.9	0	0.9	0
TOTAL SEATS		150		150		150		150		150		150		150		155		155		155		157

Papua New Guinea

A constitutional monarchy, the role of the British monarch being filled by a governor-general appointed on the advice of the Papua New Guinea government. Formerly under Australian rule, it became independent in 1975.

The government is responsible to the single-chamber House of Assembly. Its 109 members are elected on a plurality basis (see page 2) for a five-year term in single-member constituencies. Each elector has two votes: one to elect a member in each of the 89 open constituencies, the other to choose a member from each of 20 provinces. Casual vacancies are filled by by-elections.

Last election: June 5–26 1982.

Next election due: June 1987.

Main political parties

It is impossible to list PNG parties in a meaningful ideological rank order. Party ties are weak and often ephemeral, local influences strong, and the pull or repulsion of personalities, particularly that of the leader of the Pangu Pati, and former prime minister, Michael T. Somare, have been potent factors.

1. Melanesian Alliance (MA)
2. National Party (NP)
3. PNG Independent Group
4. Pangu Pati
5. Papua Besena
6. United Party (UP)
7. People's Progress Party (PPP)
8. People's Democratic Movement (PDM), split off from Pangu Pati in 1985

Result of election of June 5–26 1982

	Seats	% Seats
Pangu Pati	51	46.8
National Party	15	13.8
People's Progress Party	13	11.9
United Party	9	8.3
Melanesian Alliance	8	7.4
PNG Independent Group	7	6.4
Papua Besena	3	2.8
Independents	3	2.8
TOTAL	109	

Note: Comprehensive figures of the parties' votes are unobtainable. The result in seats was as above.

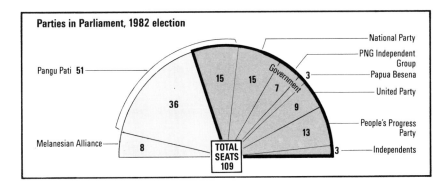

Parties in Parliament, 1982 election

Government

The present government, formed in November 1985, is a coalition of all the Papua New Guinea parties except the Melanesian Alliance and the Pangu Pati, which split, with 15 members joining the government. The prime minister is Paias Wingti (PDM).

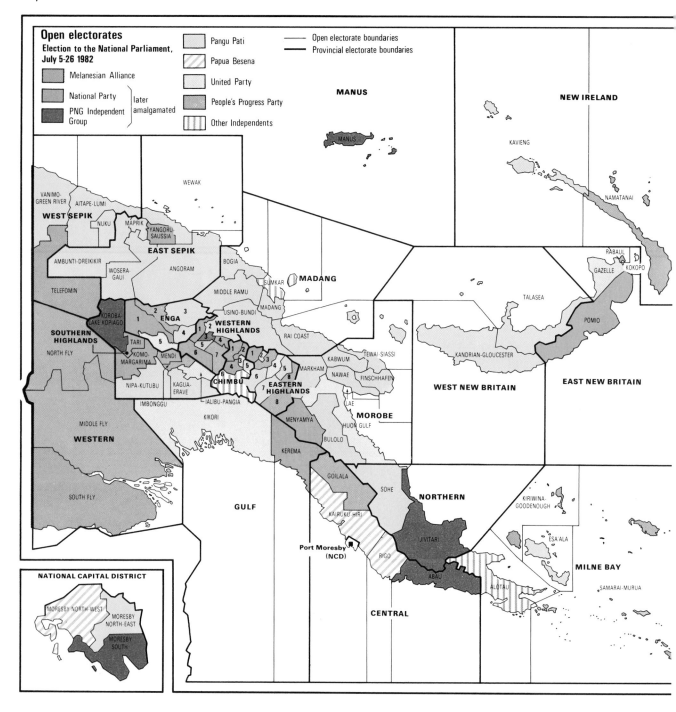

Open electorates

Election to the National Parliament, July 5-26 1982

- Melanesian Alliance
- National Party } later amalgamated
- PNG Independent Group
- Pangu Pati
- Papua Besena
- United Party
- People's Progress Party
- Other Independents

— Open electorate boundaries
— Provincial electorate boundaries

MANUS

MANUS

NEW IRELAND

KAVIENG

NAMATANAI

RABAUL

GAZELLE · KOKOPO

VANIMO-GREEN RIVER

AITAPE-LUMI

WEWAK

WEST SEPIK

NUKU

MAPRIK

YANGORU-SAUSSIA

EAST SEPIK

AMBUNTI-DREIKIKIR

WOSERA-GAUI

ANGORAM

BOGIA

MADANG

SUMKAR

MIDDLE RAMU

MADANG

TELEFOMIN

USINO-BUNDI

TALASEA

POMIO

KOROBA-LAKE KOPIAGO

1

ENGA

2

3

WESTERN HIGHLANDS

RAI COAST

SOUTHERN HIGHLANDS

TARI

5

4

3

4

1

2

KANDRIAN-GLOUCESTER

WEST NEW BRITAIN

EAST NEW BRITAIN

NORTH FLY

KOMO-MARGARIMA

MENDI

6

7

1

2

5

2

3

TEWAI-SIASSI

KABWUM

NIPA-KUTUBU

KAGUA-ERAVE

CHIMBU

5

4

6

3

4

5

8

EASTERN HIGHLANDS

4

5

MARKHAM

NAWAE

FINSCHHAFEN

IMBONGGU

IALIBU-PANGIA

6

7

8

LAE

MOROBE

HUON GULF

KIKORI

MENYAMYA

BULOLO

MIDDLE FLY

WESTERN

KEREMA

GOILALA

SOHE

NORTHERN

KIRIWINA-GOODENOUGH

SOUTH FLY

GULF

KAIRUKU-HIRI

Port Moresby (NCD)

RIGO

IJIVITARI

ESA'ALA

MILNE BAY

ABAU

ALOTAU

SAMARAI-MURUA

CENTRAL

NATIONAL CAPITAL DISTRICT

MORESBY NORTH-WEST

MORESBY NORTH-EAST

MORESBY SOUTH

108

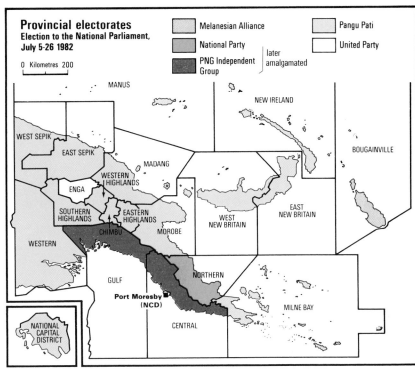

Provincial electorates
Election to the National Parliament,
July 5-26 1982

0 Kilometres 200

Legend:
- Melanesian Alliance
- National Party
- PNG Independent Group
- Pangu Pati
- United Party

later amalgamated

MANUS

NEW IRELAND

WEST SEPIK

EAST SEPIK

MADANG

BOUGAINVILLE

WESTERN HIGHLANDS

ENGA

SOUTHERN HIGHLANDS

EASTERN HIGHLANDS

CHIMBU

MOROBE

WEST NEW BRITAIN

EAST NEW BRITAIN

WESTERN

GULF

NORTHERN

Port Moresby (NCD)

MILNE BAY

CENTRAL

NATIONAL CAPITAL DISTRICT

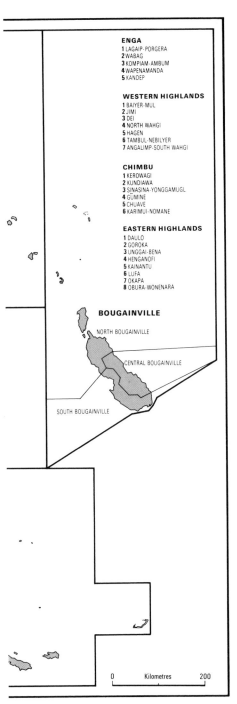

ENGA
1 LAGAIP-PORGERA
2 WABAG
3 KOMPIAM-AMBUM
4 WAPENAMANDA
5 KANDEP

WESTERN HIGHLANDS
1 BAIYER-MUL
2 JIMI
3 DEI
4 NORTH WAHGI
5 HAGEN
6 TAMBUL-NEBILYER
7 ANGALIMP-SOUTH WAHGI

CHIMBU
1 KEROWAGI
2 KUNDIAWA
3 SINASINA-YONGGAMUGL
4 GUMINE
5 CHUAVE
6 KARIMUI-NOMANE

EASTERN HIGHLANDS
1 DAULO
2 GOROKA
3 UNGGAI-BENA
4 HENGANOFI
5 KAINANTU
6 LUFA
7 OKAPA
8 OBURA-WONENARA

BOUGAINVILLE
NORTH BOUGAINVILLE
CENTRAL BOUGAINVILLE
SOUTH BOUGAINVILLE

0 Kilometres 200

Portugal

A republic, with a directly elected president who has no executive powers but has important reserve responsibilities. Democratic rule was restored in 1976, following the military takeover two years earlier. The president is elected for a five-year term on a majoritarian basis (see page 2). A second ballot is held between the two leading contenders if no candidate gains more than 50 per cent of the votes.

The government is responsible to a single-chamber parliament, the Assembly of the Republic. The Assembly, of 250 members, is elected by proportional representation, using the D'Hondt system (see page 2) in 20 multi-member constituencies. Four seats are reserved for Portuguese voters living abroad. The voters choose between rival party lists, with no possibility of expressing preferences between candidates. The minimum voting age is 18. The Assembly is elected for four years, with a possibility of early dissolution.

Last Presidential election: January 26 and February 16 1986.

Next election due: January 1991.

Last parliamentary election: October 6 1985.

Next election due: October 1989.

Result of parliamentary election of October 6 1985

Electorate: 7,619,978   Valid votes: 5,743,948 (75.4%)
Invalid votes: 150,286 (2.0%)

	Votes	%	Seats	%
Social Democratic Party	1,710,982	29.8	88	35.2
Socialist Party	1,195,439	20.8	57	22.8
Democratic Renewal Party	1,036,185	18.0	45	18.0
Communist Party and allies	893,180	15.6	38	15.2
Centre Democratic Party	559,660	9.7	22	8.8
Others	348,502	6.1	0	0.0
TOTAL	5,743,948		250	

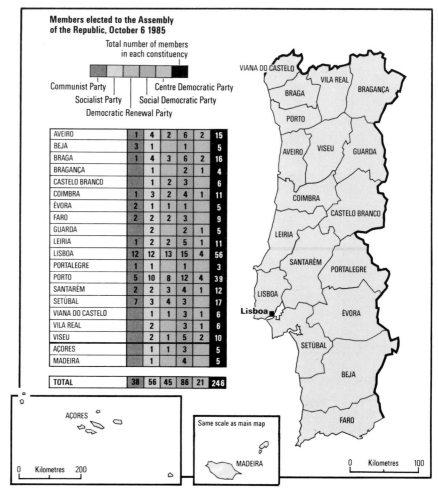

Members elected to the Assembly of the Republic, October 6 1985

Total number of members in each constituency

Communist Party | Centre Democratic Party
Socialist Party | Social Democratic Party
Democratic Renewal Party

	Communist Party	Socialist Party	Democratic Renewal Party	Social Democratic Party	Centre Democratic Party	Total
AVEIRO	1	4	2	6	2	15
BEJA	3	1		1		5
BRAGA	1	4	3	6	2	16
BRAGANÇA		1		2	1	4
CASTELO BRANCO		1	2	3		6
COIMBRA	1	3	2	4	1	11
ÉVORA	2	1	1	1		5
FARO	2	2	2	3		9
GUARDA		2		2	1	5
LEIRIA	1	2	2	5	1	11
LISBOA	12	12	13	15	4	56
PORTALEGRE	1	1		1		3
PORTO	5	10	8	12	4	39
SANTARÉM	2	2	3	4	1	12
SETÚBAL	7	3	4	3		17
VIANA DO CASTELO		1	1	3	1	6
VILA REAL		2		3	1	6
VISEU		2	1	5	2	10
AÇORES		1	1	3		5
MADEIRA		1		4		5
TOTAL	38	56	45	86	21	246

VIANA DO CASTELO

VILA REAL

BRAGANÇA

BRAGA

PORTO

AVEIRO

VISEU

GUARDA

COIMBRA

CASTELO BRANCO

LEIRIA

SANTARÉM

PORTALEGRE

LISBOA

Lisboa

ÉVORA

SETÚBAL

BEJA

FARO

AÇORES

0   Kilometres   200

Same scale as main map

MADEIRA

0   Kilometres   100

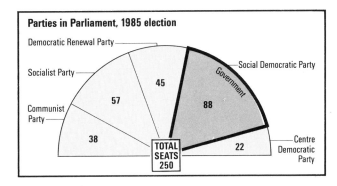

Parties in Parliament, 1985 election

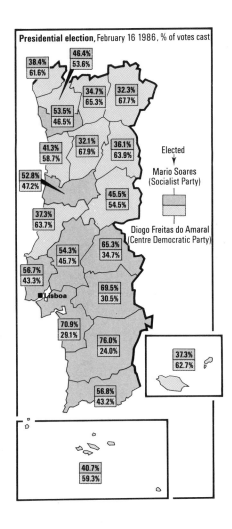

Presidential election, February 16 1986, % of votes cast

Elected
Mario Soares
(Socialist Party)

Diogo Freitas do Amaral
(Centre Democratic Party)

Main political parties

1. Communist Party (PCP)
2. Socialist Party (PSP)
3. Democratic Renewal Party (PRD)
4. Social Democratic Party (PSD),
   formerly Popular Democratic
   Party
5. Centre Democratic Party (CDS),
   Conservative

Government

The present government is a
minority Social Democratic
government, formed in October
1985. The prime minister is Anibal
Cavaco Silva. The president is Mario
Soares.

Result of Presidential election of January 26 and February 16 1986

First round

Electorate: 7,586,841   Valid votes: 5,672,142 (74.8%)
Invalid votes: 65,025 (0.9%)

	Votes	%
Diogo Freitas do Amaral (Centre Democrat)	2,625,989	46.3
Mario Soares (Socialist)	1,442,785	25.4
Salgado Zenha (Independent Socialist)	1,185,229	20.9
Maria de Lurdes Pintasilgo (Radical Catholic)	418,139	7.4
TOTAL	5,672,142	

Second round

Electorate: 7,588,297   Valid votes: 5,880,078 (77.5%)
Invalid votes: 55,216 (0.7%)

	Votes	%
Mario Soares	3,015,350	51.3
Diogo Freitas do Amaral	2,864,728	48.7
TOTAL	5,880,078	

Election results: percentage votes and seats gained since 1975

Election year	1975		1976		1979		1980		1983		1985	
Electorate	6,177,698		6,477,619		6,578,447		7,003,446		7,337,064		7,619,978	
Turnout %	85.4		79.3		87.3		82.6		75.8		75.4	
	V %	S	V %	S	V %	S	V %	S	V %	S	V %	S
Communist Party	13.5	30 ⎱	15.3	40	19.5	44	17.3	39	18.1	41	15.6	38
Democratic Movement	4.4	5 ⎰				3		2		3		
Socialist Party	40.7	116	36.7	107	28.2	74 ⎱	28.7	66	36.1	101	20.8	57
Other Democratic Left					0.7	0 ⎰		8				
Democratic Renewal Party											18.0	45
Social Democratic Party/Popular Democratic Party	28.3	81	25.2	73 ⎱	46.3	76	48.3	82	27.2	75	29.8	88
Centre Democratic Party	8.2	16	16.7	42 ⎰		42		46	12.9	30	9.7	22
Other right-wing parties	0.6		0.5			10		6	1.4	0		
Others	4.3	2	5.5	1	5.0	1	5.7	1	2.3	0	6.1	0
TOTAL SEATS		250		263		250		250		250		250

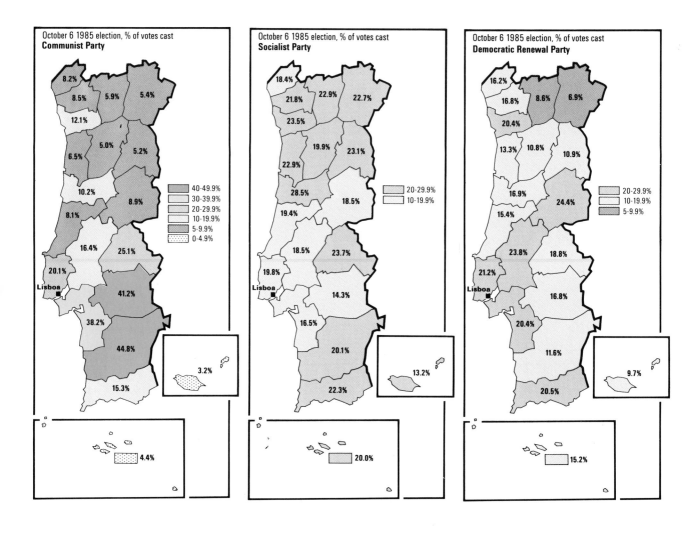

October 6 1985 election, % of votes cast
Communist Party

40-49.9%
30-39.9%
20-29.9%
10-19.9%
5-9.9%
0-4.9%

October 6 1985 election, % of votes cast
Socialist Party

20-29.9%
10-19.9%

October 6 1985 election, % of votes cast
Democratic Renewal Party

20-29.9%
10-19.9%
5-9.9%

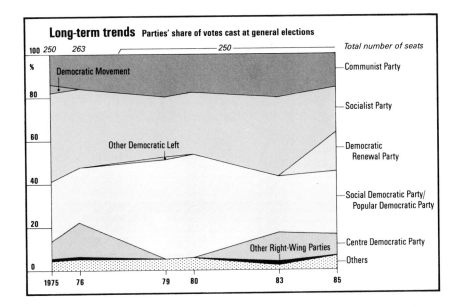

Long-term trends Parties' share of votes cast at general elections

Total number of seats

Communist Party

Socialist Party

Democratic
Renewal Party

Social Democratic Party/
Popular Democratic Party

Centre Democratic Party

Others

Democratic Movement

Other Democratic Left

Other Right-Wing Parties

1975 76 79 80 83 85

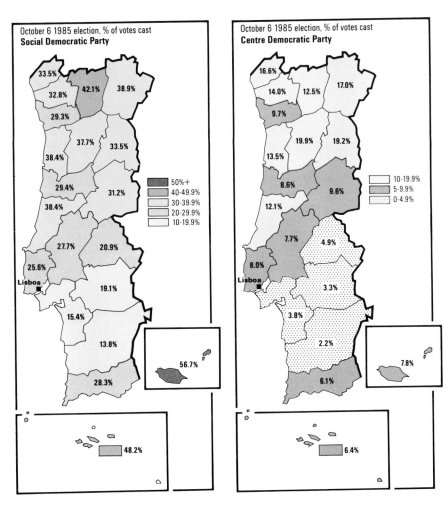

October 6 1985 election, % of votes cast
Social Democratic Party

33.5% 32.8% 42.1% 38.9% 29.3% 37.7% 33.5% 38.4% 29.4% 31.2% 38.4% 27.7% 20.9% 25.6% Lisboa 19.1% 15.4% 13.8% 28.3% 56.7% 48.2%

50%+
40-49.9%
30-39.9%
20-29.9%
10-19.9%

October 6 1985 election, % of votes cast
Centre Democratic Party

16.6% 14.0% 12.5% 17.0% 9.7% 19.9% 19.2% 13.5% 8.6% 9.6% 12.1% 7.7% 4.9% 8.0% Lisboa 3.3% 3.8% 2.2% 6.1% 7.8% 6.4%

10-19.9%
5-9.9%
0-4.9%

113

Solomon Islands

A constitutional monarchy, which became independent in 1978. The role of the British monarch is filled by a governor-general appointed on the advice of the National Parliament of the Solomon Islands.

The government is responsible to the single-chamber National Parliament. There are 38 members elected on a plurality basis (see page 2) in single-member constituencies. The term of office is four years, with the possibility of early dissolution. All adults are entitled to vote.

Last election: October 24 1984.

Next election due: October 1988.

Main political parties

1. People's Alliance Party (PAP)
2. National Democratic Party (NADEPA)
3. Solomon and Sagufenua Party (SAS)
4. United Party (SIUPA)
5. Solomon Islands Cultural Traditional Leaders Movement (SITCLM)

Government

The present government, a coalition between the SIUPA and SAS parties, with some independents, was formed in November 1984. The prime minister is Peter Kenilorea (SIUPA).

Result of election of October 24 1984

	Votes	%	Seats	%
People's Alliance Party	15,553	23.6	11	28.9
United Party	14,987	22.8	13	34.2
Solomon and Sagufenua Party	5,190	7.9	4	10.5
National Democratic Party	4,654	7.1	1	2.6
Independents and others	25,253	38.4	8	21.0
Vacant	–	–	1	2.6
TOTAL	65,637		38	

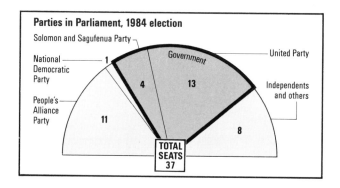

Parties in Parliament, 1984 election

Solomon and Sagufenua Party

National Democratic Party — 1

People's Alliance Party — 11

4

Government

13

United Party

Independents and others

8

TOTAL SEATS 37

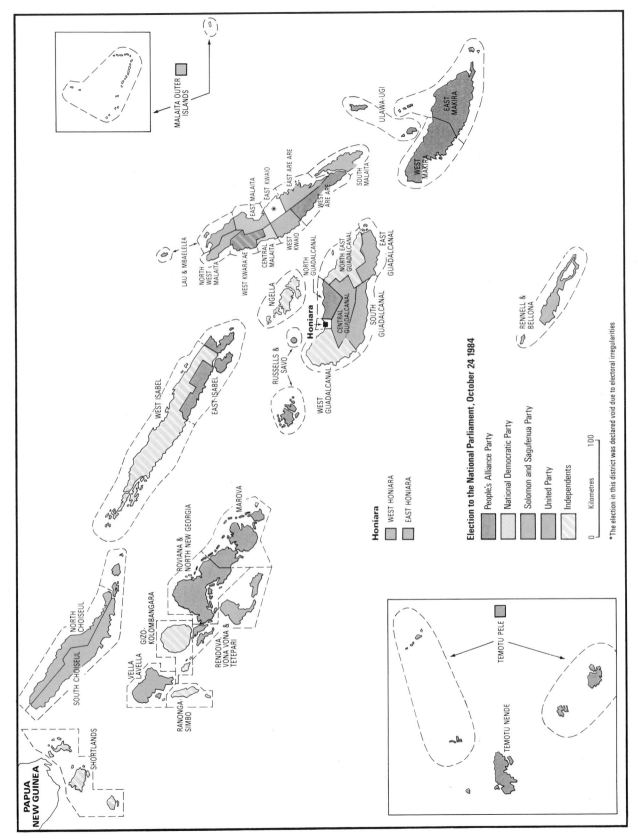

MALAITA OUTER ISLANDS

PAPUA NEW GUINEA

SHORTLANDS

NORTH CHOISEUL

SOUTH CHOISEUL

VELLA LAVELLA

GIZO-KOLOMBANGARA

RANONGA-SIMBO

RENDOVA VONA VONA & TETEPARI

ROVIANA & NORTH NEW GEORGIA

MAROVA

WEST ISABEL

EAST ISABEL

RUSSELLS & SAVO

NGELLA

WEST GUADALCANAL

CENTRAL GUADALCANAL

SOUTH GUADALCANAL

NORTH GUADALCANAL

NORTH EAST GUADALCANAL

EAST GUADALCANAL

Honiara

LAU & MBAELELEA

NORTH WEST MALAITA

WEST KWARA AE

CENTRAL MALAITA

EAST MALAITA

WEST KWAIO

EAST KWAIO

EAST ARE ARE

WEST ARE ARE

SOUTH MALAITA

ULAWA-UGI

WEST MAKIRA

EAST MAKIRA

RENNELL & BELLONA

Honiara

WEST HONIARA

EAST HONIARA

Election to the National Parliament, October 24 1984

People's Alliance Party

National Democratic Party

Solomon and Sagufenua Party

United Party

Independents

Kilometres

0   100

*The election in this district was declared void due to electoral irregularities

TEMOTU PELE

TEMOTU NENDE

Spain

A constitutional monarchy. Democratic rule was restored in 1976. The government is responsible to a two-chamber parliament, the *Cortes*. The upper house, or Senate, of 208, is elected, for a maximum term of four years, by plurality vote (see page 2).

The lower house, or Congress of Deputies, of 350 members, is elected by proportional representation, using the D'Hondt system (see page 2). Voters choose between rival party lists in multi-member constituencies. Parties must win at least 3 per cent of the vote in the constituency to qualify

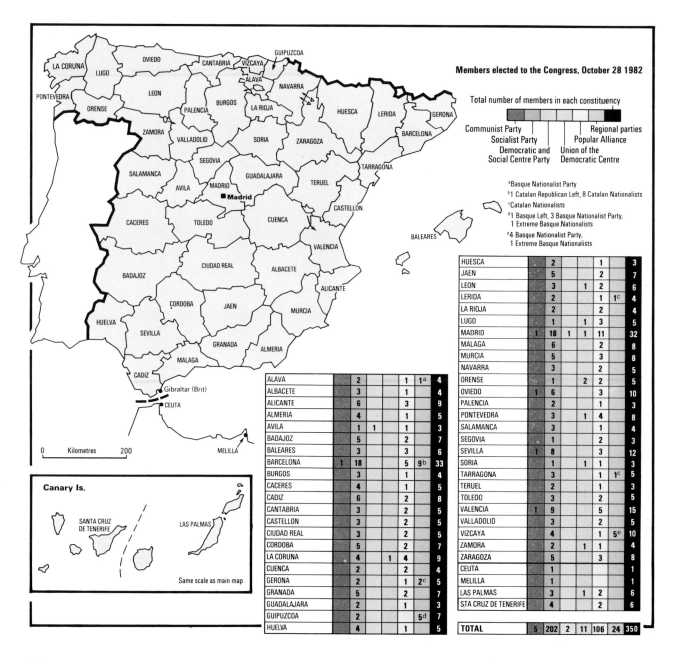

Members elected to the Congress, October 28 1982

Total number of members in each constituency

Communist Party — Socialist Party — Democratic and Social Centre Party / Regional parties — Popular Alliance — Union of the Democratic Centre

[a] Basque Nationalist Party
[b] 1 Catalan Republican Left, 8 Catalan Nationalists
[c] Catalan Nationalists
[d] 1 Basque Left, 3 Basque Nationalist Party, 1 Extreme Basque Nationalists
[e] 4 Basque Nationalist Party, 1 Extreme Basque Nationalists

Constituency	Communist Party	Socialist Party	Democratic and Social Centre Party	Union of the Democratic Centre	Popular Alliance	Regional parties	Total
ALAVA		2			1	1[a]	4
ALBACETE		3			1		4
ALICANTE		6			3		9
ALMERIA		4			1		5
AVILA		1	1		1		3
BADAJOZ		5			2		7
BALEARES		3			3		6
BARCELONA	1	18			5	9[b]	33
BURGOS		3			1		4
CACERES		4			1		5
CADIZ		6			2		8
CANTABRIA		3			2		5
CASTELLON		3			2		5
CIUDAD REAL		3			2		5
CORDOBA		5			2		7
LA CORUNA		4		1	4		9
CUENCA		2			2		4
GERONA		2			1	2[c]	5
GRANADA		5			2		7
GUADALAJARA		2			1		3
GUIPUZCOA		2				5[d]	7
HUELVA		4			1		5
HUESCA		2			1		3
JAEN		5			2		7
LEON		3		1	2		6
LERIDA		2			1	1[c]	4
LA RIOJA		2			2		4
LUGO		1		1	3		5
MADRID	1	18	1	1	11		32
MALAGA		6			2		8
MURCIA		5			3		8
NAVARRA		3			2		5
ORENSE		1		2	2		5
OVIEDO	1	6			3		10
PALENCIA		2			1		3
PONTEVEDRA		3		1	4		8
SALAMANCA		3			1		4
SEGOVIA		1			2		3
SEVILLA	1	8			3		12
SORIA		1		1	1		3
TARRAGONA		3			1	1[c]	5
TERUEL		2			1		3
TOLEDO		3			2		5
VALENCIA	1	9			5		15
VALLADOLID		3			2		5
VIZCAYA		4			1	5[e]	10
ZAMORA		2		1	1		4
ZARAGOZA		5			3		8
CEUTA		1					1
MELILLA		1					1
LAS PALMAS		3		1	2		6
STA CRUZ DE TENERIFE		4			2		6
TOTAL	**5**	**202**	**2**	**11**	**106**	**24**	**350**

Canary Is.
SANTA CRUZ DE TENERIFE — LAS PALMAS
Same scale as main map

0 Kilometres 200

Gibraltar (Brit)
CEUTA
MELILLA

116

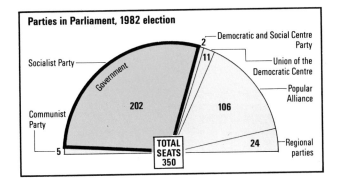

Parties in Parliament, 1982 election

Democratic and Social Centre Party — 2
Socialist Party / Government — 202
Union of the Democratic Centre — 11
Popular Alliance — 106
Communist Party — 5
Regional parties — 24
TOTAL SEATS 350

Result of election of October 28 1982

Electorate: 26,837,212   Valid votes: 21,185,948
(78.9%)   Invalid votes: 168,018 (0.6%)

	Votes	%	Seats	%
Socialist Party	9,856,531	46.5	202	57.7
Popular Alliance	5,456,218	25.8	106	30.3
Union of the Democratic Centre	1,426,263	6.7	11	3.1
Convergence and Union	823,557	3.9	12	3.4
Communist Party	861,756	4.1	5	1.4
Democratic and Social Centre Party	589,388	2.8	2	0.6
Basque Nationalist Party	398,260	1.9	8	2.3
Herri Batasuna	210,979	1.0	2	0.6
Other regional parties	1,562,996	7.4	2	0.6
TOTAL	21,185,948		350	

for the allocation of seats. Voters may not express preferences for individual candidates. Casual vacancies are filled by co-opting the runner-up in the relevant party list. The minimum voting age is 18. The term of office is four years, with the possibility of early dissolution.

Last election: October 28 1982.

Next election due: October 1986 (see Stop Press, page 160).

Main political parties

1. Communist Party (PCE)
2. Socialist Party (PSOE)
3. Democratic and Social Centre Party (CDS)
4. Union of the Democratic Centre (UCD)
5. Popular Alliance (AP), Conservative
6. Convergence and Union (CiU), Catalan regional party
7. Basque Nationalist Party (PNV)
8. Herri Batasuna (HB), extreme Basque nationalist

Government

The present government, established in October 1982, is formed by the Socialist Party. The prime minister is Felipe Gonzalez.

Election results: percentage votes and seats gained since 1977

Election year	1977		1979		1982	
Electorate	23,616,421		26,836,500		26,837,212	
Turnout %	75.6		66.9		78.9	
	V %	S	V %	S	V %	S
Communist Party	9.3	20	10.8	23	4.1	5
Socialist Party	30.3	118	30.5	121	46.5	202
Democratic and Social Centre Party					2.8	2
Union of the Democratic Centre	34.8	165	35.0	168	6.7	11
Popular Alliance	8.4	16	6.5	10	25.8	106
Main Catalan regional parties	4.5	14	3.4	9	3.9	12
Main Basque regional parties	2.0	9	3.2	11	2.9	10
Other regional parties	10.6	8	10.6	8	7.4	2
TOTAL SEATS		350		350		350

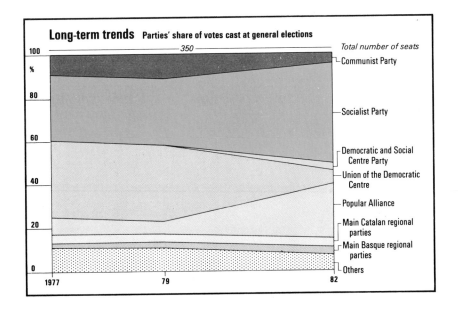

Long-term trends Parties' share of votes cast at general elections

Total number of seats — Communist Party — Socialist Party — Democratic and Social Centre Party — Union of the Democratic Centre — Popular Alliance — Main Catalan regional parties — Main Basque regional parties — Others

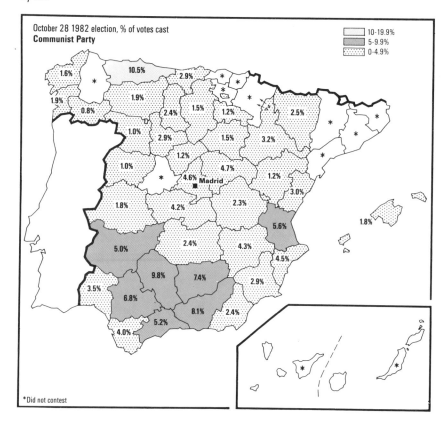

October 28 1982 election, % of votes cast
Communist Party

10-19.9%
5-9.9%
0-4.9%

*Did not contest

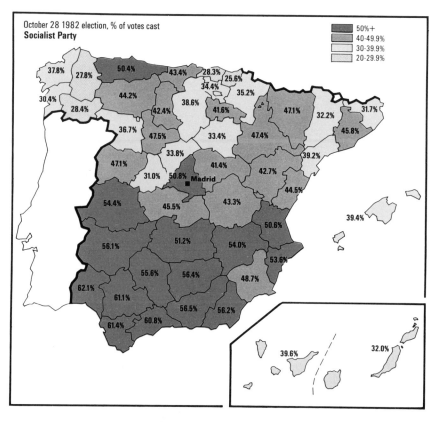

October 28 1982 election, % of votes cast
Socialist Party

50%+
40-49.9%
30-39.9%
20-29.9%

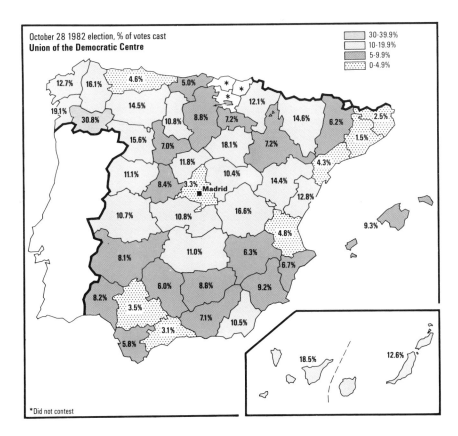

October 28 1982 election, % of votes cast
Union of the Democratic Centre

Legend:
- 30-39.9%
- 10-19.9%
- 5-9.9%
- 0-4.9%

12.7% 16.1% 4.6% 5.0% * *
* 12.1%
19.1% 14.5% 10.8% 8.8% 7.2% 14.6% 6.2% 2.5%
30.8% 1.5%
15.6% 7.0% 18.1% 7.2% 4.3%
11.8%
11.1% 10.4% 14.4%
8.4% 3.3% Madrid 12.8%
10.7% 10.8% 16.6% 9.3%
4.8%
8.1% 11.0% 6.3%
6.7%
6.0% 8.8% 9.2%
8.2% 3.5% 7.1% 10.5%
3.1%
5.8%

18.5% 12.6%

*Did not contest

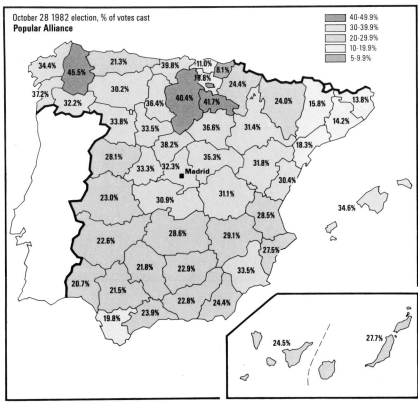

October 28 1982 election, % of votes cast
Popular Alliance

Legend:
- 40-49.9%
- 30-39.9%
- 20-29.9%
- 10-19.9%
- 5-9.9%

34.4% 21.3% 39.8% 11.0% 8.1%
45.5% 18.8% 24.4%
37.2% 30.2% 36.4% 40.4% 41.7% 24.0% 15.8% 13.8%
32.2% 36.6% 31.4% 14.2%
33.8% 33.5% 18.3%
38.2% 35.3% 31.8%
28.1% 30.4%
33.3% 32.3% Madrid
23.0% 30.9% 31.1% 34.6%
28.5%
22.6% 28.6% 29.1% 27.5%
21.8% 22.9% 33.5%
20.7% 21.5% 22.8% 24.4%
23.9%
19.8%

24.5% 27.7%

119

Sweden

A constitutional monarchy. The government is responsible to a single-chamber parliament, the *Riksdag*, with 349 members.

Parliament is elected for a three-year term, with a circumscribed right of dissolution (the new Riksdag is elected only for the balance of the unexpired term).

The Riksdag is elected on a basis of proportional representation, using the modified Sainte-Laguë system (see page 3), in 28 multi-member constituencies. There is a two-stage distribution of seats: 310 are allocated on a constituency basis; the remaining 39 seats are divided nationally and then reallocated to constituencies. To benefit from the national allocation a party must either have polled 4 per cent nationally or 12 per cent in any one constituency. Voters choose between party lists, with the opportunity of expressing preferences between candidates. Casual vacancies are filled by the co-option of substitutes. The minimum voting age is 18.

Last election: September 15 1985.

Next election due: September 1988.

Main political parties

1. Communist Party (SKP)
2. Social Democratic Party (SAP)
3. Centre Party
4. Christian Democratic Party
5. Liberal Party (FP)
6. Moderate Party, Conservative

Government

The present government is formed by the Social Democratic Party. It was reconstituted in March 1986, following the assassination of the prime minister, Olof Palme. The prime minister is now Ingvar Carlsson.

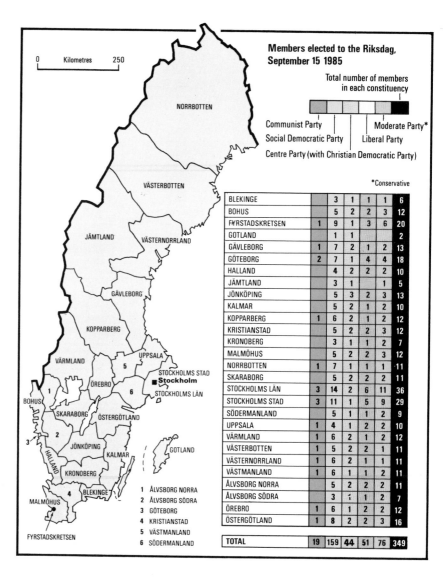

Members elected to the Riksdag, September 15 1985

Total number of members in each constituency

Communist Party — Social Democratic Party — Centre Party (with Christian Democratic Party) — Liberal Party — Moderate Party* — *Conservative

	Communist	Social Democratic	Centre	Liberal	Moderate	Total
BLEKINGE		3	1	1	1	6
BOHUS		5	2	2	3	12
FYRSTADSKRETSEN	1	9	1	3	6	20
GOTLAND		1	1			2
GÄVLEBORG	1	7	2	1	2	13
GÖTEBORG	2	7	1	4	4	18
HALLAND		4	2	2	2	10
JÄMTLAND		3	1		1	5
JÖNKÖPING		5	3	2	3	13
KALMAR		5	2	1	2	10
KOPPARBERG	1	6	2	1	2	12
KRISTIANSTAD		5	2	2	3	12
KRONOBERG		3	1	1	2	7
MALMÖHUS		5	2	2	3	12
NORRBOTTEN	1	7	1	1	1	11
SKARABORG		5	2	2	2	11
STOCKHOLMS LÄN	3	14	2	6	11	36
STOCKHOLMS STAD	3	11	1	5	9	29
SÖDERMANLAND		5	1	1	2	9
UPPSALA	1	4	1	2	2	10
VÄRMLAND	1	6	2	1	2	12
VÄSTERBOTTEN	1	5	2	2	1	11
VÄSTERNORRLAND	1	6	2	1	1	11
VÄSTMANLAND	1	6	1	1	2	11
ÄLVSBORG NORRA		5	2	2	2	11
ÄLVSBORG SÖDRA		3	1	1	2	7
ÖREBRO	1	6	1	2	2	12
ÖSTERGÖTLAND	1	8	2	2	3	16
TOTAL	19	159	44	51	76	349

0 Kilometres 250

Map labels: NORRBOTTEN, VÄSTERBOTTEN, JÄMTLAND, VÄSTERNORRLAND, GÄVLEBORG, KOPPARBERG, VÄRMLAND, UPPSALA, STOCKHOLMS STAD, Stockholm, ÖREBRO, STOCKHOLMS LÄN, BOHUS, SKARABORG, ÖSTERGÖTLAND, JÖNKÖPING, KALMAR, GOTLAND, HALLAND, KRONOBERG, KRISTIANSTAD, BLEKINGE, MALMÖHUS, FYRSTADSKRETSEN

1 ÄLVSBORG NORRA
2 ÄLVSBORG SÖDRA
3 GÖTEBORG
4 KRISTIANSTAD
5 VÄSTMANLAND
6 SÖDERMANLAND

120

Election results: percentage votes and seats gained since 1948

Election year	1948		1952		1956		1958		1960		1964		1968	
Electorate	4,707,783		4,805,216		4,902,114		4,992,421		4,972,177		5,095,850		5,445,333	
Turnout %		82.4		78.7		79.1		77.0		85.6		83.3		88.7
	V %	S	V %	S	V %	S	V %	S	V %	S	V %	S	V %	S
Communist Party	6.3	8	4.3	5	5.0	6	3.4	5	4.5	5	5.2	8	3.0	3
Social Democratic Party	46.1	112	46.0	110	44.6	106	46.2	111	47.8	114	47.3	113	50.1	125
Centre (Agrarian) Party	12.4	30	10.7	26	9.5	19	12.7	32	13.6	34	13.2	33	15.7	37
Christian Democratic Party											1.8	0	1.5	0
Liberal (People's) Party	22.7	57	24.4	58	23.8	58	18.2	38	17.5	40	17.0	42	14.3	32
Moderate (Conservative) Party	12.3	23	14.4	31	17.1	42	19.5	45	16.6	39	13.7	32	12.9	29
Others	0.1	0	0.1	0	0.1	0	0.0	0	0.1	0	1.8	5	2.6	7
TOTAL SEATS		230		230		231		231		232		233		233

Election year	1970		1973		1976		1979		1982		1985	
Electorate	5,645,804		5,690,933		5,947,077		6,040,461		6,130,993		6,249,445	
Turnout %		88.1		90.7		91.4		90.2		90.6		89.1
	V %	S	V %	S	V %	S	V %	S	V %	S	V %	S
Communist Party	4.8	17	5.3	19	4.8	17	5.6	20	5.6	20	5.4	19
Social Democratic Party	45.3	163	43.6	156	42.7	152	43.2	154	45.6	166	44.7	159
Centre (Agrarian) Party	19.9	71	25.1	90	24.1	86	18.1	64	15.5	56 ⎤	12.4	44
Christian Democratic Party	1.8	0	1.8	0	1.4	0	1.4	0	1.9	0 ⎦		
Liberal (People's) Party	16.2	58	9.4	34	11.1	39	10.6	38	5.9	21	14.2	51
Moderate (Conservative) Party	11.5	41	14.3	51	15.6	55	20.3	73	23.6	86	21.3	76
Others	0.5		0.5		0.3		0.8		2.0	0	2.0	0
TOTAL SEATS		350		350		349		349		349		349

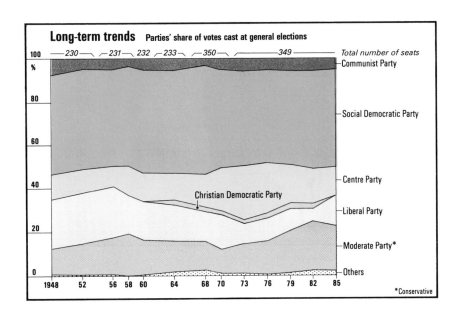

Long-term trends — Parties' share of votes cast at general elections

*Conservative

Result of election of September 15 1985

Electorate: 6,249,445   Valid votes: 5,567,022 (89.1%)
Invalid votes: 48,220 (0.8%)

	Votes	%	Seats	%
Social Democratic Party	2,487,551	44.7	159	45.6
Moderate Party	1,187,335	21.3	76	21.8
Liberal Party	792,268	14.2	51	14.6
Centre Party[a]	691,258	12.4	44	12.6
Communist Party	298,419	5.4	19	5.4
Others	110,191	2.0	0	0.0
TOTAL	5,567,022		349	

[a] Including Christian Democratic Party.

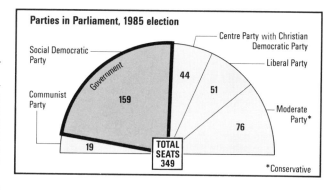

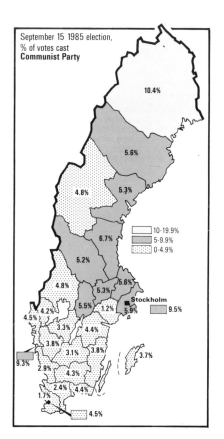

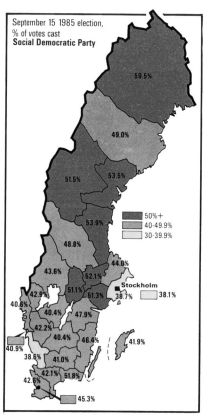

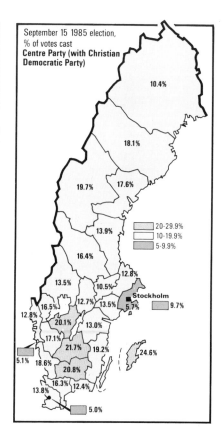

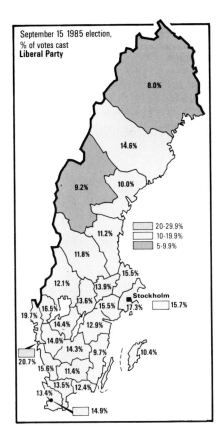

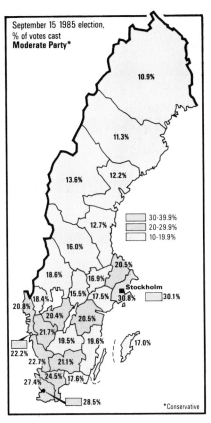

Switzerland

A confederal republic. The presidency rotates on a yearly basis among the seven members of the Federal Council (*Bundesrat*), the government. The members of the Bundesrat are chosen individually by a joint meeting of the two houses of the Federal Parliament at the beginning of each legislative term or whenever a vacancy occurs.

The upper house of the parliament, the Council of States (*Ständerat*), consists of 46 members who are chosen, mostly by plurality election (see page 2) in whichever way each *Canton* decides.

The lower house, or National Council (*Nationalrat*) with 200 members, is elected for a four-year term by proportional representation, using the Hagenbach-Bischoff quota (see page 3). In the smallest cantons, with only one member, the election is by plurality. In normal circumstances, an early dissolution of the Nationalrat is not possible.

The voter has as many votes as there are members to elect. He may choose between rival party lists, or distribute his votes among two or more lists, or even give two votes (but no more) to one candidate. The minimum voting age is 18. Casual vacancies are filled by co-opting the runner-up in the relevant party list.

The functions of the Swiss Parliament, as well as of the government (Bundesrat), are circumscribed to a greater extent than in other democratic countries, not only by the confederal provisions of the Swiss constitution, but by the very frequent use of referenda and citizens' initiatives.

Last election: October 23 1983.

Next election due: November 1987.

Main political parties

1. Communist Party (PdA)
2. Progressives (Poch)
3. Social Democratic Party (SPS)
4. Greens
5. Protestant People's Party (EVP)
6. People's Party (SVP)

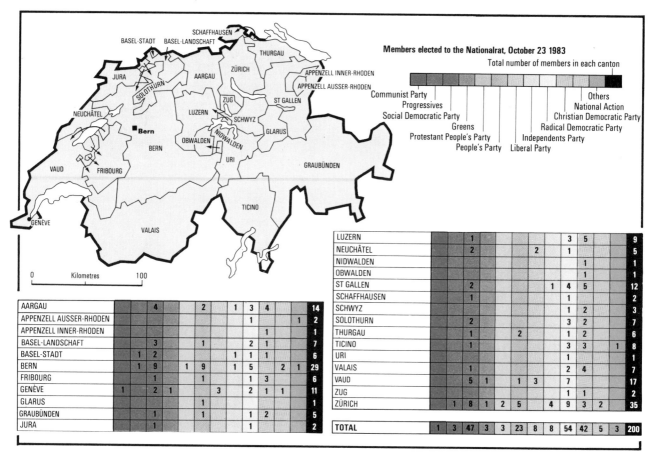

Members elected to the Nationalrat, October 23 1983

Total number of members in each canton

Communist Party · Progressives · Social Democratic Party · Greens · Protestant People's Party · People's Party · Liberal Party · Independents Party · Radical Democratic Party · Christian Democratic Party · National Action · Others

	Communist Party	Progressives	Social Democratic Party	Greens	Protestant People's Party	People's Party	Liberal Party	Independents Party	Radical Democratic Party	Christian Democratic Party	National Action	Others	Total
AARGAU			4			2		1	3	4			14
APPENZELL AUSSER-RHODEN									1			1	2
APPENZELL INNER-RHODEN										1			1
BASEL-LANDSCHAFT			3			1			2	1			7
BASEL-STADT		1	2				1	1	1				6
BERN		1	9	1	9		1	5		2	1		29
FRIBOURG			1			1			1	3			6
GENÈVE	1		2	1			3		2	1	1		11
GLARUS						1							1
GRAUBÜNDEN			1			1			1	2			5
JURA			1							1			2
LUZERN			1						3	5			9
NEUCHÂTEL			2				2		1				5
NIDWALDEN										1			1
OBWALDEN										1			1
ST GALLEN			2					1	4	5			12
SCHAFFHAUSEN			1						1				2
SCHWYZ									1	2			3
SOLOTHURN			2						3	2			7
THURGAU			1			2			1	2			6
TICINO			1						3	3		1	8
URI									1				1
VALAIS			1						2	4			7
VAUD			5	1		1	3		7				17
ZUG									1	1			2
ZÜRICH		1	8	1	2	5		4	9	3	2		35
TOTAL	1	3	47	3	3	23	8	8	54	42	5	3	200

0 Kilometres 100

7. Liberal Party (LPS)
8. Independents Party (LdU)
9. Radical Democratic Party (FDP)
10. Christian Democratic Party (CVP)
11. National Action (NA), extreme Right

The initials given for the parties come from the German original. Most parties have a different abbreviation in French.

Government

The government is a semi-permanent coalition between the four largest parties. The Radical Democrats, Social Democrats and Christian Democrats have two members each in the Bundesrat and the People's Party has one.

Result of election to Nationalrat of October 23 1983

Electorate: 4,068,532   Valid votes: 1,959,915 (48.2%)
Invalid votes: 30,097 (0.7%)

	Votes	%	Seats	%
Radical Democratic Party	457,864	23.4	54	27.0
Social Democratic Party	447,925	22.9	47	23.5
Christian Democratic Party	399,929	20.4	42	21.0
People's Party	217,219	11.1	23	11.5
Independents Party	78,523	4.1	8	4.0
National Action	67,698	3.5	5	2.5
Greens	56,165	2.9	3	1.5
Liberal Party	55,340	2.8	8	4.0
Progressives	43,668	2.2	3	1.5
Protestant People's Party	40,851	2.1	3	1.5
Communist Party	17,497	0.9	1	0.5
Others	77,236	3.9	3	1.5
TOTAL	1,959,915		200	

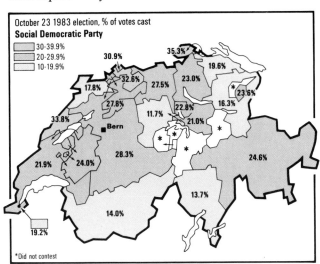

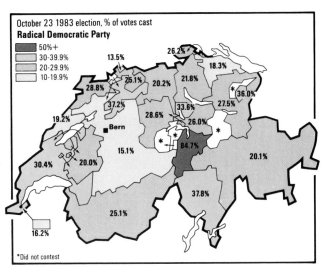

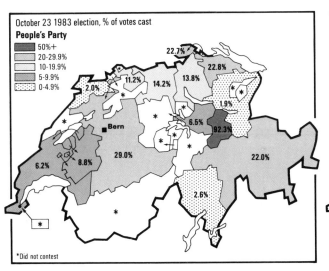

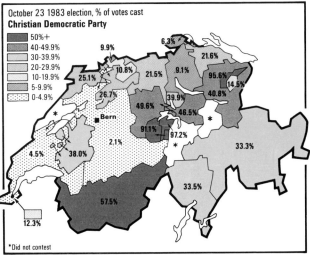

125

Election results: percentage votes and seats gained since 1947

Election year	1947 V%	1947 S	1951 V%	1951 S	1955 V%	1955 S	1959 V%	1959 S	1963 V%	1963 S	1967 V%	1967 S	1971 V%	1971 S	1975 V%	1975 S	1979 V%	1979 S	1983 V%	1983 S
Electorate	1,374,740		1,414,308		1,453,807		1,473,155		1,531,164		1,599,479		3,548,860		3,733,113		3,863,169		4,068,532	
Turnout %	70.3		68.4		67.5		67.1		63.3		62.6		56.6		51.7		47.5		48.2	
Communist Party	5.1	7	2.7	5	2.6	4	2.7	3	2.2	4	2.9	5	2.6	5	2.4	4	2.1	3	0.9	1
Progressives															1.0	0	1.7	3	2.2	3
Social Democratic Party	26.2	48	26.0	49	27.0	53	26.4	51	26.6	53	23.5	51	22.9	46	24.9	55	24.4	51	22.9	47
Greens																			2.9	3
Protestant People's Party	0.9	1	1.0	1	1.1	1	1.4	2	1.6	6	1.6	3	2.1	3	2.0	3	2.2	3	2.1	3
People's Party	12.1	21	12.6	23	12.1	22	11.6	23	11.4	22	11.0	21	11.0	23	9.9	21	11.6	23	11.1	23
Liberal Conservative Party	3.2	7	2.6	5	2.2	5	2.3	5	2.2	6	2.3	6	2.2	6	2.4	6	2.8	8	2.8	8
Independents Party	4.4	8	5.1	10	5.5	10	5.5	10	5.0	10	9.1	16	7.6	13	6.1	11	4.1	8	4.1	8
Radical Democratic Party	23.0	52	24.0	51	23.3	50	23.7	51	23.9	51	23.2	49	21.7	49	22.2	47	24.1	51	23.4	54
Christian Democratic Party	21.2	44	22.5	48	23.2	47	23.3	47	23.4	48	22.1	45	20.7	44	21.1	46	21.5	44	20.4	42
National Action											0.6	1	3.2	4	2.4	2	1.3	2	3.5	5
Others	3.9	6	3.6	4	3.2	4	3.2	4	3.6	4	3.7	3	6.0	7	5.6	5	4.2	4	3.9	3
TOTAL SEATS		194		196		196		196		200		200		200		200		200		200

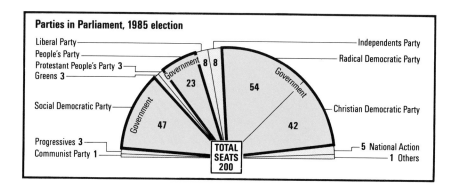

Parties in Parliament, 1985 election

Liberal Party
People's Party
Protestant People's Party **3**
Greens **3**
Social Democratic Party
Progressives **3**
Communist Party **1**

Government 47 — Government 23 — 8 — 8 — Government 54 — Government 42

Independents Party
Radical Democratic Party
Christian Democratic Party
5 National Action
1 Others

TOTAL SEATS 200

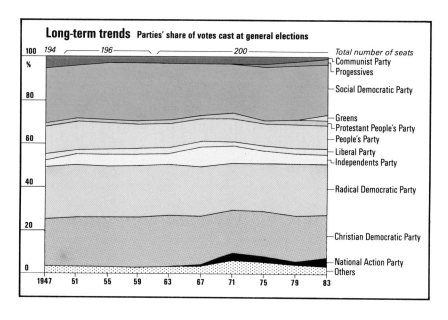

Long-term trends Parties' share of votes cast at general elections

Total number of seats
Communist Party
Progessives
Social Democratic Party
Greens
Protestant People's Party
People's Party
Liberal Party
Independents Party
Radical Democratic Party
Christian Democratic Party
National Action Party
Others

1947 51 55 59 63 67 71 75 79 83

Trinidad and Tobago

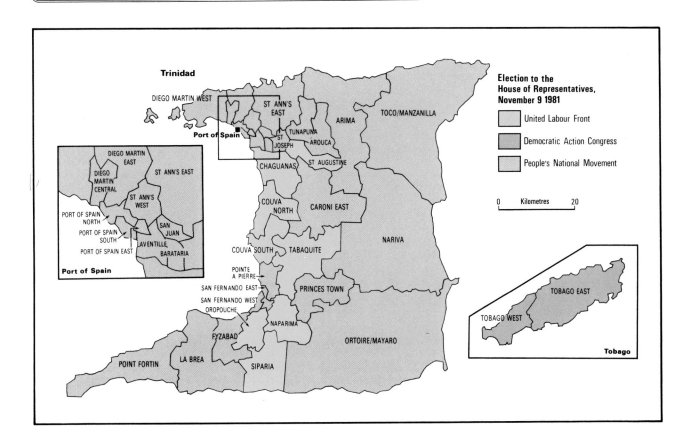

Trinidad

DIEGO MARTIN WEST

ST ANN'S EAST

Port of Spain

TUNAPUNA

ST JOSEPH

AROUCA

ARIMA

TOCO/MANZANILLA

ST AUGUSTINE

CHAGUANAS

COUVA NORTH

CARONI EAST

NARIVA

COUVA SOUTH

TABAQUITE

POINTE A PIERRE

SAN FERNANDO EAST

PRINCES TOWN

SAN FERNANDO WEST

OROPOUCHE

NAPARIMA

FYZABAD

ORTOIRE/MAYARO

POINT FORTIN

LA BREA

SIPARIA

Port of Spain

DIEGO MARTIN EAST

DIEGO MARTIN CENTRAL

ST ANN'S EAST

ST ANN'S WEST

PORT OF SPAIN NORTH

SAN JUAN

PORT OF SPAIN SOUTH

LAVENTILLE

PORT OF SPAIN EAST

BARATARIA

Election to the House of Representatives, November 9 1981

- United Labour Front
- Democratic Action Congress
- People's National Movement

0   Kilometres   20

TOBAGO EAST

TOBAGO WEST

Tobago

Result of election to the House of Representatives of November 9 1981

Electorate: 736,104   Valid votes: 415,416 (56.4%)
Invalid votes: 2,638 (0.4%)

	Votes	%	Seats	%
People's National Movement	218,557	52.6	26	72.2
Organisation for National Reconstruction	91,704	22.1	0	0.0
United Labour Front	59,613	14.3	8	22.2
Democratic Action Congress	15,390	3.7	2	5.5
Others	30,152	7.3	0	0.0
TOTAL	415,416		36	

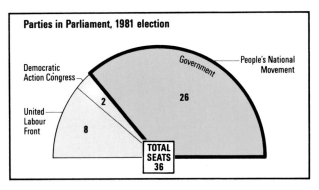

Parties in Parliament, 1981 election

Democratic Action Congress

United Labour Front

Government

People's National Movement

26

2

8

TOTAL SEATS 36

Trinidad and Tobago

A republic, with an indirectly elected president without executive powers. The government is responsible to a two-chamber parliament. The upper house, or Senate, with 31 members, is a wholly nominated body.

The lower house, or House of Representatives, with 36 members, is elected on a plurality basis (see page 2). Its term of office is five years. The minimum voting age is 18. Casual vacancies are filled by by-elections.

Last election: November 9 1981.

Next election due: by February 1987.

Main political parties

1. United Labour Front (ULF)
2. Democratic Action Congress (DAC)
3. Organisation for National Reconstruction (ONR)
   Nos. 2 and 3 recently combined with others to form the National Alliance for Reconstruction.
4. People's National Movement

Government

The present government is formed by the People's National Movement. The prime minister is George Chambers.

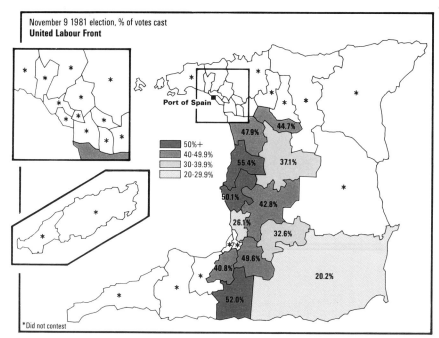

November 9 1981 election, % of votes cast
United Labour Front

- 50%+
- 40-49.9%
- 30-39.9%
- 20-29.9%

*Did not contest

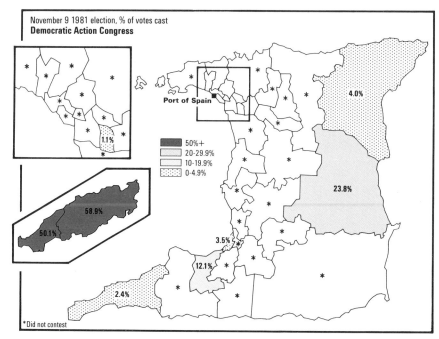

November 9 1981 election, % of votes cast
Democratic Action Congress

- 50%+
- 20-29.9%
- 10-19.9%
- 0-4.9%

*Did not contest

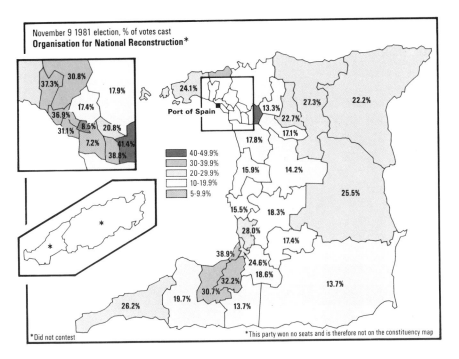

November 9 1981 election, % of votes cast
Organisation for National Reconstruction*

Port of Spain

40-49.9%
30-39.9%
20-29.9%
10-19.9%
5-9.9%

*Did not contest

*This party won no seats and is therefore not on the constituency map

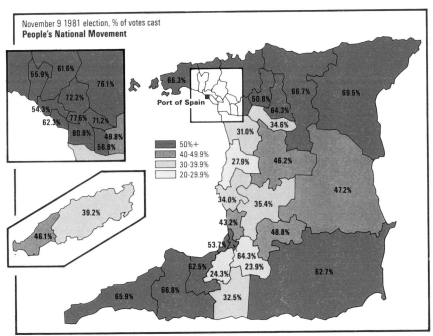

November 9 1981 election, % of votes cast
People's National Movement

Port of Spain

50%+
40-49.9%
30-39.9%
20-29.9%

United Kingdom

The United Kingdom of Great Britain and Northern Ireland is a constitutional monarchy. The government is responsible to a two-chamber parliament. The upper chamber, or House of Lords, with a nominal membership of around 1,200, is partly hereditary and partly nominated for life.

The lower house, or House of Commons, is elected on a plurality basis (see page 2) in 650 single-member constituencies. Its term of office is five years, with early dissolution possible. Casual vacancies are filled by by-elections. The minimum voting age is 18.

Last election held: June 9 1983.

Next election due: June 1988.

Main political parties

1. Communist Party
2. Labour Party
3. Green Party, called Ecology Party until 1985
4. Social Democratic Party
5. Liberal Party
   Nos. 4 and 5 constitute The Alliance
6. Conservative Party
7. National Front
8. Scottish National Party
9. Plaid Cymru, Welsh nationalist
10. Social Democratic and Labour Party
11. Official Unionist Party
12. Democratic Unionist Party
13. Provisional Sinn Fein
    Nos. 10–13 are Northern Irish parties.

Government

The present government is formed by the Conservative Party. It was reconstituted after the June 1983 general election. The prime minister is Margaret Thatcher.

Result of election of June 9 1983

Electorate: 42,192,999   Valid votes: 30,671,137 (72.7%)   Invalid votes: 51,104 (0.1%)

	Votes	%	Seats	%
Conservative Party	13,012,316	42.4	397	61.1
Labour Party	8,456,934	27.6	209	32.2
Liberal Party }The Alliance	7,780,949	25.4	17	2.6
Social Democratic Party			6	0.9
Scottish National Party	331,975	1.1	2	0.3
Official Unionist Party	259,952	0.8	11	1.7
Democratic Unionist Party	152,749	0.5	3	0.5
Social Democratic and Labour Party	137,012	0.4	1	0.2
Plaid Cymru	125,309	0.4	2	0.3
Provisional Sinn Fein	102,701	0.3	1	0.2
Ecology Party	53,848	0.2	0	0.0
National Front	27,065	0.1	0	0.0
Ulster Popular Unionist Party	22,861	0.1	1	0.2
Communist Party	11,606	0.0	0	0.0
Others	195,860	0.6	1	0.2
TOTAL	30,671,137		650	

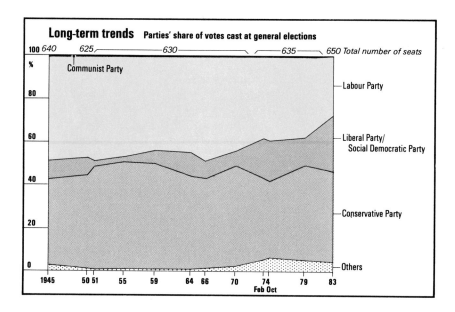

Long-term trends   Parties' share of votes cast at general elections

130

Election results: percentage votes and seats gained since 1945

Election year	1945		1950		1951		1955		1959		1964	
Electorate	33,240,391		34,412,255		34,919,331		34,852,179		35,397,304		35,894,054	
Turnout %		72.6		83.6		81.9		76.8		78.7		77.1
	V %	S	V %	S	V %	S	V %	S	V %	S	V %	S
Communist Party	0.4	2	0.3	0	0.1	0	0.1	0	0.1	0	0.2	0
Labour Party	48.0	393	46.1	315	48.8	295	46.4	277	43.8	258	44.1	317
Social Democratic Party												
Liberal Party	9.0	12	9.1	9	2.6	6	2.7	6	5.9	6	11.2	9
Conservative Party and allies	39.6	210	43.4	298	48.0	321	49.7	345	49.4	365	43.4	304
National Front												
Scottish National Party	0.1	0	0.0	0	0.0	0	0.0	0	0.1	0	0.2	0
Plaid Cymru	0.1	0	0.1	0	0.0	0	0.2	0	0.3	0	0.3	0
Social Democratic and Labour Party												
Ulster Unionist and Loyalist parties	0.4	2	0.5	2	0.4	3	0.6	2	0.2	0	0.4	0
Irish Republican Party/Sinn Fein												
Others	2.4	21	0.5	1	0.1	0	0.2	0	0.2	1	0.2	0
TOTAL SEATS		640		625		625		630		630		630

Election year	1966		1970		1974 (Feb.)		1974 (Oct.)		1979		1983	
Electorate	35,957,245		39,342,013		39,753,863		40,072,970		41,095,649		42,192,999	
Turnout %		75.8		72.0		78.8		72.8		76.0		72.7
	V %	S	V %	S	V %	S	V %	S	V %	S	V %	S
Communist Party	0.2	0	0.1	0	0.1	0	0.1	0	0.1	0	0.0	0
Labour Party	48.0	364	43.1	288	37.2	301	39.2	319	36.9	269	27.6	209
Social Democratic Party											25.4 {	6
Liberal Party	8.5	12	7.5	6	19.3	14	18.3	13	13.8	11	42.4	17
Conservative Party and allies	41.9	253	46.4	330	37.9	297	35.9	277	43.9	339	42.4	397
National Front			0.0		0.2		0.4		0.6		0.1	0
Scottish National Party	0.5	0	1.1	1	2.0	7	2.9	11	1.6	2	1.1	2
Plaid Cymru	0.2	0	0.6	0	0.6	2	0.6	3	0.4	2	0.4	2
Social Democratic and Labour Party					0.5	1	0.5	1	0.4	1	0.4	1
Ulster Unionist and Loyalist parties					1.5	11	1.5	10	1.3	10	1.4	15
Irish Republican Party/Sinn Fein	0.5	1	0.6	3	0.2	0	0.2	1	0.2	1	0.3	1
Others	0.2	0	0.6	2	0.5	2	0.5	0	0.7	0	0.8	0
TOTAL SEATS		630		630		635		635		635		650

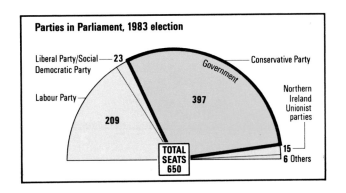

Parties in Parliament, 1983 election

Liberal Party/Social Democratic Party — 23

Labour Party — 209

Government

Conservative Party — 397

Northern Ireland Unionist parties — 15

6 Others

TOTAL SEATS 650

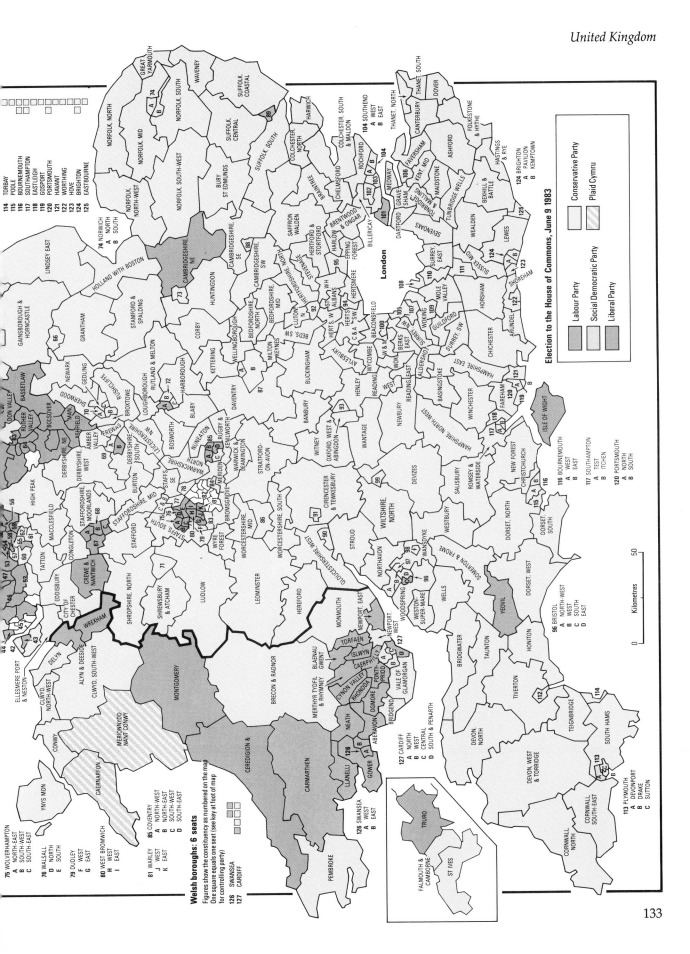

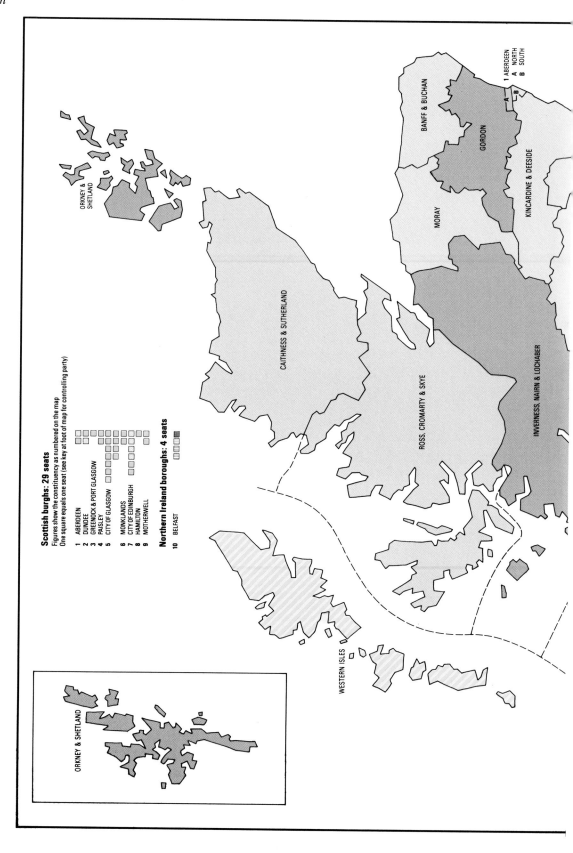

Scottish burghs: 29 seats
Figures show the constituency as numbered on the map
One square equals one seat (see key at foot of map for controlling party)

1 ABERDEEN
2 DUNDEE
3 GREENOCK & PORT GLASGOW
4 PAISLEY
5 CITY OF GLASGOW

6 MONKLANDS
7 CITY OF EDINBURGH
8 HAMILTON
9 MOTHERWELL

Northern Ireland boroughs: 4 seats

10 BELFAST

ORKNEY & SHETLAND

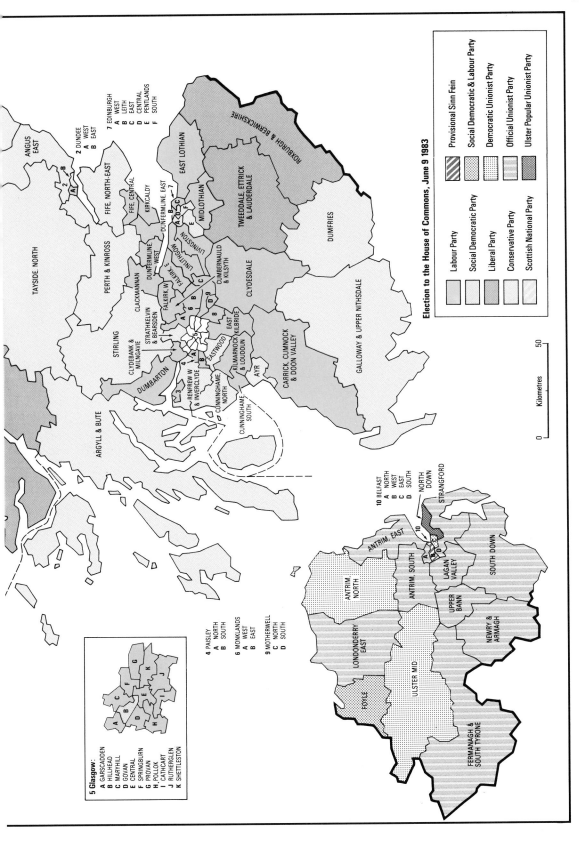

5 Glasgow:
A GARSCADDEN
B HILLHEAD
C MARYHILL
D GOVAN
E CENTRAL
F SPRINGBURN
G PROVAN
H POLLOK
I CATHCART
J RUTHERGLEN
K SHETTLESTON

4 PAISLEY
A NORTH
B SOUTH

6 MONKLANDS
A WEST
B EAST

9 MOTHERWELL
C NORTH
D SOUTH

2 DUNDEE
A WEST
B EAST

7 EDINBURGH
A WEST
B LEITH
C EAST
D CENTRAL
E PENTLANDS
F SOUTH

10 BELFAST
A NORTH
B WEST
C EAST
D SOUTH

Election to the House of Commons, June 9 1983

Labour Party	Provisional Sinn Fein
Social Democratic Party	Social Democratic & Labour Party
Liberal Party	Democratic Unionist Party
Conservative Party	Official Unionist Party
Scottish National Party	Ulster Popular Unionist Party

Kilometres

0   50

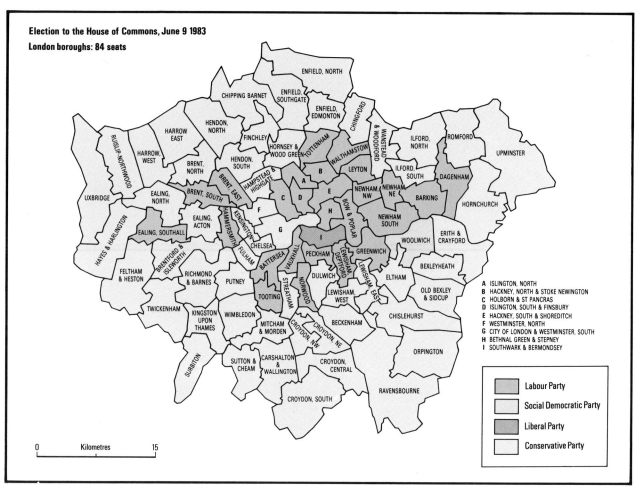

Election to the House of Commons, June 9 1983

London boroughs: 84 seats

A ISLINGTON, NORTH
B HACKNEY, NORTH & STOKE NEWINGTON
C HOLBORN & ST PANCRAS
D ISLINGTON, SOUTH & FINSBURY
E HACKNEY, SOUTH & SHOREDITCH
F WESTMINSTER, NORTH
G CITY OF LONDON & WESTMINSTER, SOUTH
H BETHNAL GREEN & STEPNEY
I SOUTHWARK & BERMONDSEY

Labour Party

Social Democratic Party

Liberal Party

Conservative Party

0   Kilometres   15

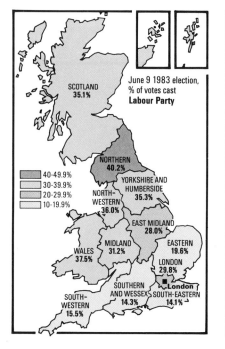

June 9 1983 election,
% of votes cast
Labour Party

SCOTLAND 35.1%
NORTHERN 40.2%
YORKSHIRE AND HUMBERSIDE 35.3%
NORTH-WESTERN 36.0%
EAST MIDLAND 28.0%
MIDLAND 31.2%
EASTERN 19.6%
WALES 37.5%
LONDON 29.8%
London
SOUTHERN AND WESSEX 14.3%
SOUTH-EASTERN 14.1%
SOUTH-WESTERN 15.5%

40-49.9%
30-39.9%
20-29.9%
10-19.9%

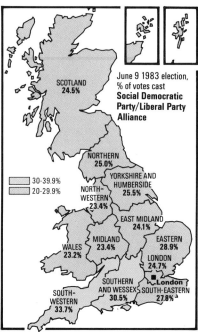

June 9 1983 election,
% of votes cast
Social Democratic Party/Liberal Party Alliance

SCOTLAND 24.5%
NORTHERN 25.0%
YORKSHIRE AND HUMBERSIDE 25.5%
NORTH-WESTERN 23.4%
EAST MIDLAND 24.1%
MIDLAND 23.4%
EASTERN 28.9%
WALES 23.2%
LONDON 24.7%
London
SOUTHERN AND WESSEX 30.5%
SOUTH-EASTERN 27.8%
SOUTH-WESTERN 33.7%

30-39.9%
20-29.9%

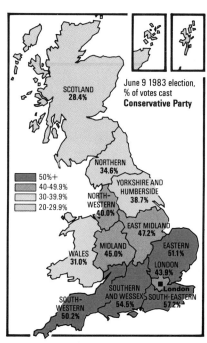

June 9 1983 election,
% of votes cast
Conservative Party

SCOTLAND 28.4%
NORTHERN 34.6%
YORKSHIRE AND HUMBERSIDE 38.7%
NORTH-WESTERN 40.0%
EAST MIDLAND 47.2%
MIDLAND 45.0%
EASTERN 51.1%
WALES 31.0%
LONDON 43.9%
London
SOUTHERN AND WESSEX 54.5%
SOUTH-EASTERN 57.2%
SOUTH-WESTERN 50.2%

50%+
40-49.9%
30-39.9%
20-29.9%

United States of America

A republic, whose president has executive powers. For most practical purposes he is directly elected, though the actual choice is made by an Electoral College. The members of the Electoral College are pledged (but not legally bound) to support the candidate in whose name they themselves were elected.

This device is one of the elements of the federal system of the United States of America. The Electoral College is made up of representatives of the 50 states and the District of Columbia, and all the College members from a state vote the same way even if the result within the state is very close. Within each state the Presidential election is conducted on a plurality basis (see page 2). In the Electoral College, majoritarian rules apply (see page 2), and there would, if necessary, be a series of ballots until one candidate secured 269 of the 537 Electoral College votes.

The president is elected for a four-year term. Each presidential candidate has a running mate, or vice-presidential candidate, who succeeds the president in the event of death, resignation or incapacity.

The two houses of Congress, of which the upper house, or Senate, is arguably the more powerful, are elected for terms of six and two years respectively. The whole of the lower house, or House of Representatives, of 435 members, is elected at the same time as the president, and then again (in so-called mid-term elections) two years later. Non-voting delegates to the House are also elected from the District of Columbia, Puerto Rico, Guam, the Virgin Islands and American Samoa.

One-third of the Senate's 100 members retire every two years and they are elected for six-year terms simultaneously with the president, and with the House, in mid-term years. Elections to both houses are conducted on a plurality basis in single-member constituencies. In the case of the Senate, the constituency is the entire area of the state. House constituencies are subdivisions of states except in the case of six states with small populations. There is no power of early dissolution.

Casual vacancies are filled by by-elections, except in the case of the Senate where, if authorised by the state legislature, the state governor may appoint a temporary replacement. The minimum voting age is 18.

Last Presidential and Congressional elections: November 6 1984.

Next Presidential election: November 8 1988.

Next Congressional elections (mid-term): November 4 1986.

Result of elections of November 6 1984

Votes

	Total Vote	Democrat Votes	%	Republican Votes	%	Others Votes	%
President	92,652,793	37,577,137	40.5	54,455,074	58.8	620,582	0.7
US House	82,404,820	42,961,688	52.1	38,714,659	47.0	728,473	0.9
US Senate	45,464,401	22,219,850	48.9	22,851,440	50.2	393,111	0.9

Seats

a) Senate seats: Democrats, elected 16, total members 47 (47%)
Republicans, elected 17, total members 53 (53%)
Total Senators: 100

b) House of Representatives' seats (Congressmen):
Democrats, 253 (58.2%) (including one disputed seat in the Indiana 8th District)
Republicans, 182 (41.8%)
Total Congressmen, 435

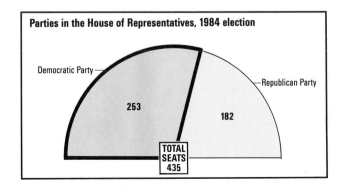

Parties in the House of Representatives, 1984 election

Democratic Party — 253

Republican Party — 182

TOTAL SEATS 435

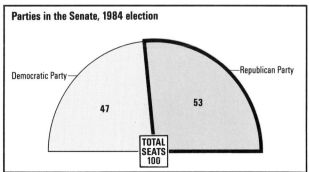

Parties in the Senate, 1984 election

Democratic Party — 47

Republican Party — 53

TOTAL SEATS 100

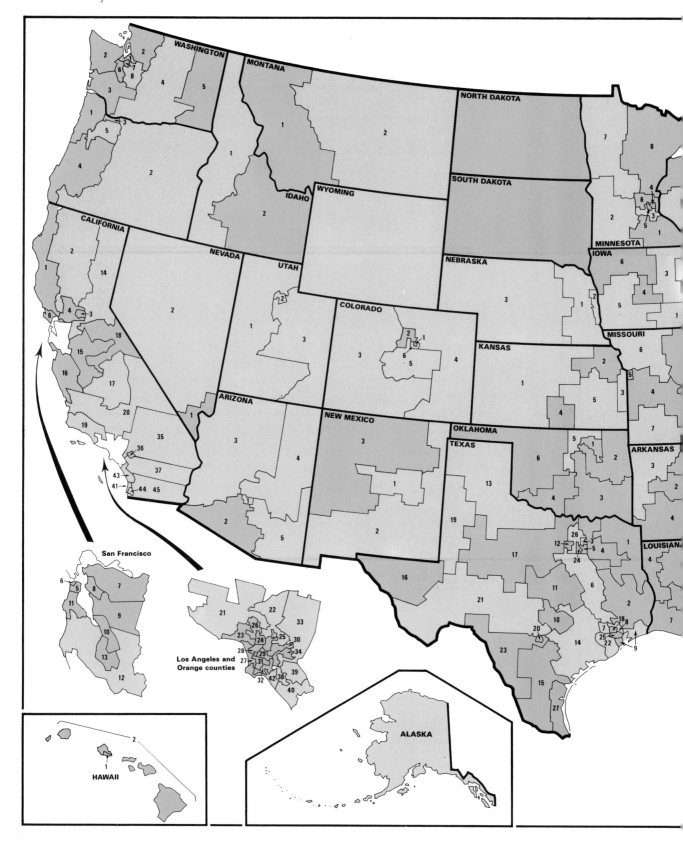

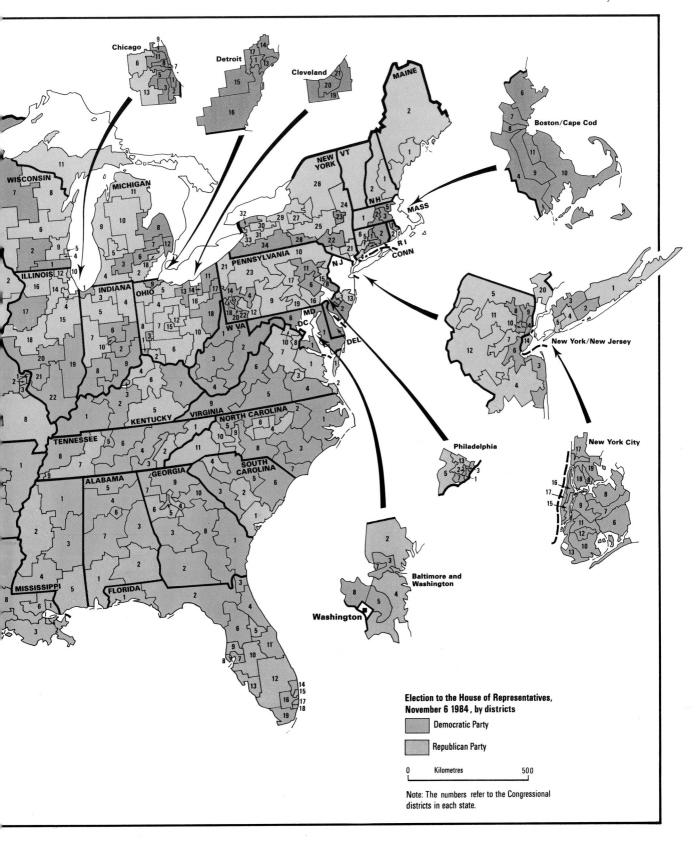

Election to the House of Representatives, November 6 1984 , by districts

Democratic Party

Republican Party

0   Kilometres   500

Note: The numbers refer to the Congressional districts in each state.

Presidential election results: percentage and electoral college votes since 1948

Election year	1948 V%	1948 EC	1952 V%	1952 EC	1956 V%	1956 EC	1960 V%	1960 EC	1964 V%	1964 EC	1968 V%	1968 EC	1972 V%	1972 EC	1976 V%	1976 EC	1980 V%	1980 EC	1984 V%	1984 EC
Electorate	91,408,000		96,466,000		100,524,000		105,292,000		111,612,000		117,438,000		136,162,000		146,219,000		156,973,000		175,147,000[a]	
Turnout %	53.3		63.7		65.6		65.4		63.3		62.3		57.1		55.8		55.1		52.9	
Democratic Party	49.5	303	44.4	89	42.0	73	49.7	303	61.1	486	42.7	191	37.5	17	50.1	297	41.0	49	40.6	525
Republican Party	45.1	189	55.1	442	57.4	457	49.5	219	38.5	52	43.4	301	60.7	520	48.0	240	50.7	489	58.8	13
Progressive (H. Wallace)	2.4	0	0.2	0																
Independent (J. Anderson)																	6.6	0		
States Rights (S. Thurmond)	2.4	39																		
American Independent Party (G. Wallace)											13.5	46	1.4	0	0.2	0	0.0	0		
Others	0.6	0	0.2	0	0.7	1	0.8	15	0.5	0	0.3	0	0.3	1	1.7	1	1.6	0	0.7	0
TOTAL electoral college votes		531		531		531		537		538		538		538		538		538		538

[a] Estimated.

Election results: composition of US Congress since 1946

Election year Congress	1946 80th Seats	1948 81st Seats	1950 82nd Seats	1952 83rd Seats	1954 84th Seats	1956 85th Seats	1958 86th Seats	1960 87th Seats	1962 88th Seats	1964 89th Seats	1966 90th Seats	1968 91st Seats	1970 92nd Seats	1972 93rd Seats	1974 94th Seats	1976 95th Seats	1978 96th Seats	1980 97th Seats	1982 98th Seats	1984 99th Seats
Senate																				
Democratic Party	45	54	48	46	48	49	64	64	67	68	64	58	54	56	61	61	58	46	45	47
Republican Party	51	42	47	48	47	47	34	36	33	32	36	42	44	42	37	38	41	53	55	53
Others			1	2	1								2	2	2	1	1	1		
TOTAL SEATS	96	96	96	96	96	96	98	100	100	100	100	100	100	100	100	100	100	100	100	100
House of Representatives																				
Democratic Party	188	263	234	213	232	234	283	262	258	295	248	243	255	242	291	292	277	243	267	253
Republican Party	246	171	199	221	203	201	153	175	176	140	187	192	180	192	144	143	158	192	168	182
Others	1	1	2	1										1						
Vacant									1											
TOTAL SEATS	435	435	435	435	435	435	436	437	435	435	435	435	435	435	435	435	435	435	435	435

Main political parties

1. Democratic Party
2. Republican Party

President

The president is Ronald Reagan, who was elected for a second term in November 1984.

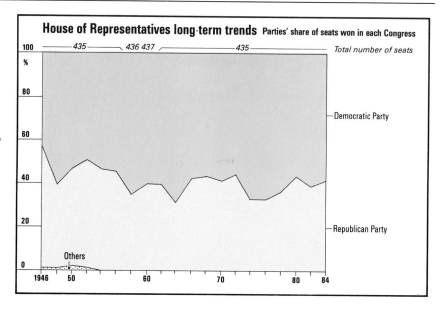

House of Representatives long-term trends — Parties' share of seats won in each Congress

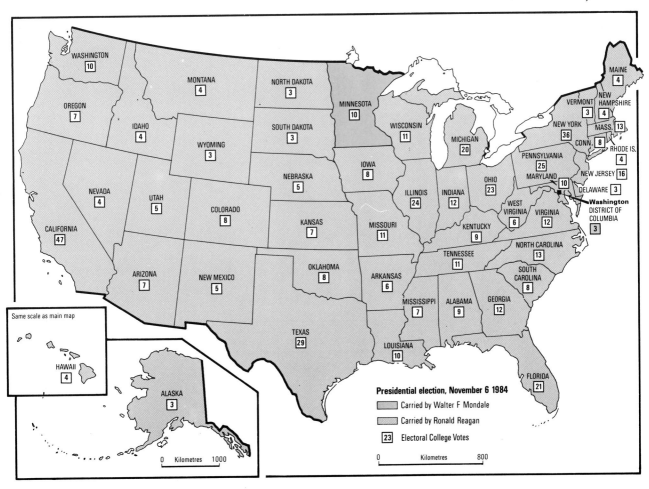

Presidential election, November 6 1984

Carried by Walter F Mondale

Carried by Ronald Reagan

23 Electoral College Votes

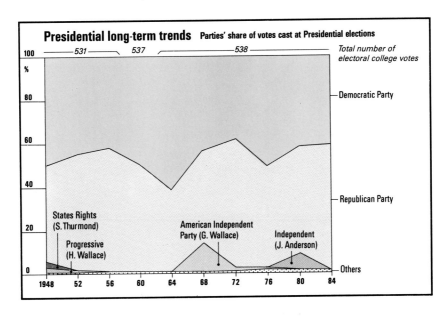

Presidential long-term trends   Parties' share of votes cast at Presidential elections

Total number of electoral college votes

Democratic Party

Republican Party

States Rights (S. Thurmond)

Progressive (H. Wallace)

American Independent Party (G. Wallace)

Independent (J. Anderson)

Others

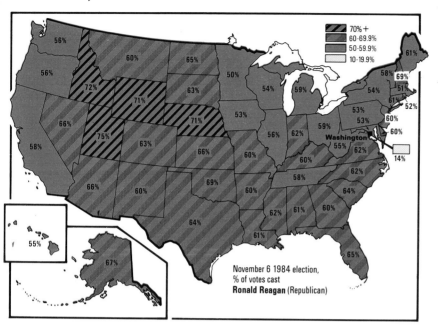

November 6 1984 election,
% of votes cast
Ronald Reagan (Republican)

Legend:
- 70% +
- 60-69.9%
- 50-59.9%
- 10-19.9%

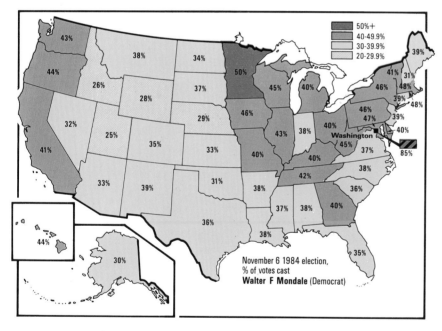

November 6 1984 election,
% of votes cast
Walter F Mondale (Democrat)

Legend:
- 50% +
- 40-49.9%
- 30-39.9%
- 20-29.9%

Footnote to table on p. 143
[a] Others receiving votes: Richards (Populist), 66,336; Serrette (Independent Alliance), 46,852; Hall (Communist), 36,386; Mason (Socialist Workers), 24,706; Holmes (Workers' World), 17,985; Dennis (American), 13,161; Winn (Workers' League), 10,801; Dodge (Prohibition), 4,242; Anderson (National Unity), 1,486; Baker (Big Deal), 892; Lowry (United Sovereign Citizens), 825; scattered write-ins, 17,589.
[b] Write-in vote.

Result of Presidential election of November 6 1984

Total popular vote: 92,652,793   Reagan's plurality: 16,877,937

	Ronald Reagan (Republican)		Walter F. Mondale (Democrat)		David Bergland (Libertarian)		Lyndon H. LaRouche (Independent)		Sonia Johnson (Citizens)		Other[a]	
	Votes	%	Votes	%	Votes	%	Votes	%	Votes	%	Votes	%
Alabama	872,849	60.5	551,899	38.3	9,504	0.7					7,461	0.5
Alaska	138,377	66.7	62,007	29.9	6,378	3.1					843	0.4
Arizona	681,416	66.4	333,854	32.5	10,585	1.0			18[b]		24[b]	
Arkansas	534,774	60.5	338,646	38.3	2,221	0.3	1,890	0.2	960	0.1	5,915	0.7
California	5,467,009	57.5	3,922,519	41.3	49,951	0.5			26,297	0.3	39,647	0.4
Colorado	821,817	63.4	454,975	35.1	11,257	0.9	4,662	0.4	23[b]		2,646	0.2
Connecticut	890,877	60.7	569,597	38.8	204[b]				14[b]		6,208	0.4
Delaware	152,190	59.8	101,656	39.9	268	0.1			121	0.1	337	0.1
District of Columbia	29,009	13.7	180,408	85.4	279	0.1	127	0.1			1,465	0.7
Florida	2,730,350	65.3	1,448,816	34.7	754[b]				58[b]		73[b]	
Georgia	1,068,722	60.2	706,628	39.8	152[b]		34[b]		4[b]		580[b]	
Hawaii	185,050	55.1	147,154	43.8	2,167	0.7	654	0.2			821	0.2
Idaho	297,523	72.4	108,510	26.4	2,823	0.7					2,288	0.6
Illinois	2,707,103	56.2	2,086,499	43.3	10,086	0.2			2,716	0.1	12,684	0.3
Indiana	1,377,230	61.7	841,481	37.7	6,741	0.3					7,617	0.3
Iowa	703,088	53.3	605,620	45.9	1,844	0.1	6,248	0.5			3,005	0.2
Kansas	677,296	66.3	333,149	32.6	3,329	0.3					8,217	0.8
Kentucky	821,702	60.0	539,539	39.4			1,776	0.1	599		5,729	0.4
Louisiana	1,037,299	60.8	651,586	38.2	1,876	0.1	3,552	0.2	9,502	0.6	3,007	0.2
Maine	336,500	60.8	214,515	38.8							2,129	0.4
Maryland	879,918	52.5	787,935	47.0	5,721	0.3			18[b]		2,299	0.1
Massachusetts	1,310,936	51.2	1,239,606	48.4							8,893	0.3
Michigan	2,251,571	59.2	1,529,638	40.2	10,055	0.3	3,862	0.1	1,191		5,341	0.1
Minnesota	1,032,603	49.5	1,036,364	49.7	2,996	0.1	3,865	0.2	1,219	0.1	7,402	0.4
Mississippi	582,377	61.9	352,192	37.4	2,336	0.3	1,001	0.1			3,198	0.3
Missouri	1,274,188	60.0	848,583	40.0					2[b]		10	
Montana	232,450	60.5	146,742	38.2	5,185	1.4						
Nebraska	460,054	70.6	187,866	28.8	2,079	0.3					2,091	0.3
Nevada	188,770	65.9	91,655	32.0	2,292	0.8					3,950	1.4
New Hampshire	267,050	68.7	120,347	30.9	735	0.2	467	0.1			418	0.1
New Jersey	1,933,630	60.1	1,261,323	39.2	6,416	0.2			1,247		15,246	0.5
New Mexico	307,101	59.7	201,769	39.2	4,459	0.9			455	0.1	586	0.1
New York	3,664,763	53.8	3,119,609	45.8	11,949	0.2					10,489	0.2
North Carolina	1,346,481	61.9	824,287	37.9	3,794	0.2					799	
North Dakota	200,336	64.8	104,429	33.8	703	0.2	1,278	0.4		0.1	1,857	0.6
Ohio	2,678,560	58.9	1,825,440	40.1	5,886	0.1	10,693	0.2			27,040	0.6
Oklahoma	861,530	68.6	385,080	30.7	9,066	0.7						
Oregon	685,700	55.9	536,479	43.7							4,348	0.4
Pennsylvania	2,584,323	53.3	2,228,131	46.0	6,982	0.1					3,839	0.1
Rhode Island	212,080	51.8	197,106	47.9	277	0.1			240	0.1	789	0.2
South Carolina	615,539	63.6	344,459	35.6	4,359	0.5					4,172	0.4
South Dakota	200,267	63.0	116,113	36.5							1,487	0.5
Tennessee	990,212	57.8	711,714	41.6	3,072	0.2	1,852	0.1	978	0.1	4,166	0.2
Texas	3,433,428	63.6	1,949,276	36.1			14,613	0.3	87[b]		167[b]	
Utah	469,105	74.5	155,369	24.7	2,447	0.4			844	0.1	1,891	0.4
Vermont	135,865	57.9	95,730	40.8	1,002	0.4	423	0.2	264	0.1	1,277	0.5
Virginia	1,337,078	62.3	796,250	37.1			13,307	0.6				
Washington	1,051,670	55.8	807,352	42.9	8,844	0.5	4,712	0.3	1,891	0.1	9,441	0.5
West Virginia	405,483	55.1	328,125	44.6							2,134	0.3
Wisconsin	1,198,584	54.2	995,740	45.0	4,883	0.2	3,791	0.2	1,456	0.1	7,235	0.3
Wyoming	133,241	70.5	53,370	28.2	2,357	1.3						
TOTAL	54,455,074	58.8	37,577,137	40.6	228,314	0.2	78,807	0.1	72,200	0.1	241,261	0.3

United States of America

Senate membership on November 6 1984
- Represented by two Democratic Senators
- Represented by two Republican Senators
- One Democratic Senator and one Republican Senator

Same scale as main map

HAWAII

ALASKA

0 Kilometres 1000

0 Kilometres 800

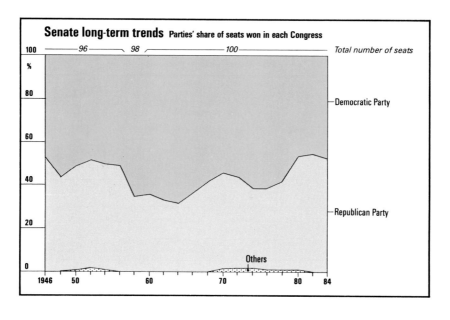

Senate long-term trends Parties' share of seats won in each Congress

Total number of seats

Democratic Party

Republican Party

Others

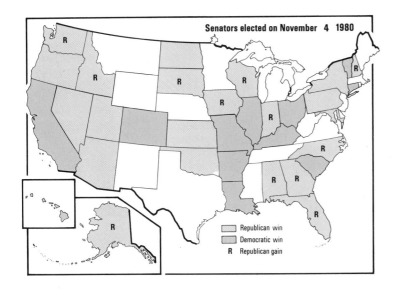

Senators elected on November 4 1980

Republican win
Democratic win
R Republican gain

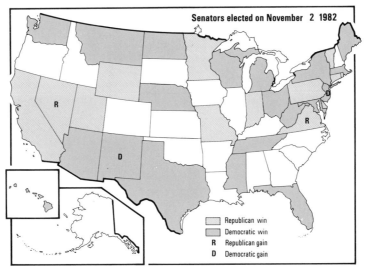

Senators elected on November 2 1982

Republican win
Democratic win
R Republican gain
D Democratic gain

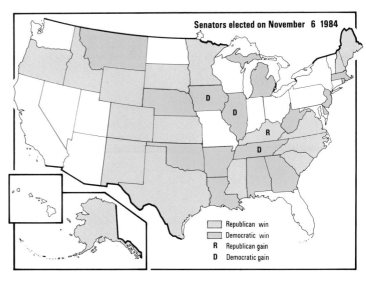

Senators elected on November 6 1984

Republican win
Democratic win
R Republican gain
D Democratic gain

Venezuela

A republic, with a directly elected president with executive powers. Democratic rule, in modern times, dates from the overthrow of the Jimenez dictatorship in 1958.

The president is elected for a five-year term by plurality vote (see page 2). He is restricted to a single consecutive term, but may run again after a ten-year gap.

The two houses of Congress, the Senate (46 members) and the Chamber of Deputies (200 members), are elected at the same time as the president, for five-year terms. Each house is elected on the basis of proportional representation, using the Hare quota (see page 2). There are two stages of seat allocation, the first being made at the provincial level, which constitutes 23 multi-member constituencies. Surplus votes and seats are transferred to a national pool, whose object is to compensate parties which have been under-represented at provincial level. The 'national' seats are then re-allocated to the constituencies.

The voters choose between rival party lists, with no possibility of varying the order of candidates. The minimum voting age is 18.

Last election: December 4 1983.

Next election due: December 1988.

President
The president is Jaime Lusinchi (Democratic Action), elected in December 1983.

Result of Presidential election of December 4 1983

Electorate: 7,777,892   Valid votes: 6,653,317 (85.5%)
Invalid votes: 171,863 (2.2%)

	Votes	%
Jaime Lusinchi (Democratic Action)	3,773,341	56.7
Rafael Caldera (COPEI)	2,298,176	34.5
Teodoro Petkoff (Movement towards Socialism)	277,498	4.2
Jose Vicente Rangel (People's Electoral Movement)	221,918	3.3
9 other candidates – total	82,384	1.2
TOTAL valid votes	6,653,317	

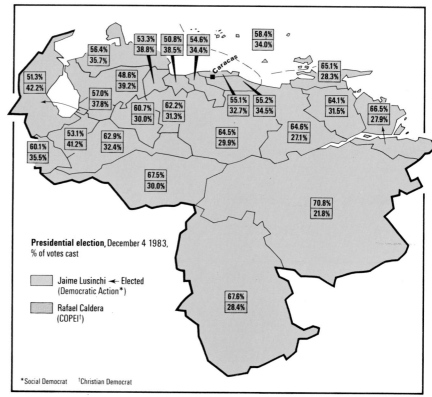

Presidential election, December 4 1983, % of votes cast

Jaime Lusinchi ◄ Elected (Democratic Action*)

Rafael Caldera (COPEI†)

*Social Democrat   †Christian Democrat

Main political parties

1. Socialist League (LS)
2. Communist Party (PCV)
3. Movement towards Socialism (MAS)
4. People's Electoral Movement (MEP)
5. New Alternative Party (NA)
6. Democratic Action (AD), Social Democrat
7. Democratic Republican Party (URD)
8. COPEI, Christian Democrat
9. National Opinion Party (OPINA), right-wing

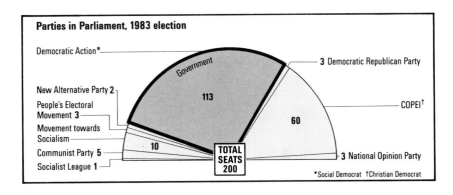

Parties in Parliament, 1983 election

Democratic Action* — Government — 113
3 Democratic Republican Party
COPEI† 60
New Alternative Party 2
People's Electoral Movement 3
Movement towards Socialism
Communist Party 5
Socialist League 1
10
TOTAL SEATS 200
3 National Opinion Party

*Social Democrat †Christian Democrat

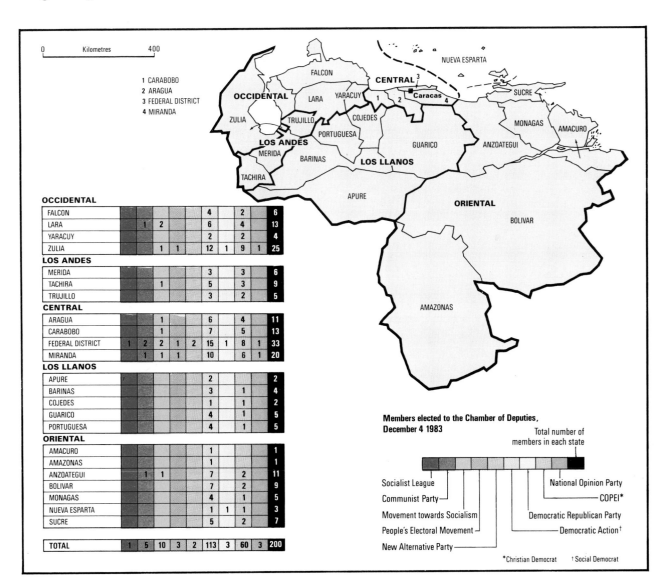

0 — Kilometres — 400

1 CARABOBO
2 ARAGUA
3 FEDERAL DISTRICT
4 MIRANDA

	LS	PCV	MAS	MEP	NA	AD	URD	COPEI	OPINA	Total
OCCIDENTAL										
FALCON						4		2		6
LARA		1	2			6		4		13
YARACUY						2		2		4
ZULIA			1	1		12	1	9	1	25
LOS ANDES										
MERIDA						3		3		6
TACHIRA			1			5		3		9
TRUJILLO						3		2		5
CENTRAL										
ARAGUA			1			6		4		11
CARABOBO			1			7		5		13
FEDERAL DISTRICT	1	2	2	1	2	15	1	8	1	33
MIRANDA		1	1	1		10		6	1	20
LOS LLANOS										
APURE						2				2
BARINAS						3		1		4
COJEDES						1		1		2
GUARICO						4		1		5
PORTUGUESA						4		1		5
ORIENTAL										
AMACURO						1				1
AMAZONAS						1				1
ANZOATEGUI		1	1			7		2		11
BOLIVAR						7		2		9
MONAGAS						4		1		5
NUEVA ESPARTA						1	1	1		3
SUCRE						5		2		7
TOTAL	1	5	10	3	2	113	3	60	3	200

Members elected to the Chamber of Deputies, December 4 1983

Total number of members in each state

Socialist League
Communist Party
Movement towards Socialism
People's Electoral Movement
New Alternative Party
National Opinion Party
COPEI*
Democratic Republican Party
Democratic Action†

*Christian Democrat   † Social Democrat

147

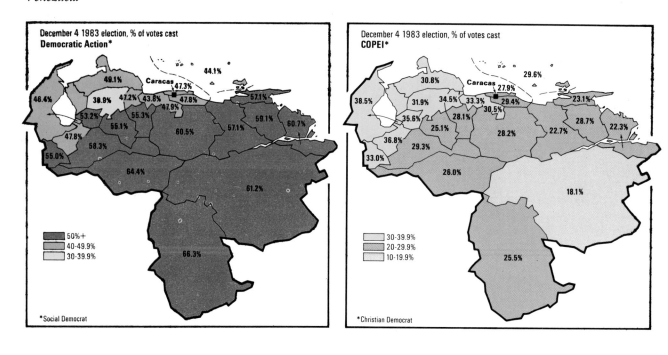

December 4 1983 election, % of votes cast
Democratic Action*

*Social Democrat

December 4 1983 election, % of votes cast
COPEI*

*Christian Democrat

Result of election to the Chamber of Deputies of December 4 1983

Electorate: 7,777,892   Valid votes: 6,580,899 (84.6%)
Invalid votes: 244,281 (3.1%)

	Votes	%	Seats	%
Democratic Action	3,284,166	49.9	113	56.5
COPEI	1,887,226	28.7	60	30.0
Movement towards Socialism	377,795	5.7	10	5.0
Communist Party	219,085	3.3	5	2.5
National Opinion	130,022	1.9	3	1.5
People's Electoral Movement	129,263	2.0	3	1.5
Democratic Republican Party	125,458	1.9	3	1.5
New Alternative Party	122,235	1.9	2	1.0
Socialist League	95,174	1.5	1	0.5
Others	210,475	3.2	0	0.0
TOTAL	6,580,899		200	

The European Parliament

The European Parliament has grown out of the Common Assembly of the European Coal and Steel Community, founded in 1952. It is now intended to give the European Economic Community's 250 million voters a direct say in the development of the Community and to provide democratic control over its other institutions. The reality falls somewhat short of these aspirations, as the powers of the Parliament are severely limited.

Since 1979, the Parliament has been directly elected simultaneously in all the member states. The term of office is five years, with no provision for early dissolution. There should be a common electoral system for all member states, but so far agreement on this has not been reached. Consequently, each member state has used its own system which, in most cases, resembles that used for the election of its own national Parliament.

There have, so far, been two direct elections: in June 1979 and in June 1984. The 1979 election was held in nine member states. Greece, which joined the Community on January 1 1981, subsequently elected 24 members on October 18 1981.

The 1984 election was held in ten member states. Portugal and Spain, which joined the Community on January 1 1986, appointed 24 and 60 members respectively, from their national parliaments, to represent them on a temporary basis. Elections are planned for later in 1986.

The elections have been contested in each member state by the main national political parties. But within the parliament the elected members have joined together in trans-national political groups and they sit in these groups, rather than in national delegations, inside the

Result of first election to the European Parliament of June 7–10 1979

Votes, percentages and seats

	Total	Belgium	Denmark	France	West Germany	Republic of Ireland	Italy	Luxembourg[b]	Netherlands	United Kingdom
Socialists	29,523,692	1,274,778	387,605	4,763,026	11,370,045	193,898	5,381,218	(37,053)	1,722,240	4,393,829
	26.6%	23.4%	22.1%	23.6%	40.8%	14.5%	15.4%	21.7%	30.4%	32.7%
	113	7	4	22	35	4	13	1	9	18
Christian Democrats	33,036,236	2,053,865		(1,788,433)[a]	13,700,205	443,652	12,970,693	(61,644)	2,017,743	
	29.8%	37.7%		(8.8%)	49.2%	33.1%	37.0%	36.1%	35.6%	
	107	10		8	42	4	30	3	10	
Conservatives	6,986,761		353,099							6,633,662
	6.3%		20.1%							49.3%
	64		3							60
Communists	14,960,785	145,804	81,991	4,153,710	112,055		10,361,344	(8,538)	97,343	
	13.5%	0.7%	4.7%	20.5%	0.4%		29.6%	5.0%	1.7%	
	44	0	1	19	0		24	0	0	
Liberals	11,512,455	885,212	252,767	(3,800,418)[a]	1,662,621	89,838	2,167,298	(47,983)	914,787	1,691,531
	10.4%	16.3%	14.4%	(18.8%)	6.0%	6.7%	6.2%	28.1%	16.2%	12.6%
	40	4	3	17	4	1	5	2	4	0
Gaullists and allies	4,114,969		100,702	3,301,980		464,451				
	3.7%		5.7%	16.3%		34.7%				
	22		1	15		5				
Others (Represented)	5,722,036	738,981	365,760			81,522	3,853,118		511,967	418,524
	5.1%	13.6%	20.9%			6.1%	10.9%		9.0%	3.1%
	20	3	4			1	9		2	3
Others (Unrepresented)	5,095,554	344,227	212,414	2,434,780	1,002,183	65,711	308,930	(15,541)	403,223	308,545
	4.6%	6.3%	12.1%	12.1%	3.6%	4.9%	0.9%	9.1%	7.1%	2.3%
	0	0	0	0	0	0	0	0	0	0
TOTAL (V)	110,952,518	5,442,867	1,754,338	20,242,347	27,847,109	1,339,072	35,042,601	171,272	5,667,303	13,446,091
TOTAL (S)	410	24	16	81	81	15	81	6	25	81

[a] UFE (Simone Veil): split between Christian Democrats and Liberals, 8:17.
[b] In Luxembourg every voter had six votes, so totals divided by six.

149

chamber. In the first elected Parliament there were six main political groups (in order of size): Socialists, Christian Democrats, Conservatives, Communists, Liberals and Progressive Democrats (mostly Gaullists).

In the second elected parliament, these have been joined by an extreme right-wing group, the Group of the European Right, and a Rainbow Group, consisting of Ecologists and other heterodox parties. The Christian Democratic group is known as the European People's Party, the Conservative group as the European Democratic Group and the predominantly Gaullist group as the Group of the European Democratic Alliance.

The results of the 1979 election are shown in tabulated form on page 149.

Those for 1984 are shown in greater detail, along with electoral maps for each of the ten countries that took part. The current (spring 1986) membership of each of the political groups in the Parliament is shown below.

The electoral system used in 1984 and the number of members per country were as follows.

Belgium: PR, regional lists. 24 members.
Denmark: PR, national lists. 15 members.
Greenland: plurality. 1 member. When Greenland left the EEC on January 1 1985 this member was replaced by an additional member from metropolitan Denmark.
France: PR, national lists. 81 members.
West Germany: PR, regional lists. 78 members. (West Berlin: 3 appointed members.)
Greece: PR, national lists. 24 members.
Republic of Ireland: PR, single transferable vote (STV). 15 members.
Italy: PR, regional lists. 81 members.
Luxembourg: PR, national lists. 6 members.
Netherlands: PR, national lists. 25 members.
United Kingdom: plurality. 78 members. (Northern Ireland: PR, single transferable vote. 3 members.)

Political groups on May 1 1986

Country	S	PPE	ED	COM	L	RDE	ARC	DR	NI	Total
Belgium	8	6	–	–	5	–	4	–	1	24
Denmark	3	1	4	2	2	–	4	–	–	16
France	20	9	–	10	12	20	–	10	–	81
West Germany	33	41	–	–	–	–	7	–	–	81
Greece	10	9	–	4	–	–	–	1	–	24
Republic of Ireland	–	6	–	–	1	8	–	–	–	15
Italy	12	27	–	27	5	–	2	5	3	81
Luxembourg	2	3	–	–	1	–	–	–	–	6
Netherlands	9	8	–	–	5	–	2	–	1	25
United Kingdom	33	–	46	–	–	1	–	–	1	81
TOTAL elected	130	110	50	43	31	29	19	16	6	434
Portugal	6	2	–	3	9	4	–	–	–	24
Spain	36	7	13	–	2	–	1	–	1	60
TOTAL	172	119	63	46	42	33	20	16	7	518

Abbreviations

S	Socialist Group
PPE	Group of the European People's Party (Christian Democratic Group)
ED	European Democratic Group (Conservative Group)
COM	Communist and allies Group
L	Liberal and Democratic Group
RDE	Group of the European Democratic Alliance
ARC	Rainbow Group
DR	Group of the European Right
NI	Non-attached

Note: The abbreviations used for the groups in the European Parliament are derived from the French form of their titles.

Results of elections of June 1984

Belgium

Seats: 24   Turnout: 92.1%

Party	Votes	%	Seats
Socialist parties (PS/SP)	1,741,995	30.4	9
Christian parties (PSC/CVP)	1,568,790	27.4	6
Liberal parties (PRL/PVV)	1,034,887	18.0	5
Volksunie (VU)	484,404	8.5	2
Ecolo/Agalev	467,375	8.2	2
Front Démocratique Francophone (FDF)	142,879	2.5	–
Communist Party (PCB/KPB)	87,379	1.5	–
Vlaams Blok	73,171	1.3	–
Others	120,921	2.1	–

Names of parties and membership of political groups in the European Parliament

PS	French-speaking Socialist Party	S
SP	Flemish-speaking Socialist Party	S
PSC	Social Christian Party	PPE
CVP	Christian Democratic Party	PPE
PRL	French-speaking Liberal Party	L
PVV	Flemish-speaking Liberal Party	L
VU	Volksunie	ARC
Ecolo	French-speaking Ecologist Party	ARC
Agalev	Flemish-speaking Ecologist Party	ARC

Denmark

Seats: 16 (including 1 for Greenland)   Turnout: 52.4%

Party	Votes	%	Seats
Conservative Party (KF)	414,177	20.8	4
Popular Movement against EEC	413,808	20.8	4
Social Democratic Party (S)	387,098	19.4	3
Liberal Party (V)	248,397	12.5	2
Left Socialist Party (SF)	183,580	9.2	1[a]
Centre Democratic Party (CD)	131,984	6.6	1
Progress Party	68,747	3.5	–
Others	142,489	7.2	–

Greenland

Seat: 1   Turnout: 35.6%

Party	Votes	%	Seats
Siumut	7,364	59.7	1[a]
Atassut	4,241	34.4	–
Others	737	6.0	–

Names of parties and membership of political groups in the European Parliament

	Popular Movement against EEC	ARC
S	Social Democratic Party	S
V	Liberal Party	L
KF	Conservative Party	ED
CD	Centre Democratic Party	PPE
SF	Socialistisk folkeparti (Left Socialist Party)	COM
	Siumut (Greenland)	S

[a] Greenland left the Community on December 31 1984 and its seat in Parliament went to the Left Socialist Party with effect from January 1 1985.

France

Seats: 81   Turnout: 56.7%

Party	Votes	%	Seats
Union of Opposition	8,883,596	43.0	41
Socialist Party (PS)	4,188,875	20.7	20
Communist Party (PCF)	2,261,312	11.2	10
National Front (FN)	2,210,334	10.9	10
Greens	680,080	3.4	–
Others	2,156,657	10.7	–

Names of parties and membership of political groups in the European Parliament

	Union of Opposition[a]	PPE/L/RDE
PS	Socialist Party	S
PCF	Communist Party	COM
FN	National Front	DR

[a] A combined list of the Rally for the Republic (RPR) and the Union for French Democracy (UDF)

West Germany

Seats: 81   Turnout: 56.8%

Party	Votes	%	Seats
Christian Democratic Union (CDU)	9,308,411	37.5	34
Christian Social Union (CSU)	2,109,130	8.5	7
Social Democratic Party (SPD)	9,296,417	37.4	33
Greens	2,025,972	8.2	7
Free Democratic Party	1,192,624	4.8	–
Others	918,817	3.6	–

Names of parties and membership of political groups in the European Parliament

CDU	Christian Democratic Union	PPE
CSU	Christian Social Union	PPE
SPD	Social Democratic Party	S
	Greens	ARC

Greece

Seats: 24   Turnout: 77.2%

Party	Votes	%	Seats
Panhellenic Socialist Movement (PASOK)	2,477,445	41.6	10
New Democracy Party (ND)	2,266,088	38.0	9
Communist Party of Greece (KKE)	693,466	11.6	3
Communist Party of Greece – Interior (KKE–Es)	203,671	3.4	1
National Political Union (EPEN)	136,623	2.3	1
Others	181,473	3.0	–

Names of parties and membership of political groups in the European Parliament

PASOK	Panhellenic Socialist Movement	S
ND	New Democracy Party	PPE
KKE	Communist Party of Greece	COM
KKE–Es	Communist Party of Greece – Interior	COM
EPEN	National Political Union	DR

Republic of Ireland

Seats: 15   Turnout: 63.5%

Party	Votes	%	Seats
Fianna Fáil (FF)	438,946	39.2	8
Fine Gael (FG)	361,034	32.2	6
Independent (Ind)	113,067	10.1	1
Labour Party	93,656	8.4	–
Sinn Fein	54,672	4.9	–
Workers' Party	48,449	4.3	–
Others	10,592	0.9	–

Names of parties and membership of political groups in the European Parliament

FF	Fianna Fáil	RDE
FG	Fine Gael	PPE
Ind	Independent	L

Italy

Seats: 81   Turnout: 83.4%

Party	Votes	%	Seats
Communist Party (PCI)	1,714,428	33.3	27
Christian Democracy (DC)	1,583,787	33.0	26
Socialist Party (PSI)	3,940,445	11.2	9
Italian Social Movement (MSI/DN)	2,274,556	6.5	5
Liberal Party/Republican Party PLI/PRI	2,140,502	6.1	5
Social Democratic Party (PSDI)	225,462	3.5	3
Radical Party (PR)	199,876	3.4	3
Proletarian Democracy	506,753	1.4	1
South Tyrol People's Party (SVP)	198,220	0.6	1
Union of Val d'Aosta/Sardinian Action Party (PSdA)	193,430	0.5	1
Liga Veneta	164,115	0.5	–

Names of parties and membership of political groups in the European Parliament

PCI	Italian Communist Party	COM
DC	Christian Democracy Party	PPE
PSI	Italian Socialist Party	S
MSI/DN	Italian Social Movement/National Right	DR
PLI/PRI	Italian Liberal Party/Italian Republican Party	L
PSDI	Italian Social Democratic Party	S
PR	Radical Party	NI
DP	Proletarian Democracy Party	ARC
SVP	South Tyrol People's Party	PPE
UV/PSdA	Union of Val d'Aosta/Sardinian Action Party	ARC

Luxembourg

Seats: 6   Turnout: 88.8%

Party	Votes	%	Seats
Christian Social Party (PCS)	345,586	34.9	3
Socialist Party (POSL)	296,382	29.9	2
Democratic Party (DP)	218,481	22.1	1
The Green Alternative	60,152	6.1	–
Communist Party	40,395	4.1	–
Others	29,146	2.9	–

Names of parties and membership of political groups in the European Parliament

PCS	Christian Social Party	PPE
POSL	Socialist Party	S
DP	Democratic Party	L

Netherlands

Seats: 25   Turnout: **50.57%**

Party	Votes	%	Seats
Labour Party (PvdA)	1,785,399	33.70	9
Christian Democratic Appeal (CDA)	1,590,601	30.02	8
Liberal Party (VVD)	1,002,825	18.93	5
Green Progressive Alliance (left-wing and ecologist parties) (CPN/GPN/FPR/PSP)	296,516	5.60	2
Calvinist parties (SGP/RPF/GPV)	275,824	5.21	1
Centre Party	134,888	2.55	–
Democrats '66	120,848	2.28	–
Greens	67,423	1.27	–
'God with us'	23,297	0.44	–

Names of parties and membership of political groups in the European Parliament

CDA	Christian Democratic Appeal	PPE
PvdA	Labour Party	S
VVD	Liberal Party	L
PPR/PSP	Radical Party/Pacifist Socialist Party	ARC
SGP	Calvinist Party	NI

United Kingdom

Seats: 81 (including 3 for Northern Ireland) Turnout: 32.6%

Great Britain

Seats: 78   Turnout: 31.8%

Party	Votes	%	Seats
Conservative Party	5,426,856	40.76	45
Labour Party	4,865,224	36.55	32
Scottish National Party	230,594	1.73	1
Social Democratic Party/Liberal Party Alliance	2,591,635	19.47	–
Others	198,562	1.49	–

Northern Ireland

Seats: 3   Turnout: 86.5%

Party	Votes	%	Seats
Democratic Unionist Party	230,251	33.59	1
Social Democratic and Labour Party	151,399	22.09	1
Ulster Unionist Party	147,169	21.47	1
Others	156,498	22.83	–

Names of parties and membership of political groups in the European Parliament

Cons.	Conservative and Unionist Party	ED
Lab.	Labour Party	S
SNP	Scottish National Party	RDE
DUP	Democratic Unionist Party	NI
SDLP	Social Democratic and Labour Party	S
UUP	Ulster Unionist Party	ED

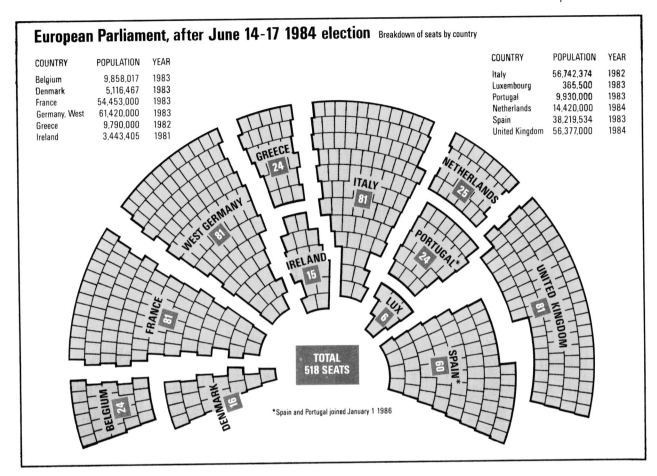

European Parliament, after June 14-17 1984 election
Breakdown of seats by country

COUNTRY	POPULATION	YEAR
Belgium	9,858,017	1983
Denmark	5,116,467	1983
France	54,453,000	1983
Germany, West	61,420,000	1983
Greece	9,790,000	1982
Ireland	3,443,405	1981

COUNTRY	POPULATION	YEAR
Italy	56,742,374	1982
Luxembourg	365,500	1983
Portugal	9,930,000	1983
Netherlands	14,420,000	1984
Spain	38,219,534	1983
United Kingdom	56,377,000	1984

GREECE 24 · WEST GERMANY 81 · ITALY 81 · NETHERLANDS 25 · PORTUGAL* 24 · IRELAND 15 · FRANCE 81 · LUX 6 · SPAIN* 60 · UNITED KINGDOM 81 · BELGIUM 24 · DENMARK 16

TOTAL 518 SEATS

*Spain and Portugal joined January 1 1986

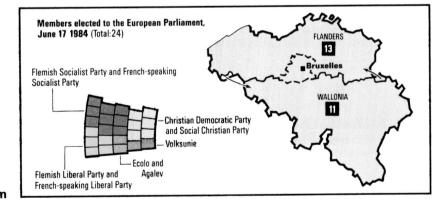

Members elected to the European Parliament, June 17 1984 (Total:24)

Flemish Socialist Party and French-speaking Socialist Party
Christian Democratic Party and Social Christian Party
Volksunie
Ecolo and Agalev
Flemish Liberal Party and French-speaking Liberal Party

FLANDERS 13 · Bruxelles · WALLONIA 11

Belgium

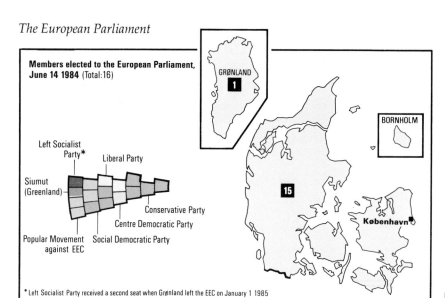

Members elected to the European Parliament, June 14 1984 (Total:16)

Left Socialist Party*

Liberal Party

Siumut (Greenland)

Conservative Party

Centre Democratic Party

Popular Movement against EEC

Social Democratic Party

GRØNLAND **1**

BORNHOLM

15

København

* Left Socialist Party received a second seat when Grønland left the EEC on January 1 1985

Denmark

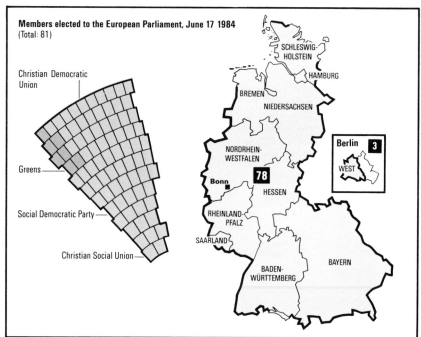

Members elected to the European Parliament, June 17 1984 (Total: 81)

Christian Democratic Union

Greens

Social Democratic Party

Christian Social Union

SCHLESWIG-HOLSTEIN

HAMBURG

BREMEN

NIEDERSACHSEN

NORDRHEIN-WESTFALEN

Bonn

HESSEN

RHEINLAND-PFALZ

SAARLAND

BADEN-WÜRTTEMBERG

BAYERN

78

Berlin **3** WEST

West Germany

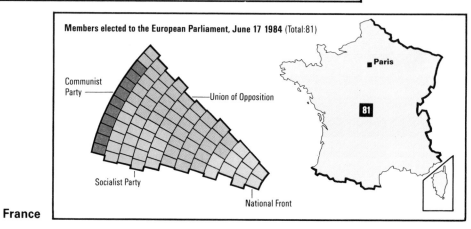

Members elected to the European Parliament, June 17 1984 (Total:81)

Communist Party

Union of Opposition

Socialist Party

National Front

Paris

81

France

154

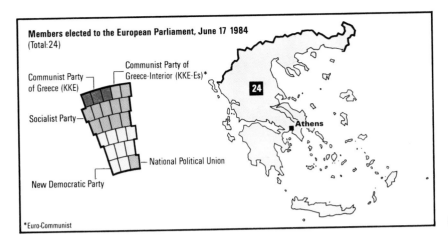

Members elected to the European Parliament, June 17 1984
(Total: 24)

Communist Party of Greece (KKE)

Communist Party of Greece-Interior (KKE-Es)*

Socialist Party

National Political Union

New Democratic Party

24

Athens

*Euro-Communist

Greece

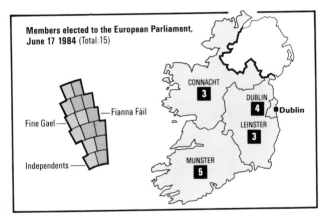

Members elected to the European Parliament, June 17 1984 (Total: 15)

Fine Gael

Fianna Fáil

Independents

CONNACHT
3

DUBLIN
4
Dublin

LEINSTER
3

MUNSTER
5

Republic of Ireland

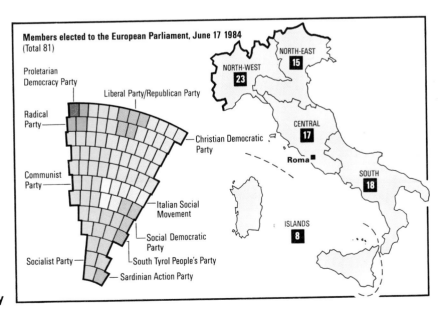

Members elected to the European Parliament, June 17 1984
(Total 81)

Proletarian Democracy Party

Liberal Party/Republican Party

Radical Party

Christian Democratic Party

Communist Party

Italian Social Movement

Social Democratic Party

Socialist Party

South Tyrol People's Party

Sardinian Action Party

NORTH-WEST
23

NORTH-EAST
15

CENTRAL
17

Roma

SOUTH
18

ISLANDS
8

Italy

opposite **United Kingdom**

Members elected to the European Parliament, June 17 1984 (Total 6)

Christian Social Party

Socialist Workers Party

Democratic Party *

*Liberal

6

Luxembourg City

Luxembourg

Netherlands

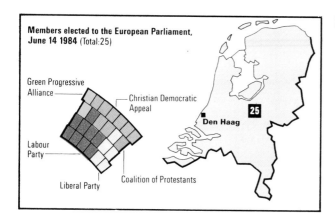

Members elected to the European Parliament, June 14 1984 (Total:25)

Green Progressive Alliance

Christian Democratic Appeal

Labour Party

Liberal Party

Coalition of Protestants

Den Haag

25

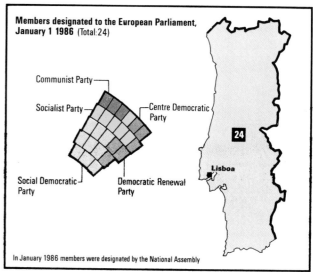

Members designated to the European Parliament, January 1 1986 (Total:24)

Communist Party

Socialist Party

Centre Democratic Party

Social Democratic Party

Democratic Renewal Party

Lisboa

24

In January 1986 members were designated by the National Assembly

Portugal

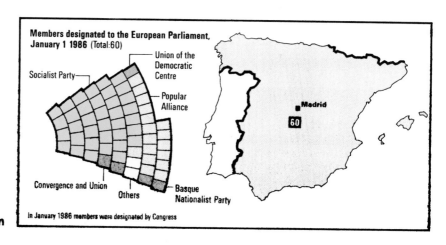

Members designated to the European Parliament, January 1 1986 (Total:60)

Socialist Party

Union of the Democratic Centre

Popular Alliance

Convergence and Union

Others

Basque Nationalist Party

Madrid

60

In January 1986 members were designated by Congress

Spain

156

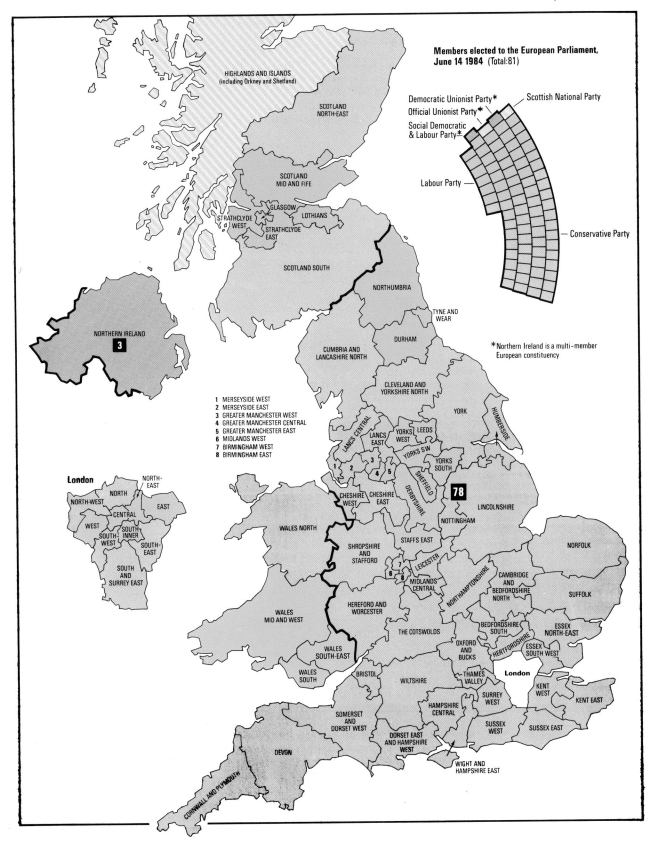

**Members elected to the European Parliament,
June 14 1984** (Total: 81)

Democratic Unionist Party *
Official Unionist Party *
Social Democratic & Labour Party *

Scottish National Party

Labour Party

Conservative Party

* Northern Ireland is a multi-member
European constituency

HIGHLANDS AND ISLANDS
(including Orkney and Shetland)

SCOTLAND
NORTH-EAST

SCOTLAND
MID AND FIFE

GLASGOW

STRATHCLYDE
WEST

LOTHIANS

STRATHCLYDE
EAST

SCOTLAND SOUTH

NORTHUMBRIA

TYNE AND
WEAR

DURHAM

NORTHERN IRELAND
3

CUMBRIA AND
LANCASHIRE NORTH

CLEVELAND AND
YORKSHIRE NORTH

YORK

HUMBERSIDE

1 MERSEYSIDE WEST
2 MERSEYSIDE EAST
3 GREATER MANCHESTER WEST
4 GREATER MANCHESTER CENTRAL
5 GREATER MANCHESTER EAST
6 MIDLANDS WEST
7 BIRMINGHAM WEST
8 BIRMINGHAM EAST

LANCS CENTRAL
LANCS
EAST
YORKS
WEST
LEEDS
YORKS SW
YORKS
SOUTH

London

NORTH-
EAST
NORTH
NORTH-WEST
CENTRAL
EAST
WEST
SOUTH-
INNER
SOUTH-
WEST
SOUTH-
EAST
SOUTH
AND
SURREY EAST

CHESHIRE
WEST
CHESHIRE
EAST
DERBYSHIRE
SHEFFIELD
78
LINCOLNSHIRE
NOTTINGHAM

WALES NORTH

STAFFS EAST

SHROPSHIRE
AND
STAFFORD

7
6 8
LEICESTER
MIDLANDS
CENTRAL
NORTHAMPTONSHIRE
NORFOLK
CAMBRIDGE
AND
BEDFORDSHIRE
NORTH
SUFFOLK

WALES
MID AND WEST

HEREFORD AND
WORCESTER

THE COTSWOLDS

BEDFORDSHIRE
SOUTH
HERTFORDSHIRE
ESSEX
NORTH-EAST
ESSEX
SOUTH WEST

WALES
SOUTH-EAST

OXFORD
AND
BUCKS

WALES
SOUTH

BRISTOL
WILTSHIRE

THAMES
VALLEY
London

KENT
WEST
KENT EAST

SURREY
WEST

HAMPSHIRE
CENTRAL

SUSSEX
WEST
SUSSEX EAST

SOMERSET
AND
DORSET WEST

DEVON

DORSET EAST
AND HAMPSHIRE
WEST

WIGHT AND
HAMPSHIRE EAST

CORNWALL AND PLYMOUTH

Stop Press

Elections were held in a number of countries while this book was going through the press. Official figures were not immediately available, and the following – in some cases – partial results came from unofficial sources.

Austria

Result of Presidential election of May–June 1986

First round, May 4 1986

	Votes	%
Kurt Waldheim (People's Party)	2,343,227	49.6
Kurt Steyrer (Socialist Party)	2,060,652	43.7
Freda Meissner-Blau (Independent Green)	259,448	5.5
Otto Scrinzi (Right-wing Nationalist)	56,618	1.2

Second round, June 8 1986

	Votes	%	
Kurt Waldheim (People's Party)	2,460,203	53.9	elected
Kurt Steyrer (Socialist Party)	2,105,118	46.1	

Fred Sinowatz resigned as chancellor on June 9 1986. His place was taken by Franz Vranitsky (Socialist Party).

Barbados

Result of parliamentary election of May 28 1986

	Votes	%	Seats	%
Democratic Labour Party	80,050	59.4	24	88.9
Barbados Labour Party	54,467	40.4	3	11.1
Others	227	0.2	0	0.0
TOTAL	134,744		27	

Errol Barrow, leader of the Democratic Labour Party, became prime minister of a new government formed by the Democratic Labour Party on May 29 1986.

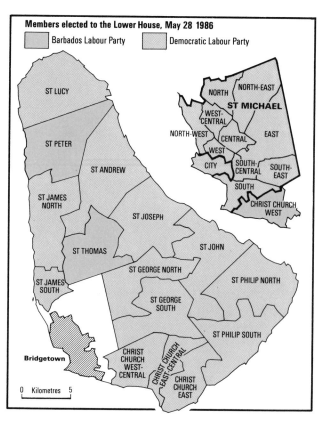

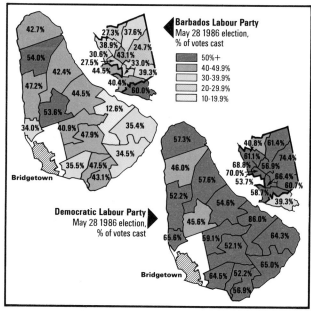

Colombia

Result of election to House of Representatives of March 9 1986

	Votes	%
Liberal Party	3,168,937	48.9
Conservative Party	2,440,281	37.7
New Liberalism	446,160	6.9
Patriotic Union	94,781	1.5
Others	324,468	5.0
TOTAL valid votes	6,473,971	

Result of Presidential election of May 25 1986

	Votes	%	
Virgilio Barco (Liberal Party)	4,211,826	58.3	elected
Alvaro Gomez (Conservative Party)	2,578,667	35.8	
Jaime Pardo (Left)	328,641	4.5	
Regina Betancourt (Independent)	46,811	0.6	
TOTAL valid votes	7,225,875		

Costa Rica

Result of Presidential election of February 2 1986

	Votes	%	
Oscar Arias (National Liberation Party)	620,314	52.3	elected
Rafael Angel Calderon (Social Christian Unity Party)	542,434	45.8	

Four other candidates polled less than 2 per cent.

Result of election to the Legislative Assembly of February 2 1986

	Seats
National Liberation Party	29
Social Christian Unity Party	25
United People's Coalition (Communist Party)	2
Others	1
TOTAL	57

Dominican Republic

Result of Presidential election of May 16 1986

	Votes	%	
Joaquin Balaguer (Reformist Party)	857,942	41	elected
Jacobo Majluta (Revolutionary Party)	814,716	39	
Juan Bosch (Liberation Party)	379,269	18	

Other candidates polled around 2 per cent.

Ecuador

A partial election for 59 out of the 71 seats in Congress was held on June 1 1986. Leftist and Left-of-centre parties, opposed to President Febres-Cordero, were reported to have made a net gain of 2 seats, leaving them with 43 seats out of the 71. No further details were available as the book went to press.

France

On July 8 1986 the Constitutional Court invalidated the results for the Haute-Corse and Haute-Garonne *départements* in the elections held on March 16 1986. By-elections to fill the ten seats involved were to be held later in 1986.

In June 1986 the French electoral law was changed. Future elections to the Chamber of Deputies will be held under the traditional majoritarian two-ballot system (see page 2) rather than by proportional representation, as in March 1986.

Japan

Result of election to the House of Representatives of July 6 1986

Electorate: 86,426,845 Valid votes: 61,707,095 (71.4%)

	% Votes	Seats	% Seats
Liberal Democratic Party	49.4	300	58.6
Japan Socialist Party	17.2	85	16.0
Clean Government Party	9.4	56	10.9
Japan Communist Party	8.8	26	5.1
Democratic Socialist Party	6.4	26	5.1
New Liberal Club	1.8	6	1.2
Others	6.9	13[a]	2.5
TOTAL		512	

[a] Including 4 seats for the Social Democratic Federation and 9 Independents.

Netherlands

Result of election to Second Chamber of May 21 1986

Valid votes: 9,167,335 (85.7%)

	Votes	%	Seats	%
Christian Democratic Appeal	3,170,081	34.6	54	36.0
Labour Party	3,052,268	33.3	52	34.6
Liberal Party	1,595,377	17.5	27	18.0
Democrats '66	561,865	6.1	9	6.0
State Reform Party	159,897	1.8	3	2.0
Radical Party	115,009	1.3	2	1.3
Pacifist Socialist Party	110,331	1.2	1	0.7
Reformed Political Association	88,006	1.0	1	0.7
Reformational Political Federation	83,269	0.9	1	0.7
Communist Party	57,840	0.6	0	0.0
Others	173,392	1.8	0	0.0
TOTAL	9,167,335		150	

Spain

Result of election of June 22 1986
(based on 99.9% of votes counted)

Turnout: 70.7%

	% Votes	Seats	% Seats
Socialist Party	44.1	184	52.6
Popular Coalition (inc. Popular Alliance)	26.2	105	30.0
Democratic and Social Centre	9.3	19	5.4
Convergence and Union	4.7	18	5.1
United Left (inc. Communist Party)	4.6	7	2.0
Basque Nationalist Party	1.6	6	1.7
Herri Batasuna	1.2	5	1.4
Basque Left	0.5	2	0.6
Others	7.8	4	1.1
TOTAL		350	